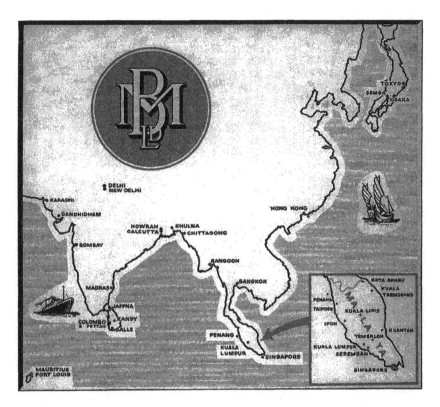

Frontispiece   Locations of principal overseas branches of the Mercantile Bank, 1959

The Paradise Bank

For our parents

The Paradise Bank

The Mercantile Bank of India, 1893–1984

EDWIN GREEN and SARA KINSEY

Routledge
Taylor & Francis Group

LONDON AND NEW YORK

First published 1999 by Ashgate Publishing

Published 2016 by Routledge
2 Park Square, Milton Park, Abingdon, Oxon OX14 4RN
711 Third Avenue, New York, NY 10017, USA

Routledge is an imprint of the Taylor & Francis Group, an informa business

British Library Cataloguing in Publication Data

Green, Edwin, 1948–
    The Paradise Bank: The Mercantile Bank of India, 1893–1984
    (Studies in Banking History)
    1. Mercantile Bank.   2. Mercantile Bank—History.   3. Banks and
    banking—India.
    I. Title.   II. Kinsey, Sara.
    332.1'0954

Library of Congress Cataloging-in-Publication Data

Green, Edwin.
    The paradise bank: the Mercantile Bank of India, 1893–1984/Edwin
    Green and Sara Kinsey
        (Studies in Banking History)
    Includes bibliographical references and index.
    ISBN 1-84014-685-0 (hbk: acid-free paper)
    1. Mercantile Bank of India—History.   2. Banks and banking,
    British—India—History.   I. Kinsey, Sara, 1969–   . II. Title.
    III. Series.
    HG3288.M74G74   1999
    332.1'5'0954—dc21   99–16515
                                                                    CIP

Transfered to Digital Printing in 2012

ISBN 9781840146851 (hbk)
ISBN 9781138268852 (pbk)

Contents

Contents

Tables

Figures

Plates

Appendices

Conventions

Countries and places are referred to in the text by names which are historically accurate and were commonly used by English speakers at that time. Thus, for example, what is now Malaysia is referred to as Malaya in the period before 1957. Where this historic form is not widely known, today's name is given in brackets – for instance, Jakarta is referred to in the text as Batavia (Jakarta).

The main player in the story, the Mercantile Bank of India, is usually referred to in the text by its abbreviated name, the Mercantile. Similarly, the Hongkong and Shanghai Banking Corporation is usually referred to as the Hongkong Bank.

Amounts in the text are given in sterling unless otherwise stated. Hong Kong dollars are denoted HK$. Where figures are quoted in Indian rupees, large numbers are given in millions of rupees.

References: sources and abbreviations

All original sources are from the Mercantile Bank collection (MBH) of the Archives of the HSBC Group unless otherwise stated. There are also many references to items from the Hongkong Bank, head office collections (GHO), in Chapters Seven and Eight.

Muirhead   Muirhead, Stuart (1996), *Crisis Banking in the East: The History of the Chartered Mercantile Bank of India, London and China 1853–93*, Aldershot: Scolar Press.

King I   King, Frank H. H. (1987), *The History of The Hongkong and Shanghai Banking Corporation, The Hongkong Bank in Late Imperial China, 1864–1902: On an Even Keel*, Cambridge: Cambridge University Press.

King II   King, Frank H. H. (1988), *The History of The Hongkong and Shanghai Banking Corporation, The Hongkong Bank in the Period of Imperialism and War, 1895–1918: Wayfoong, the Focus of Wealth*, Cambridge: Cambridge University Press.

King III   King, Frank H. H. (1988), *The History of The Hongkong and Shanghai Banking Corporation, The Hongkong Bank between the Wars and the Bank Interned, 1919–1945: Return from Grandeur*, Cambridge: Cambridge University Press.

King IV   King, Frank H. H. (1991), *The History of The Hongkong and Shanghai Banking Corporation, The Hongkong Bank in the Period of Development and Nationalism, 1941–1984: From Regional Bank to Multinational Group*, Cambridge: Cambridge University Press.

Introduction

The main title of this history is taken from the telegraphic address, PARADISE, which the Mercantile Bank of India used at its head office and branch offices from 1893 to 1984. In international banking in the nineteenth and early twentieth centuries, a telegraphic address was a business essential and not an ornament; from the late 1860s onwards, a high proportion of the transactions and decisions of any overseas bank was transmitted by telegraph. However, the choice of cable address could be an arbitrary affair. Most companies and institutions could adopt abbreviated or stylized versions of their own names or choose from a list of available names offered by the postal authorities. In the world of business, the selection of these names might bear no relation to the title of the firm or company. For example, the State Bank of India used THISTLE and the Banco America do Sul of Brazil chose GINKO; telegraphs to the National Mutual Life Assurance Society were sent to the splendid address of UNDOUBTED while the United Kingdom Provident Association preferred PRECAUTION.

The Mercantile Bank's PARADISE was one of the best-known and most easily remembered of these telegraphic titles. It was inherited from its forerunner, the Chartered Mercantile Bank of India, London and China, which had begun to use this cable address in about 1875. It was also an apt title. The address was a reminder that the bank's offices included some distant and exotic locations in the East, even where working conditions could not be described as paradise. It was also fitting for a bank which generated the real affection of its customers, shareholders, staff and pensioners around the world.

The history of the Mercantile Bank itself reflects the great diversity in the origin and upbringing of modern banks. Financial history is rich in distinct traditions. Retail or 'high street' banking, investment and merchant banking, overseas banking and trade finance, money market business and savings banks have all contributed in different measures to the composition of modern banks. Those traditions may no longer be obvious in the names and addresses of banks but they remain a source of experience, expertise and reputation.

International banking shares this diversity of tradition. One of the long-standing characteristics of overseas banking was the abundance of banks which were linked to a specific region or country. In the 1950s and 1960s in London, for example, banks such as the Standard Bank of South Africa and the National Bank of New Zealand concentrated on the markets named in their titles. Parallel examples could be found in

Paris, Amsterdam, Brussels, Madrid, Lisbon and Hong Kong. The Banque Indo-Suez of Paris or the Banco Hispano Americano of Madrid were explicitly associated with particular regions and trading routes. Many such banks were linked with the territories or former territories of the European empires but the 'regional' tradition in overseas banking also included banks such as the Bank of London and South America and the Deutsche Asiatische Bank, which operated without a direct link to a colonial background.

By the end of the twentieth century this specialist tradition had been absorbed into the larger setting of multinational banking and it was no longer an independent and visible part of the banking scene. However, the tradition continued to contribute to international banking. The Mercantile Bank of India, established in 1893 and acquired by the Hongkong and Shanghai Banking Corporation in 1959, epitomized the regional tradition. Still operating in its own name as recently as 1984 and with its former branches and personnel continuing to play a part in the HSBC Group in the late 1990s, the Mercantile was also an especially durable example of this distinctive genre in overseas banking.

This book places the Mercantile's contribution to the world of banking on record and in context. The book appears in a series devoted to banking history and, as a result, it is intended to be a research contribution to the history of overseas banking in general and the history of the HSBC Group in particular. We cannot pretend that this history covers in any detail the more personal aspects of the Mercantile Bank – the career experiences and anecdotes of bankers in the East – but in the text and illustrations we have attempted to show the business setting for those careers.

As the bank was not newly-minted when it was incorporated in 1893, we begin with a summary of the career of the predecessor bank, the Chartered Mercantile Bank of India, London and China, from its formation in 1853 to its reconstruction as the Mercantile Bank of India in 1893. A full history of the Chartered Mercantile by the late Stuart Muirhead was published in 1996 and this history is its sequel and companion volume.[1] For the Mercantile's history after 1893, we have adopted a simple chronological arrangement. The covering dates of the chapters reflect the principal periods of office of the bank's chief managers. For a relatively small bank such as the Mercantile, the appointment of chief manager was of pivotal importance as it affected other senior appointments, relationships between directors, managers and staff as well as the style and purpose of management of the bank. In these important areas, changes in management provide a more natural pattern for assessing the performance and character of the bank than other internal or external events.

Within this framework our priorities have been to trace the performance of the Mercantile and compare it with competitors in Eastern banking; to assess the role of the business and branches of the bank; and to identify the distinctive features of the bank, its management and staff. We have also compared the Mercantile's experience with common assumptions about banks of this type, particularly the notion that most British overseas banks were moderate performers and that they lacked ambition and enterprise. Even in the earliest stages of research for this project, it was clear that the history of the Mercantile did not fit such a simple pattern. We were repeatedly surprised by the difference between the bank's modest public demeanor and its actual, spirited achievements in different Eastern markets. This element of 'discovery' of the real performance of the Mercantile has provided a continuous theme of our research for this history. To that end, information about the bank's earnings and branch performance is provided in more detail than is usually possible in bank histories.

We have been fortunate in the range of sources available for research. The archives of the Mercantile Bank are relatively plentiful, thanks to the efforts of successive controllers of the archives of the Hongkong Bank (Brian Ogden, Stuart Muirhead and Ian Donaldson) and Margaret Lee, manager of the archives of the Hongkong Bank.[2] The collection, which since 1993 has been in the care of the HSBC Group Archives in London, includes full sets of board minutes and financial records, extensive correspondence between the head office and branches, and detailed records of the bank's Eastern staff and premises. These records are valuable for research on a wide range of topics beyond the scope of this book, including the political and social history of territories where the bank operated; the economic and monetary history of the sub-continent and the East; and the history of commodities and individual firms in international trade. In addition, the database which we have compiled to analyse the careers of the bank's staff will have applications for other research topics in the future or, more simply, for family history.

A special feature of the Mercantile Bank archives is the set of oral histories comprising taped and transcribed interviews with former members of staff and their families. These interviews were recorded in 1980–81 by Frank and Catherine King and Christopher Cook as part of the much larger programme of oral histories for the Hongkong Bank history.[3] These archives provide a vivid human picture of the lives and careers of bankers in the East. They are also a fruitful source of anecdotal information and, although we have not been able to use these anecdotes to any great extent in tackling the more basic tasks of this history, they are an indispensable source for future historians of the culture and social milieu of expatriate business communities.

As with any collection of business archives, there are also weaknesses in the sources. While there is no shortage of references to the bank's customers, for example, the surviving records do not include any single source which gives a continuous view of changes in the clientele of the bank. The bank's archives also give a head office view rather than a local view of transactions, as relatively few records of the branch offices (especially those in India) have survived. Similarly the extant records do not provide a continuous view of the shareholders of the bank. Perhaps the most serious drawback, however, is the paucity of information about the local staff of the bank. This is a deficiency in the archive collections of other overseas banks and it is a neglected area of banking development which deserves future attention and research effort from archivists and historians.

We have been especially fortunate in the quality and range of published work on Eastern banking. King's four-volume history of the Hongkong Bank dominates this sector of banking history and is a unique achievement in the wider field of business history.[4] That history has been invaluable not only for comparative purposes but also for its account of the Hongkong Bank's relations with the Mercantile during and after the acquisition in 1959. Other outcomes of the Hongkong Bank's history project – especially the *Eastern Banking* essays and Geoffrey Jones's two-volume history of the British Bank of the Middle East[5] – have greatly strengthened the comparative base for the project. Jones has also come to the aid of all banking historians with his wide-ranging study of British multinational banking, a definitive guide to the strategies and performance of far-flung overseas banks and an indispensable compilation of statistics for this distinctive group of banks.[6]

Stuart Muirhead's *Crisis Banking in the East*, the history of the Mercantile's forerunner bank from 1853 to 1893, has been a core source and influence on this project. That history, which we helped to prepare for publication after Stuart's sudden death in 1993, is especially valuable for its detailed analysis of the business and staff of an overseas bank. The chapter on the mechanics of the bank's business, which has been described as 'truly outstanding',[7] is an insider's guide to the workings of an Eastern exchange bank. As a former member of the Mercantile's staff, Stuart Muirhead had also been assiduous in collecting the bank's records during his tenure as controller of the archives of the Hongkong Bank between 1981 and 1986. We are very grateful to Sheila Muirhead for making available her husband's notes and statistics both for *Crisis Banking* and for the sequel volume which he had hoped to add. These papers included the analysis of the Chartered Mercantile's sources of earnings which appears in Chapter One of this book and which had not come to light when *Crisis Banking* went to press.

We have received many other forms of help and encouragement in our work on this history. Sir William Purves, formerly Group Chairman of HSBC Holdings, gave us permission and indispensable support both to prepare Stuart Muirhead's history for publication and to embark on this project. Bob Tennant, General Manager of Group Human Resources, and his staff made it possible for us to contact former members of the Mercantile's staff and also hosted our meetings in the early stages of the work. Mary Jo Jacobi, Adviser to the Board of the HSBC Group, has supported us throughout our time with the Mercantile history project and has also encouraged us in our continuing research on the history and archives of the Group. Margaret Lee, Manager of the Archives of the Hongkong Bank in Hong Kong, has taken generous interest in this and our other current projects. We are also grateful to Brian Ogden, who established the archives of the Hongkong Bank while he was Secretary and was then Controller of Archives between 1979 and 1981, for his hospitality and for his guidance on the later history and character of the Mercantile Bank. We have also been encouraged by the interest of colleagues throughout the Group. We are especially indebted to Rachel Huskinson, Assistant Archivist. She has not only been patient when the Mercantile project edged out other concerns but she has also contributed a special study of the Bank of Mauritius (the first for that bank, which became part of the Mercantile in 1916) in the appendices to this history.

Outside the Group, Professor Frank King and the late Catherine King have been inspirational for all our work on the archives of the Hongkong and Mercantile banks. They were enthusiastic and helpful in discussing this project and bringing their earlier work on the Mercantile (particularly the oral histories) into lively perspective. We are also grateful to Frank King for reading and commenting on our Chapter Seven, which covers the period of the 1959 acquisition; he found time for reading that chapter in the midst of his continuing research travels in the Far East. We have also learned from and appreciated comments and advice from other historians, notably regular visitors to the HSBC Group Archives such as Dr Raj Brown, Professors Phil Cottrell and Geoffrey Jones, Drs David Kynaston and Lucy Newton, and Professor Shin-ichi Nishimura.

The interest and support of former members of staff of the Mercantile Bank and the Hongkong Bank has been unprecedented in our own experience of business history. Former officials and their families have contributed papers, reminiscences and photographs which will be of value to the HSBC Group's archives for many years to come. We were also very fortunate in being able to meet and interview Peter and Marian Fletcher, Paul Lamb, Ian Macdonald, Sunil Singh Roy and Janie

Stewart. Our interviews with them were not only very enjoyable but also helped to clarify the modern history of the Mercantile in a way which would have been impossible from the archives alone. The results of Paul Lamb's own research in the early 1970s on the history of the Mercantile were an additional asset.

Our greatest debt, however, is to the panel of advisers which was formed at the outset of the project. Frank Reid, Hamish Stewart and John Wright represent different generations of the Mercantile's staff but they have each brought their own rich experience and their enthusiasm to the project. Frank Reid, in addition to these duties, also played a key role in establishing the project and then in maintaining contact with other former members of the Mercantile's staff. The panel of advisers has met regularly throughout our programme of research and writing and has read and commented on each successive plan and draft of our work. We are extremely grateful to them for their constant support and for their concern for the Mercantile's history and archives; the errors, omissions and misunderstandings which remain are our own. This wide range of interest and support has made it a privilege to work on the history of such a distinctive business as the Mercantile Bank.

CHAPTER ONE

Reprise, 1853–93

When the Mercantile Bank of India opened its doors for business on 4 February 1893 its branches and staff began with the benefit of 40 years' experience of Eastern exchange banking. Its predecessor, the Chartered Mercantile Bank of India, London and China, was a well-established business with branches throughout India, the Straits and the Chinese treaty ports. The bank had used the shortened form of its name, 'the Mercantile', since its inception and bequeathed this recognized and respected corporate identity to its successor.

The Chartered Mercantile had started life as the Mercantile Bank of Bombay in 1853.[1] At that stage Indian trade was dominated by its triangular commercial relationship with Britain and China. Its principal exports were raw cotton, opium to China, and grain and indigo; it was an economy in which jute and tea, staples of trade in the next generation, barely featured. In return the Indian market was dominated by imports from Britain of manufactured goods, large-scale bullion imports (especially silver) and the 'invisible' services of shipping and insurance.[2] The finance of this trade prior to the 1850s was largely in the hands of the East India Company and the agency houses. These houses were merchant firms which had been established with British and Indian capital and which had benefited from the end of the East India Company's monopoly of Indian trade in 1813 and Chinese trade in 1834. The agency houses, which also set up small banks of their own, suffered severely in the financial crises of 1826, 1834 and 1846–47. The many failures amongst the merchant community left a gap in the market for the finance of Eastern trade. Other institutions could not fill the vacuum. The three presidency banks, in which the Indian government participated and which were carrying out treasury functions, were expressly excluded from exchange banking. Indian banks, which were traditionally more concerned with inland trade and moneylending, were suffering in the same period as a result of the East India Company's introduction of the standard rupee in 1835. These banks showed little sign of moving across into trade finance; the chettiar bankers of Ceylon and South India were exceptions as they had been undertaking significant bill business since the early years of the nineteenth century.

Into this opening came the first Eastern exchange banks and, in particular, the Oriental Bank Corporation. This was the first bank with a head office in London, a network of branches stretching across the

East to China, and a business which was primarily the financing of international trade. The bank had initially been founded in Bombay in 1842 but swiftly moved its headquarters to London and was granted a royal charter in 1851, allowing it to operate in all the territories under the control of the East India Company. Its establishment and structure provided a blueprint for similar establishments, and its success inspired others to follow.

There ensued a wave of promotions of Eastern exchange banks in the 1850s. Some were London creations whose promoters were often men prominent in the City with connections with Eastern trade; their first priority was to gain a royal charter. Others were devised locally with the impetus provided by members of the business community in India. The Mercantile Bank of Bombay fell into the latter category. In October 1853, Cowasjee Nanabhoy, a Bombay Parsee merchant, called on his friend and business colleague, Edwin Heycock, and discussed with him the opportunities that existed for a new bank in Bombay. Heycock later recalled: 'I took a day to consider the subject, and on the next an advertisement was issued which led to the formation of the bank.'

Their optimism about the prospects for a new bank seemed well founded: shares in the new bank were quickly taken up and business commenced on 3 January 1854 in Rampart Row, Bombay. The early shareholders were divided almost equally between European and Indian residents, with the Parsees the largest body of proprietors. The first board of directors showed a balanced composition with three British and two Parsee directors. Between conception and opening, the bank had changed its name to the Mercantile Bank of India, London and China, demonstrating its early ambition and determination to expand beyond Bombay.

Despite the strong Bombay connections, it was the bank's intention from the outset to obtain a royal charter which would entail a change of domicile to London. This charter conferred certain benefits: prestige, the advantages of limited liability and a pool of London shareholders and directors. In 1854 the bank opened negotiations with the Chartered Bank of Asia with a view to a proposed amalgamation which would bring with it chartered status and a proprietary in London. However, the negotiations eventually failed when the Treasury in London refused to grant an altered charter for the proposed merged bank.

Undaunted, the Mercantile applied for a charter under its own auspices; this was granted in September 1857. The business of the old Mercantile was wound up and transferred to the new bank, the Chartered Mercantile Bank of India, London and China, which commenced business on 1 July 1858. The rupee capital was converted into £500 000 and transferred to London. The new court of directors in London contained two members of the old Bombay board and two members of the old London board. The bank's business continued undisturbed. By the time the head office transferred to London, the bank had established a network of nine branches in India, Ceylon, Singapore and China.

Throughout the remainder of the decade the bank built up its business, its reserves and its branch network. By 1860 it had added Mauritius to its roll call of branches and the reserves had reached £50 000, mainly invested in Indian government securities. This prosperous and expansionist period continued into the early 1860s. The first half of the 1860s was dominated by the increase in the price of cotton due to the disruption of supplies from America as a result of the civil war. The Indian cotton market, centred on Bombay, benefited greatly from the rise in price and demand for its products, and experienced a buoyant period. The bank prospered from this boom and by 1862 reserves had reached £100 000. Record profits followed in 1863, of which the most substantial amount was contributed by the Bombay branch. Business success encouraged the bank to expand its branch network yet further, reaching Japan in 1863 and adding new branches in Ceylon and India. The bank also took this opportunity to increase its capital to £750 000 by issuing 10 000 new shares which were mostly taken up in London.

However, by the late summer of 1864 there was unease in the Indian economy. The cotton price was falling on the news of peace negotiations in America. The exchange banks were also under pressure from new competitors which, having started up in the prosperity of the early years of the decade, were now forcing established banks to cut margins to retain business share. The Chartered Mercantile shut those branches, like Mauritius, which were not paying their way, and kept liquidity high to combat potential crises in confidence. At the same time, a number of merchant houses in Bombay and beyond failed in 1865 and cotton, tea and silk prices continued to fall. Worse was to follow in 1866 when the crash of the discount house of Overend, Gurney & Co. in London caused shock waves throughout the merchant community in the East. The financial turmoil spread and by the end of the year 21 banks connected with India and the East had either suspended payment or were in the process of liquidating. The Chartered Mercantile was one of the few to withstand the storm.

The Chartered Mercantile survived the crisis by prudence. The bank had built up large reserves during the years of prosperity and had remained liquid to forestall any run. Public confidence had remained in the bank. Although large amounts of bad debts were incurred during the crisis (and were not written off until the end of the decade), the bank was in a strong position: many of its competitors had gone to the wall and it had proved itself able to weather a crisis. By 1870, on the strength of its total assets, it was the third largest Eastern bank after the Oriental Bank and the newly founded and vigorous Hongkong and Shanghai Banking Corporation.

The 1870s brought new problems. Periodically the bank suffered considerable losses from the failures of trading firms and internal frauds. A more serious and long-term problem was the decline in the price of silver. In 1872 the price began to fall as new supplies of silver were discovered in Nevada and as European countries such as Germany substituted gold for silver currencies. The countries where the bank operated used silver currencies – the rupee, the Straits dollar and the Chinese tael – whose exchange value was highly dependent on the price of silver. Since the bank had been established the silver price had remained stable at 20 rupees to one pound sterling but now the bank had to learn to operate in a much more dynamic exchange-rate environment. The depreciation of these Eastern currencies had serious implications for banks whose capital had been paid in sterling but was subsequently remitted to the East and converted into local currencies as capital for branches. This erosion of capital required Eastern banks to establish special reserve funds to provide for any future exchange losses.

Trade depression and the silver depreciation took their toll on the bank's results. After the City of Glasgow Bank crisis in 1878 the bank was forced to announce that for the first time in its history it was unable to pay a dividend for the half-year. Additionally it had to transfer the entire reserve fund into a special reserve fund to cover the fall in silver and loss in value of rupee securities. Although business improved in the following years, the bank again had to announce that no dividend would be paid in the latter half of 1881. The losses of the bank in this year could be blamed partly on decisions of the directors, who had misjudged the outcome of discussion of the silver problem at the Paris monetary conference of 1881. Anticipating that the result would restore some measure of stability to silver, the board had led managers in the East to accept business which would have been better avoided. However, the price of silver fell after the conference and the bank incurred large losses – in effect the result of speculation.

In common with many other bankers and merchants dealing with India and the East, some of the directors and prominent shareholders of the Chartered Mercantile were firm believers in bimetallism. Bullen, a director between 1874 and 1893, was a member of the Bimetallist League, as were Samuel Montagu and Sir Alexander Wilson, who were to play an important part in the reconstruction of the bank. The League sought to persuade the government of the benefits of a double monetary standard of gold and silver which they hoped would help to check the fall in the price of silver. This economic doctrine may have influenced the outlook and judgement of the bank at a time when it needed to be realistic about the future of silver.

The mistakes of 1881 were compounded by the decision in the autumn of that year to make large purchases of 4 per cent and 4.5 per cent rupee paper (Indian government securities). The value of these holdings dropped quickly, not only because of the fall in silver but also because interest rates rose to 8 per cent soon after their purchase; they were a poor investment and could only be sold at a loss. Unfortunately, the bank had invested around £770 000 in these purchases and the depreciation of this amount needed to be covered by additional transfers to special reserves. Further declines in the exchange rate led the board to abandon their previous optimistic attitude towards silver and from 1883 the bank announced its intention of only holding a small proportion, if any, of its London reserves in silver.

This change of heart may have stemmed from the change in management in 1882. In that year the long-standing chairman, George Garden Nicol, stepped down, to be replaced by a chairmanship held in rotation by members of the board. Simultaneously, the bank's chief manager, David Robertson, resigned, to be replaced by William Jackson, who had served the bank for many years (including a stint as the bank's inspector). The shareholders' discontent with the board was vociferous in the early 1880s and culminated in the resignation of the entire board in 1883: they sought and obtained re-election *en bloc* to demonstrate that they could still command shareholder confidence.

Despite the periodic losses and the silver problem, the 1870s and 1880s were periods of steady business for the Chartered Mercantile. The bank had pursued its business cautiously and built up reserves to counteract the effects of the depreciation of its capital; by 1890 it had amassed reserves of £250 000. This process was aided by the bank's announcement in 1884 that dividends would be limited to 5 per cent per annum until the depreciation of capital had been made up. Although the total number of the branches remained the same, the bank closed its outlying agencies in Yokohama, Foochow and Hankow, and opened up new offices in Rangoon, Batavia (Jakarta) and Malacca.

Some of the bank's competitors had not been so conservative. The Oriental Bank Corporation, one of the largest exchange banks, had been plagued by bad debts and had incurred large losses in the aftermath of the 1878 depression which wiped out its reserves. None the less it had continued to pay its traditionally high dividends. It struggled into the 1880s but eventually failed in 1884 and was reconstructed as the New Oriental Bank Corporation. Its failure highlighted the wisdom of the Chartered Mercantile's management in taking a prudent, conservative approach. On the other hand, while pursuing its steady course, the bank had been overtaken by some of its rivals – for instance the Chartered Bank of India, London and Australia, whose total assets overtook those of the Chartered Mercantile during the 1870s. By 1890 the bank was still the third largest Eastern bank, behind the Hongkong Bank and the Chartered but ahead of rivals such as the Agra Bank and the National Bank of India.

A combination of depressed market conditions, management misjudgement and bad luck eventually resulted in the need to reconstruct the bank in 1892. A sudden fall in the price of silver and several failures among the merchant firms made 1891 a disastrous year for the Eastern trades. By June 1891 the bank had to appropriate around £125 000, half of the reserve fund, to cover losses which had been incurred mainly at the Singapore branch. This situation was compounded by the collapse of the New Oriental Bank Corporation, which was already being anticipated in the early part of 1892; the bank eventually stopped payment in June 1892. Inevitably all the Eastern banks suffered from the drop in public confidence and the subsequent run on the banks. The Mercantile was especially vulnerable to this drain in support, given its bad losses the previous year, between December 1891 and June 1892 the total value of current deposits kept with the bank halved in value.

Added to this already precarious situation, the bank was unlucky enough to be the victim of a massive fraud in the first half of 1892. An old and established customer, Beyts, Craig & Co. of Bombay and London, had sold bills to the bank that were backed up by false bills of lading. Although the Bombay agent of the bank had been given a limit by head office on bills drawn on the London office of Beyts, Craig & Co., he had continued to take bills drawn on third parties. The bank brought proceedings against the partners of the firm and, although these resulted in prison sentences for those involved, the bank still sustained losses in the region of £75 000.

By the summer of 1892 it was obvious to the directors that to continue business under the present charter was impossible. Apart from the huge erosion of the bank's capital in terms of sterling, there was a loss of confidence in the bank which was significantly reducing deposits, note issue and business generally. Unfortunately, the terms of the bank's charter did not allow it to raise fresh capital easily: the paid-up capital could not be written down as a precursor to issuing new shares, nor could the bank issue preference shares. The chief manager and directors conferred with the bank's solicitors and in October 1892 a circular was sent out to shareholders outlining a suggested reconstruction scheme.

This scheme was discussed by the shareholders at the half-yearly meeting in October. The major points of the scheme were the establishment of a new bank registered under the Companies Acts which would take over the current business, assets and liabilities of the existing bank. The new bank's capital of £1.5 million would be composed of shares in the old bank (which would be converted into B shares) and new A shares which would be entitled to a preferential dividend of 5 per cent. The meeting appointed a reconstruction committee composed of some of the most powerful and prestigious shareholders to consider the proposals. After some minor modifications the committee approved the scheme and the old shareholders rallied round. By 31 December 1892 all 15 000 new A shares were placed, of which over 90 per cent were bought by existing shareholders.

The Mercantile Bank of India Ltd held its first board meeting on 2 December 1892. The winding up of the Chartered Mercantile Bank by voluntary liquidation began on 3 February 1893; the liquidation included the surrender of the royal charter and the right to issue bank notes. By agreement with the liquidators, the business and goodwill of the old bank passed to the Mercantile Bank which commenced trading the next day. In addition to the physical buildings, the staff and the customers that the old bank bequeathed to its successor, it also passed on less tangible assets: its culture, procedures, administration and its attitude to risk.

The bank's centre of control was the management at head office in London and the board of directors. The directors were traditionally men who were closely involved with Eastern trading businesses and whose expertise and knowledge were spread over the geographical areas in which the bank operated. Thus, for instance, the board often included a director involved in the Ceylon tea trade, another with interests in China, someone with Singapore connections and at least two from Indian trading houses. In addition to these business connections, there was often one member of the board with a strong colonial government pedigree. The directors met every week to discuss a wide range of business, including the approval of branch limits for certain transactions such as bills purchased, staff matters such as appointments, and property issues. Additionally, committees of two or three directors were often appointed to inspect in more detail certain aspects of the bank's business, including branch returns.

The day-to-day running of the bank was in the hands of the London management, comprising the chief manager, the secretary, sub-manager, chief accountant and often a roving inspector of branches. This small group was the pivot for the overall control and direction of the bank's operations in all its offices. Guidelines were issued for the direction of business, and operations were carefully monitored to ensure that they conformed to these guidelines and to the limits laid down for various types of business. These limits included the amount each branch could be exposed to a single customer and for how long loans could be made. As the bank matured, these procedures were improved and refined whenever weakness became apparent, for instance, in response to bad losses or fraud. After the losses of the 1860s the bank was anxious to curtail expenditure and appointed a committee of the board to examine minutely the expenses of each branch. From 1866 each branch was required to produce a fortnightly statement, which was sent to head office detailing all operations down to the cost of the last postage stamp. This close checking of expenditure was a routine which became entrenched in the bank's procedures and culture.

The patterns of staff recruitment, training, promotion, pay and conditions were also firmly in place by the 1890s. From the 1860s all executive staff were recruited through the London office, where they remained for a period of around three years before being sent to their first posting in the East. Many of those recruited already had experience in a bank or commercial firm and were often introduced by directors or senior officers. A significant number of the recruits were Scots with experience in a Scottish bank – between 1882 and 1891 17 of the 33 officers who joined the bank in London with some banking or commercial experience were Scots. Officers could expect promotion to the rank of accountant after around ten years in the East and after another five could begin to be considered for the post of manager or agent. The executive staff all shared similar backgrounds and the common experience as London juniors. Their numbers never exceeded 50 after the 1860s and they were a close-knit group who were expected to imbue the bank overseas with its particularly 'British' flavour.

In addition to these executive officers, there were hundreds of local staff whose positions ranged from head clerks and ledger-keepers to messengers and watchmen. The most important member of the local staff was the shroff (in India and the Straits) or compradore (in China), who was the intermediary between the bank and the local business community. The shroff was generally a prominent and wealthy member of this group and was responsible for introducing new business, for which he was often paid a commission. Additionally, the shroff was in charge of the cash department and was required to guarantee the fidelity of his staff. By 1893 each branch had many long-serving members of local staff who were knowledgable about the individual branch systems and day-to-day routines. They provided continuity of procedure and training to the juniors who arrived fresh, and inexperienced in local conditions and practices, from London.

The bank's core business was the finance of trade between India, the East and Europe, supporting the export of commodities such as cotton from India and tea from Ceylon, and the import of manufactured goods from Britain. Exchange business was the single most important element of the bank's business and included the purchase and discount of bills of exchange, the sale of drafts drawn in different currencies and telegraphic remittances of money. From the 1880s onwards the bank also became more involved in loans and advances which earned interest and commission (see Figure 1.1). These were often connected with the commodities whose export the bank financed – for instance the bank would advance to cotton estates on the security of crops under cultivation; the advances would be repaid on the sale of the crops to an agency house which would then use the bank for the exchange business involved in their export. However, the bank was keen to keep long-term commitments such as advances to a minimum and preferred to use money for exchange business where it could be turned over quickly and used for other transactions. This attitude was instilled in the staff so that any business undertaken needed to include an exchange element.

These banking transactions were financed by the capital allotted to each branch and the resources that they could garner locally in deposits. Branches could also supplement these sources of finance through loans from London office, from other branches or through inter-bank borrowing. In India this often meant borrowing from the three presidency banks – the Banks of Bengal, Bombay and Madras – which had all been set up with government involvement and which performed some of the functions of a central bank, including transacting government business and issuing notes. The demands of each branch for finance would fluctuate according to the seasonal demands for money, determined by the growing seasons for different crops of tea, coffee, cotton and rice. Each branch also needed to cover its exchange positions by buying, selling and holding silver coin and bullion, rupee paper and drafts in different currencies. The limits for exchange commitments were laid down by head office; it was a tenet of exchange banking instilled into officers that they had to be able to cover any forward commitments. The types of banking transactions that the bank undertook left it open to risk in two main areas: exchange-rate fluctuations and over-exposure in certain commodities. Accurate knowledge of customers, commodities and market conditions to counteract these risks was an essential part of the system.

By 1893 the Mercantile was an established part of the banking scene in India, the Straits and China, but its success beyond reconstruction could not be guaranteed. The Oriental Bank Corporation had never recovered its former glory after it was forced to reconstruct in 1884, and this memory was surely fresh in the minds of the shareholders, directors, staff and customers of the new Mercantile when it opened its

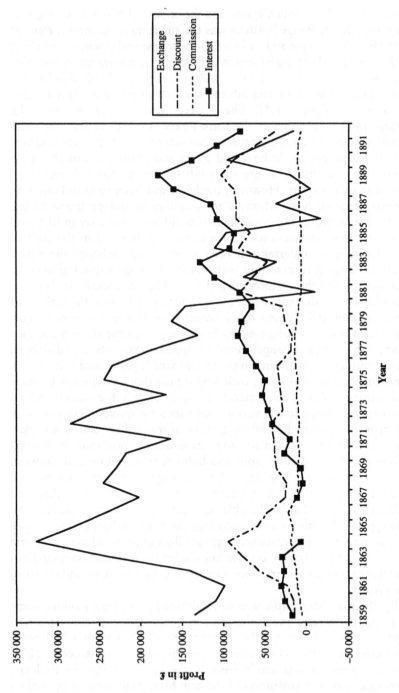

1.1 Chartered Mercantile Bank: selected profit and loss credit items, 1859–92

doors for business in February 1893. William Jackson, the last chief manager of the old Chartered Mercantile, was busy reassuring shareholders as the reconstruction took place: 'I see nothing to prevent the reconstructed bank having a prosperous future', he wrote to one shareholder early in January 1893.[3] In reality, Jackson knew that the unpredictable and volatile nature of Eastern exchange banking made it impossible to prophesy with any certainty. As he wrote to a fellow member of staff: 'I hope the management in the future will be more fortunate.'[4]

CHAPTER TWO

Rehabilitation, 1893–1913

If the shareholders of the Mercantile Bank of India had been launching an entirely new bank in 1893, they could not have chosen a less promising moment. The early 1890s were not fertile ground for new institutions in British finance. Although existing companies continued to expand their branch networks in this phase, entrepreneurs and shareholders were reluctant to establish new banks and insurance companies. Only three new banks were overseas ventures in the style of the Mercantile. The African Banking Corporation (1891), the Bank of British West Africa (1894) and the Bank of Mauritius (1894) were, like the Mercantile, typical 'free-standing' companies with British headquarters and overseas operations. Like the Mercantile, they were also closely linked to earlier projects or to local trading groups and were not entirely 'new' banks.

The Baring crisis of 1890 had seriously shaken the confidence of investors throughout the financial community in London. The downfall of Barings' international commitments also swayed markets away from overseas risks towards the apparently safer option of domestic industrial and municipal investment. The clear warnings over international involvements were underlined by the financial and political crises in South America in the early 1890s, the failure of the English Bank of the River Plate in 1891 and, in the East, the collapse of the New Oriental Bank Corporation in 1892.[1] Overseas risks became yet more obvious when, in April and May 1893, the Australian banking sector was plunged into crisis: of the 64 banks operating in Australia before the crisis, 34 closed permanently. Those which failed or were temporarily suspended included London-based banks with large numbers of shareholders, notably the English, Scottish and Australian Chartered Bank and the London Chartered Bank of Australia.

With investors' confidence so weakened, newcomers to banking could not pretend to be sure of the business outlook. In the Mercantile's sphere of activity, in particular, there was little enthusiasm for new ventures. 'There is practically no market at home just now for Indian investments', Jardine Skinner's London office told its Calcutta managers in 1892.[2] In India itself, the long- and short-term decline in silver prices was accelerating and jeopardizing the prospects for the sustained recovery of the Eastern markets. No less than 80 per cent of India's external trade was with gold-using countries and its silver rupee currency was continually prey to hoarding and speculation.[3] 'Bankers and insurance companies who have money out in the silver countries', warned the economist Robert Giffen in 1893, 'have been forced to endure a great depreciation in their silver assets, which must be recognised when the amounts are converted into gold ... and thus to face a great loss.'[4]

The immediate outlook in India was alarming. In 1893 the Herschell Committee, appointed to review the currency and exchange situation in India, recommended in its final report a number of measures which it hoped would stabilize the exchange rate. These included closing the mints to the free coining of rupees but accepting gold in exchange for rupees at a fixed rate of 1s. 4d. to the rupee. On 26 June 1893 the mints were duly closed. Unfortunately, the Mercantile Bank already had silver in transit destined for the mints. Although the bank appealed to the government to make an exception for such circumstances, these pleas fell on deaf ears and the bank ultimately lost £12 700.[5] The Indian government's reasoning was that it was impossible to discriminate between shipments of bullion in the normal course of banking business and consignments shipped by speculators.

In these circumstances it was crucial that the Mercantile was *not* a newcomer to overseas banking. Although its authorized capital of £1.5 million, with £555 000 paid up in A and B shares, represented a new start, its shareholders were essentially the same group that had subscribed to the Chartered Mercantile in its final years.[6] The B shareholders were all former investors in the old bank and no less than 91 per cent of the A shares (the new capital) was provided by ex-Chartered Mercantile shareholders. The capital structure of the new Mercantile gave the appearance of continuity, which in itself was an advantage over any new entrant to banking. The Mercantile Bank's branches and buildings were also inherited from the old bank; Rangoon branch, which closed in September 1892, was the only office that was not retained.

The more searching questions about the Mercantile's permanence related to the quality of the bank's staff and management, and its ability to retain its customers after the reconstruction. Should these factors have been in any doubt, then the capital value of the new bank and the trust of its shareholders would have quickly succumbed in the hostile banking climate of the 1890s. Here, although at least one shareholder had argued for 'a clean sweep',[7] the wholesale replacement of the directors, management and staff of the old bank was never seriously contemplated. There was a great deal that was still familiar about the face which the Mercantile Bank presented to the world. The new board comprised only six members: Sir Alexander Wilson (as chairman), R. W. Chamney, William Jackson, F. W. Lunau, J. A. Maitland and Thomas Scott. Maitland and Scott had been directors and Jackson had been chief manager of the Chartered Mercantile. Wilson, Chamney and Lunau had all been prominent shareholders.

The overhaul of management was more obvious. William Jackson, chief manager of the Chartered Mercantile, was not in any way in disgrace as a result of the liquidation. He joined the board of the new bank and remained active as a director until his death in August 1908. However, Jackson was closely identified with the old bank and, at the age of about 60 and with 36 years' service with the Chartered Mercantile, Jackson did not have youth on his side. He recruited his successor, James Campbell, in what Muirhead describes as a 'very relaxed' fashion.[8] 'The work is interesting and not over hard & I think would suit you & you it', Jackson told Campbell on 3 December 1892.[9]

James Campbell, then aged 45, brought an entirely fresh face to the leadership of the bank. After serving his apprenticeship with the Royal Bank of Scotland at Sanquhar, Dumfries, he had worked for the National Bank of India between 1867 and 1884 in Hong Kong, Shanghai and Calcutta (where he was acquainted with Sir Alexander Wilson). From 1884 he was secretary of the English, Scottish and Australian Chartered Bank in London, making him one of the small circle of senior overseas bankers in London.[10] That circle also included his brother Robert, a former inspector in the Chartered Mercantile. Robert had become joint general manager of the National Bank of India in 1877, was general manager between 1880 and 1892, and gave outstanding service as chairman of that bank from 1903 until his death in 1924.[11]

James Campbell's appointment was the only occasion in the history of the bank that an outsider had been brought in at its head. All other chief managers, both before and since, were men who had worked their way up through the bank. It was an appointment which sent a message of intent to shareholders and customers that the management of the reconstructed bank would not simply continue the methods – and mistakes – of the old bank. The arrival of a new chief manager in February 1893, nevertheless, was balanced by a remarkable continuity in the other senior management and staff. Although the senior officers of the Chartered Mercantile (including William Jackson) had been given notice of dismissal by the old bank in October 1892, they had been assured that if the reconstruction was successful, 'the notices to officers will in most cases be withdrawn'.[12] In the interim staff were discouraged from accepting outside appointments.

Valuable as the continuities were in shareholdings, management and staff, the Mercantile's most precious bequest from the old bank was its muster of contacts and customers. In the short term the loyalty of customers was made plain in the list of directors. Eastern trading houses, with interests ranging from exports and imports to insurance, shipping and utilities, dominated the boardroom. The Jardine network of companies (represented by Sir Alexander Wilson), Blyth, Greene, Jourdain and Co. (Chamney), Guthrie and Co. (Scott) and Maitland and Co. (Maitland) had all been long-standing customers of the Chartered Mercantile. Jardines, Blyths and Maitlands had also acted as the official agents of the bank.[13] Leading clients were also present in strength at shareholders' meetings during and immediately after the reconstruction of the bank. The board minutes and correspondence of the reconstructed Mercantile confirm that the old bank's customers continued to apply for and to receive the traditional facilities of an Eastern exchange bank.

Similarly, the reconstructed bank was able to rely upon the old network of bankers and agencies. The London Joint Stock Bank, which had acted as the Chartered Mercantile's banker in the capital city since 1854, continued all its correspondent facilities for the new Mercantile. While not one of the largest banks in the City, the London Joint Stock Bank had earned a solid reputation in correspondent banking, as a long-standing member of the London Clearing House, and as banker to a myriad of stockbrokers, lawyers and other City opinion-formers.[14]

The Mercantile's impressive collection of loyalties could not in itself guarantee the rehabilitation of the business. In the short run Campbell's first major challenge was to match running costs to the reduced resources and earning power in comparison with the old bank. Certainly the Chartered Mercantile's expenses of £75 000 in 1892 could not be maintained. Initially the board debated reductions in the number of branches and staff. They were especially concerned with each branch's ability to attract local deposits and to fund its own business, as they did not wish to risk any of the bank's new capital in the vulnerable silver currency areas. By May 1893 it was already obvious that the branches in China and the Straits were recovering only slowly from the crisis of confidence brought about both by the reconstruction of the bank and by the more general distrust occasioned by the Australian banking crisis. As a result the decision was taken to shut the Malacca and Batavia (Jakarta) branches.[15] The situation in China was complicated by the fact that the Hong Kong and Shanghai branches were used in exchange dealings with the Singapore branch and were also channels in the silver bullion trade. Shanghai branch was also hampered with an expensive lease on its premises in Nanking Road which was costing the bank £1300 a year. A compromise was reached: Hong Kong branch was to remain open but the manager's salary was reduced. Shanghai branch remained open with just one member of staff until the summer of 1894, when the bank appointed Jardine, Matheson & Co. to act as their agents.[16]

By 1894 the expenses for the whole bank had been reduced by a third to £50 000.[17] Further savings were achieved in 1896 by the surrender of the lease to 65 Old Broad Street, the home of the old bank since 1866. The Mercantile then moved its head office to 'other convenient and suitable offices' at 40 Threadneedle Street, where the landlords were the National Provincial Bank. The annual rent of £2000 represented a useful saving on the £6000 annual rent at Old Broad Street.[18]

Even if costs could be controlled in this way, the survival of the new bank depended upon its ability to maintain or increase earnings. Here Campbell was ready to impose a firm management approach. He judged that many of the local managers did not see that the reconstruction was a precarious, risky affair and not simply a licence to continue as before. A sharp reminder was needed.

At the time of the reconstruction the most important members of the Eastern staff were the managers of Bombay (Henry Fidler), Calcutta (Reginald Murray) and Singapore (George Murray). One of Campbell's first acts in February 1893 was to write to Fidler and Reginald Murray, informing them that they should live above their branches so that each day they could read and digest all messages from London and think over what needed to be done before going into the bank. He then told them how they should be running their branches and operating their exchange positions, guided by figures that he himself had used when he had been manager of the National Bank of India's branch in Calcutta.[19] This advice was not gratefully received by Murray in Calcutta. Murray had been with the bank since 1864, had been a manager since 1877, and may even have thought of himself as the next chief manager. His initial correspondence with Campbell was fiery. He accused Campbell of being out of touch with Indian conditions and told him that the National Bank practised unsound banking – obviously a slur on Campbell himself.[20] The clash ended with Murray's resignation in March 1893.

The branch closures and other economies of 1893 had resulted in only five job losses (excluding Reginald Murray), and by the end of 1893 the total Eastern staff numbered just under 30. This represented a significant reduction from the average level of 40 to 45 staff in the period between the mid-1860s and 1892. While continuity was maintained in the managerships of Singapore, Colombo and Madras, Murray's resignation from Calcutta now brought problems of leadership to the bank in India. Henry Fidler moved from Bombay to take up the vacant position as manager at Calcutta and his replacement was Robert Kennedy from the bank's Shanghai branch. Neither of these two senior managers could claim any great managerial experience. Fidler was only 33 and had been manager at Bombay for only a year. Kennedy was even younger at 29 and, although he had been acting manager in Shanghai for two years, he had no management experience in India. Many of Campbell's early letters to his two senior Indian managers, with their pages of instructions and coaching, demonstrate the extent to which they were newcomers to dealing with exchange. Campbell was especially displeased at Kennedy's dabbling in long-term forward contracts, which he thought amounted to speculation. Kennedy was recalled to London in 1894 to explain his actions to the directors, and eventually resigned in 1896 after he was told that the board did not consider him fit to take charge of another branch. Fidler also proved a liability to the bank in his early years as manager at Calcutta. Campbell wrote to the relief Calcutta manager in 1896 that 'All my schooling of Fidler last year did not prevent his operations proving disastrous.'[21] After a year's furlough, however, Fidler was reappointed manager in Calcutta and he remained there until his resignation in 1902. The Mercantile's small staff numbers did not leave the directors many options when it came to choosing their managers, and their early appointments in India demonstrated how this could have serious consequences for the fortunes of a branch when its manager was inexperienced or ineffectual.

Campbell was also prepared to intervene in routine lending decisions. With its reduced resources the bank was required to lower its limits for bills at each branch. With this in mind, and also as a control measure in the light of the frauds suffered in 1892, a general review of all limits was undertaken in the spring of 1893. In April Campbell advised George Murray in Singapore that 'with diminished resources we must take smaller risks and curtail limits all round'.[22] It was a policy which clearly ran the risk of antagonizing customers who wanted to retain the larger limits allowed by the old bank and could have forced the vitally needed custom to go elsewhere.

The centrepiece of these early management initiatives was Campbell's review of the quality of the branches' business. First-hand appraisal was needed and Campbell and his directors promptly invited William Jackson to tour the Eastern branches. The itinerary for the former chief manager covered all the Mercantile's branches except Kandy and Galle.

A thorough inspection of the bank's branches by a senior and respected figure in the bank was a tried and tested method to appease the anxiety of shareholders and customers. The Hongkong Bank, for example, had sent David McLean, its respected ex-Shanghai manager and then sub-manager in London, on such an inspection when the bank faced a crisis in 1874.[23] Jackson's tasks included the usual practices of checking and reviewing the limits at each branch and reporting on loans or overdrafts which had insufficient or irregular security. In addition, during his time in India Jackson was required to report to head office the opinions of the Indian managers as to the possibility of placing

Table 2.1   William Jackson's tour of inspection, 1893

Date	Branch itinerary	Date	Branch itinerary
April 15	Bombay	July 7	Batavia
April 19	Calcutta	July 31	Penang, closing branch
May 12	Penang	August 16	Colombo
May 16	Singapore	September 5	Madras
May 31	Hong Kong	September 12	Calcutta
June 9	Shanghai	September 22	Bombay
Mid-June	Singapore	October 10	London, board meeting

silver capital in India. Inevitably he reported that all managers thought it an 'inopportune' time. The letters from Campbell in London show that Jackson was charged with closing those branches deemed too costly by the board and arranging for the transfer of their staff.[24] Jackson was also given responsibility for managing the changes in staff forced by Murray's resignation in March, including the dispatch of their orders and giving advice where needed. For example, Jackson visited Bombay on his return home to discuss matters with Robert Kennedy, who had just been made manager of the branch and was inexperienced in Indian banking at a senior level. Jackson reported on the staff he encountered on his trip to the East and his recommendations prompted the dismissal of two members of staff on his return to London. Jackson's maxim was that it was not worth keeping members of staff who were not eligible for promotion on the payroll of the bank.[25]

James Campbell's direct and practical style of management slowly edged the new bank away from its high-risk beginnings towards comparative safety. Total assets, which for the Chartered Mercantile had been as high as £10.6 million in 1890, were less than £2.6 million in 1894 and Campbell warned his chairman early in 1896 that: 'I am afraid it will take in all a long time to make a respectable balance sheet.'[26] None the less the balance sheet total recovered to £3 million by 1897 and £3.6 million in 1899. On the earnings side, published profits of £16 000 each year in 1894 and 1895 were barely one-tenth of the levels which had been achieved by the old bank in the 1880s. Although these published earnings had doubled by 1898 and 1899, an annual profit of £31 000 was unremarkable. Consequently returns to shareholders were modest. Dividends of 5 per cent were awarded to A shareholders while B shareholders waited until 1895 for their first dividend of 2 per cent, a low return which did not rise to 4 per cent until 1900.

These first six years after the reconstruction provided a period of quarantine in which trust and assurance could be built up between the bank and its customers, its shareholders and its agents. In the longer run, from about 1900, the bank's performance showed a more striking improvement. Total assets increased to £4.1 million by 1903 and were then lifted to over £6.1 million in 1907 and to over £8 million in 1912 and 1913. Published profits reached £60 000 by 1904 (four times their level a decade earlier), exceeded £70 000 each year between 1906 and 1909 and then advanced from £83 000 in 1910 to £111 000 in 1913. In reality the bank's core earnings were even more substantial. 'Real' profits – after taxation and bad debts were written off but before head office adjustments and transfers to reserves – ran at an average level 17 per cent higher than the published totals between 1910 and 1913 (Appendix Two).

Shareholders now began to benefit from the recovery. While dividends from A shares were progressively raised from 5 per cent in 1906 to 8 per cent in 1912, B share dividends were at last paid at a rate equal to the A shares from 1903 onwards. A longer-term reassurance was the board's decision to make payments to a published reserve fund in 1896. The first payment into the fund was the £10 000 surplus from the 'unrealised assets account' (a contingency account created at the time of the reconstruction). Initially these published transfers were only £10 000 each year from 1898 but much larger payments were made after 1903, notably in 1907 (£40 000) and 1911 and 1912 (£50 000 in each year). These awards lifted the reserve fund from nil in 1893–96 to £465 000 in 1913. This was a larger cushion than had ever been created by the old bank, whose maximum reserve had reached only £250 000. In addition, in 1897 the directors considered the bank's performance to be robust enough to create an inner reserve or contigency account. The first payment of £22 363 in 1897 was regularly supplemented and inside funds had reached £188 032 by 1913.

The Mercantile's strong performance in the early years of the century did not place it among the giants of overseas banking. Its assets and earnings were dwarfed by the Hongkong Bank and the Chartered Bank, as Figure 2.1 demonstrates. Its ranking nevertheless improved steadily. By 1910 the Mercantile's assets of £7.59 million were in the same range as London overseas banks such as the English, Scottish and Australian (£8.73 million), the National Bank of New Zealand (£6.21 million), the Anglo-Egyptian (£5.19 million) and the Colonial (£4.10 million). Its total assets were markedly higher than those of specialist overseas banks such as the Imperial Bank of Persia (£2.75 million) and the Bank of British West Africa (£1.81 million).

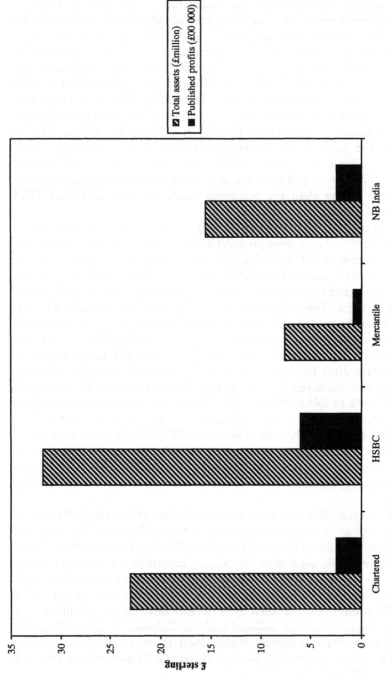

2.1 Eastern banks: total assets and published profits, 1910

The upturn in performance reflected the board and management's readiness to take on a more expansive and even opportunistic business role. That new confidence became public in 1900 when, in order to fill the gap left by the failure of the Agra Bank earlier that year, the directors agreed to open a new branch in Karachi, the first attempt at branch extension since the reconstruction in 1893. Five years later a sub-branch was opened at Penang, where the old bank had maintained an office between 1860 and 1893 and had retained Boustead and Co. as agents after 1893.

Campbell's most determined effort to win new business was the acquisition of the Bank of Calcutta in 1906. This bank had been established in 1895 and it was primarily a vehicle for the trading interests of the Yule family. The principal shareholder was David Yule, while George Yule and Co. acted as its London agent. This linkage with a single trading house was characteristic of a number of other British overseas banks of this generation. The Bank of British West Africa, for instance, was connected with Alfred Jones's Liverpool interests, and the Eastern Bank was founded in 1909 by the Sassoon family's businesses. The Bank of Calcutta, operating from its single office in Clive Row, Calcutta, held assets of Rs 14 million in 1901. Although this volume could not be compared with the business of the Allahabad Bank (Rs 28 million in assets), it was comparable with long-established banks such as Commercial Bank of India (with Rs 14 million in assets) or the Bank of Upper India (Rs 12 million).

The acquisition of the Bank of Calcutta was completed in March 1906 with remarkably little fuss and no interruption of business. The Mercantile, which paid £6667 for the goodwill directly out of that year's gross profits, was permitted to select which accounts it wished to transfer. Those chosen included the Monarch and Howrah flour mills, the Delta Jute Mills, and the tea companies managed by W. Cresswell and Co. The business of the Mercantile's branch at Calcutta doubled as a result, an achievement which was recognized in the award of a bonus of Rs 5000 to Percy Mould, manager at Calcutta, and his staff. The Bank of Calcutta was eventually placed in liquidation in March 1908, by which time the bulk of its business (but apparently not its staff) had migrated to the Mercantile's office.

The purchase of the Bank of Calcutta was a small affair in comparison with some of the great alliances then being negotiated in British domestic banking.[27] Yet for the Mercantile the acquisition brought a major gain in its Calcutta business and the valuable development of its link with the Yule empire. David Yule himself was party to the legal settlement, which specified that he should join the Mercantile board. Subsequently he became an active and influential director. He was also an important source of market information, as he kept up his habit of spending three to four months each year travelling to the East. Subsequently the Mercantile was advertised as banker to new Yule companies such as the Kelantan Copra Co. Ltd, which began life in 1913 with an open advance of £23 000 from the bank.

The gain in assets and profitability after the Calcutta acquisition enabled the directors to lift dividends to 6 per cent in 1907 – the first rise for the A shareholders since the reconstruction – and to award a 10 per cent bonus to the bank's staff. The board also renewed its interest in the branch network as stability returned to the silver currency areas and the international economy continued its remarkable and sustained growth in the years before the First World War. In the rupee areas in particular the Indian Government Currency Scheme of 1899, by making the sovereign and half-sovereign legal tender, had introduced meaningful controls over the exchange rate for the rupee.

Against this background the Mercantile's extension of its branch network was partly a return to familiar territory. The possibility of reopening in Rangoon and establishing an office at Howrah was discussed as early as October 1907 and the Rangoon branch and the Howrah sub-office to Calcutta were eventually established in the autumn of 1909. An office was also opened at Kuala Lumpur in November 1909, responding to the rapid increase in customers' exports of rubber and the multiplicity of new company formations at that time. In answer to the Singapore manager's pleas for an office in the state of Kelantan, the Mercantile was the first bank to open in Kota Bahru in 1911. In 1912 the board agreed to open a branch at Delhi, the newly designated capital of the Empire of India. Percy Mould, manager at Calcutta, was diverted from a tour of inspection to find premises in Delhi and to oversee the opening of the new branch.

This more ambitious approach to the branch network was matched by the extension of the Mercantile's official agencies. New agencies were established in 1913 at Cheriban, Java (where the agents were the Netherlands India Handelsbank) and Manila and Cebu in the Philippines (where Ker and Co. were appointed agents). A counterpart to this proliferation was the bank's willingness to act as a correspondent bank. Its new correspondent links ranged from the Anglo-Japanese Bank (1906) to the Bank of Abyssinia, Addis Ababa (1909).

Initiatives of these kinds could no longer be attempted in green-field territory. Eastern banking was increasingly competitive and international, and the Mercantile was only one of many new entrants in some of its markets. At Delhi, for example, where only five banks had been active at the beginning of the century, eleven banks were in business by 1913. The Mercantile also faced new competitors. The Eastern Bank, founded in 1909, then opened branches in Bombay and Calcutta. The Mercantile responded by raising the borrowing limits for E. D. Sassoon & Co., the prime mover in the Eastern Bank. In addition the bank found itself protecting its own name against competitors. In 1909, in order to clear up misunderstanding in Bombay, the bank published notices to disassociate itself from the Mercantile Bank of London Ltd; this British domestic bank had been formed in 1891 and was to go into liquidation in 1914. Two years later, the bank was objecting to the use of 'Mercantile' in the name of the Kanayakubja Mercantile Bank of India.

These disputes over names are a reminder that the Mercantile's markets both at home and abroad were not highly regulated. The acquisition of the Bank of Calcutta had not needed official permission in London or Calcutta. It was sufficient at this stage to ensure that audited annual accounts and other returns were in accordance with the Companies Acts. From 1911, when the bank resumed the issue of bank notes in Hong Kong, it was also necessary to report to the local authorities both the amount of notes in circulation and the bank's cover for its note issue.

The bank's growth and improved performance after 1900 owed much to the expansive tactics of acquisition, new branching and wider agency links. However, the performance of the major branches was not uniform. Throughout the history of the bank, the primacy of London branch was maintained. Its assets of £1.78 million in 1900 represented 50.6 per cent of the bank's total balance sheet and ten years later the total assets of £3.67 million took a 48.2 per cent share of the business. Similarly, London office achieved the lion's share of earnings, even though that contribution fell towards the end of this phase. Net profits of £20 401 amounted to 40.2 per cent of net branch profits in 1900 and, at £34 484, 30.5 per cent ten years later.

Certainly London office was central to the bank's pattern of business. Its managers and staff were responsible for the liquidity and financial operations of the bank, particularly the management of its accounts with the Bank of England and the London Joint Stock Bank. They were also the main point of contact for the British trading houses and companies which required finance for their shipments. However, London's assets and earnings reflected the business which was made possible by the overseas branches. Its assets were held on behalf of the branches and its profits were derived from payments to and from the branches and their customers. The more telling comparison of the source of earnings was the assets and net profits of the overseas branches themselves. In terms of total assets of the overseas branches, Bombay (24.6 per cent), Calcutta (24.5 per cent), Singapore (15.7 per cent), Hong

Kong (11.6 per cent) and Colombo (10.6 per cent) led the 1900 rankings. Ten years later Calcutta branch was clearly the largest overseas business, with 30.7 per cent of total assets as a result of the 1906 acquisition, followed by Bombay (22.0 per cent). Colombo, with 16.5 per cent of the bank's assets, had by then moved ahead of Singapore (11.7 per cent). These principal overseas branches, unlike London and the deposit-taking agency at Edinburgh, were all 'lending' offices with a significant margin of assets over liabilities.

On the earnings side, there were also changes in the position of the overseas branches in the first years of the century. Calcutta, Singapore and (to a lesser extent) Madras consistently ranked among the most profitable Mercantile branches, as they had done in the lifetime of the Chartered Mercantile Bank. Bombay, after its inconsistent long-term performance before 1893, was one of the most productive branches by 1910. It was perhaps a sign of the Mercantile's new-found solidity that the misfortunes of individual branches could now be absorbed without great effect on the overall results. Singapore office suffered losses in 1908 as a result of local Chinese firms' forward purchases on China. Hong Kong branch, which had been one of the top six earners before 1893, recorded a series of heavy losses between 1907 and 1912. In 1911 and 1912, in particular, the bank was in serious dispute with the Hong Kong compradore (the key Chinese official in the branch) and his staff, but the resulting losses made little impact on the Mercantile's overall performance.

By far the most prominent change in these rankings was the emergence of Colombo. The old bank's Ceylon business, apart from a brief spurt in the mid-1870s, had barely featured in terms of profitability. In 1889 and 1890, Colombo had incurred losses of £18 000 and £32 000 respectively, which were the worst losses incurred by a single branch since the disasters at Bombay between 1866 and 1870.[28] By 1900, in contrast, it was the most profitable overseas branch of the new bank. In 1910 its net profits of £45 000 even surpassed London's earnings of £35 000 and by 1914 the branch was achieving net profits of nearly £50 000, nearly five times the level in 1900 and 1901.

The surge in business at Colombo over the previous decade, and particularly from 1910, made Ceylon a strong element in the bank's longer-term recovery and growth in the years before the First World War. Colombo's success was built upon attracting the accounts of large tea estates, for instance the Empire of India and Ceylon Tea Company Ltd, and agency houses such as Finlay Muir and Co. and C. W. Mackie. This portfolio of business was also maintained by an ambitious and almost aggressive lending position. From about 1900 the offices at Colombo, Kandy and Galle consistently held a higher proportion of their assets in loans and overdrafts than the other Eastern branches, and in 1907 the board explicitly supported Colombo office in increasing its limits on holdings of bills. By 1910 loans and overdrafts comprised 70 per cent of Colombo's assets, in comparison with approximately 60 per cent at other overseas branches (the much smaller Penang office, with a level of 72 per cent in that year, was the one exception to this pattern). The Colombo manager was even confident enough to propose the acquisition of the local Bank of Uva in November 1909. Although the board declined this chance, it was a sign of Colombo's importance within the bank that the local manager could volunteer such an initiative.

Changes in the character of the bank's business also contributed to its growth and performance after about 1900. The great commodity trades of cotton, tea, coffee and jute continued to dominate commerce and finance in the East, with rubber from Malaya also emerging as an important export towards the end of this period. In addition to meeting the steady demand of these major commodity trades, however, the Mercantile was increasingly adventurous in the spread of its business and risks. This trend was reflected in the confirmed credits granted by the bank. These credits, which were distinct from credits given directly by the bank to importers or exporters, were agreements to honour credits given by trading firms to exporters.[29] They were a vital lubricant for international trade in this period. In effect they delegated the timing and scale of lending to trading houses and their agents and also gave assurance of payment to the exporter.[30]

The total annual value of the bank's confirmed credits grew from a level of £313 020 in 1900 to £951 748 by 1910. While this activity represented only some 10 per cent of the bank's total assets at any one time, the selection and approval of credits was treated with more care than any other aspect of its business. Each board meeting was presented with a list of credits which required confirmation and – so far as can be judged from the minutes – these decisions occupied the largest part of each meeting. The credit facilities ranged from as little as £100 to as much as £30 000 (for the Calcutta agents of the Majuli Tea Company Ltd in November 1900) and £50 000 (in favour of A. H. Alden and Co. for credits to C. W. Mackie and Co. of Colombo in December 1910). Fixed mainly in sterling, the Mercantile's credits averaged £2795 for the 112 cases in 1900, rising to an average of £5229 for the 185 cases in 1910. A period of three or six months' sight was allowed for bills presented under these credits, so as to allow time for shipment of goods. The facilities remained available to customers for six or (more commonly) twelve months.

Analysis of these credits helps to identify the bank's customers and the distribution of its business. Agency houses, as partnerships or as limited companies, dominate the lists of customers applying for credits. In 1900, for instance, the leading users of confirmed credits were: William Birch Jnr and Co. Ltd, which required eleven different credits for exporters throughout the sub-continent; Malcolm Brunker and Co. Ltd of Colombo and the Ceylon Land and Produce Company, both dealing with exports from Ceylon; Leslie and Anderson, which needed a total of seventeen credits for Calicut, Coorg, Madras, Mysore and Travancore; Henckell du Boisson and Co. of London, for business in Malaya and Travancore; and A. Wiesenfeld, for exports from Colombo, Bombay and Madras. Ten years later the business was increasingly international, with a marked rise in the number and value of credits granted to European firms. Jules Gravier of Marseilles obtained seven credits for exports from Pondicherry, while Bendit Limburger – also from Marseilles – were granted seven credits for Madras, Cuddalore and Pondicherry. The largest single customer in 1910, however, was T. Middleton and Co., which obtained sixteen credits, mostly in favour of Vencatakistnamah Chetty and Co., a Madras Chettiar banker.

The distribution of credits reflected the new importance of Ceylon exports in the business of the reconstructed bank. Ceylon was by far the largest destination for confirmed credits, with 40 per cent of the total number granted in 1900 and 32 per cent in 1910. Madras, with 19 per cent of the business in 1900 and 16 per cent in 1910, and Calcutta, with 12.5 per cent in 1900 and 11 per cent in 1910, followed well behind the Ceylon lead. Even so, in the first years of the century there was a small but significant shift to more distant markets. Whereas in 1900 all credits were devoted to the sub-continent (with the exception of single shipments from Hong Kong and Penang), ten years later the scope of business was much wider. By then the Mercantile was financing exports from Batavia (Jakarta) (eight credits), Hong Kong (six), Kuala Lumpur (eight), Singapore (five) and Beira in Mozambique (five credits). The sub-continent's share had fallen appreciably to 83 per cent of all confirmed credits.

This diversification was a sign of the bank's greater confidence in taking on new business. A similar change was evident in the Mercantile's handling of securities or collateral for the confirmed credits which it granted. Knowledge of its customers and their trade was a powerful influence on all the bank's lending decisions, to the extent that a high proportion of its credits were granted without any security. In 1900, 37.5 per cent of credits were given in this way and by 1910 that proportion had increased to 44 per cent. When these 'open' credits were not appropriate, the bank's preferred securities were bills of lading and letters of hypothecation (pledges mostly for delivery of tea, coffee or sugar) or shipping documents (for export of other produce). By 1910 there was also a greater variety of export products and shipping routes cited in the bank's securities. Examples included the export of decorticated groundnuts from Pondicherry, rubber from Colombo to New York, white Java sugar from Batavia to Karachi, and rice from Saigon to Reunion or Mauritius. The board considered each of these securities in great detail, even recording whether the shipments were by sail or by steamship.

The Mercantile Bank, like its competitors in Eastern banking, preferred actual possession of commodities when they were offered as security. This was in contrast with domestic banking where, with the exception of the special conditions of cotton trade finance, documentary proof of shipment was sufficient as a form of security. The Mercantile's managers usually insisted on 'earmarking' crops or produce and physically transferring them to the bank's own godowns or warehouses. Such securities were not always the bulky staple goods of the plantations. In June 1910, for example, the bank acquired up to £20 000 in bills 'covered by parcels of pearls to be sent to our Paris agents and held by them until payment of the bills'. In contrast, the bank was averse to many types of property security. In June 1911 – an extreme example perhaps – the board declined to lend 100 000 Hong Kong dollars on the mortgage of a Chinese theatre in Hong Kong as it 'was not of a nature for the bank to make advances upon'.

In the broader view the Mercantile Bank, by allowing an increasing number of credits without security and by being prepared to accept more variation in securities, was showing more assurance in the management of risks than had ever been possible in the earlier phases of reconstruction. By 1913 the bank was also building up customer relationships outside the traditional formula of British-linked exporters and importers. Major international shippers, in contrast to specialist firms working out of single ports, were now emerging as customers. In June 1913, for instance, the Mercantile provided a discount facility of £100 000 for the East Asiatic Company, drawing bills on the Danske Landsmanbank, Copenhagen. The company had been founded by H. N. Andersen in 1897 and by 1913 it was operating a fleet of 21 steamships as well as holding a strong hand in the trade of Burma, Siam and Malaya.[31] Later the same year and in 1914 the bank provided overdrafts at its Bombay office for Mitsui Bussan Kaisha. This offspring of Mitsui had been created in Osaka in 1876 and, in the period since setting up a shipping section in 1897, it was the pioneer of the *sogo shosha* form of diversified trading company. By 1914 Mitsui Bussan Kaisha had over 30 branches, including offices in key Eastern markets such as Shanghai, Hong Kong and Singapore.[32]

In these cases the Mercantile was establishing its credentials with a new generation of trading houses which were highly mobile and

international in their reach. Twenty years after the reconstruction of
1893 this increasingly outward-looking stance was shaping a new and
more robust identity for the bank. None the less, while the bank's
business preferences were changing, the pattern of staff and management was remarkably stable. The recruitment, training and management
of personnel continued in the new bank as it had in the old. At the
bank's overseas branches, the local staff were recruited and managed by
the shroff (or compradore in the Far East). The shroff or compradore
was responsible for as many as 50 local staff at major branches such as
Bombay and Calcutta and as few as ten at smaller branches such as
Galle in Ceylon. Clerical staff made up approximately half this complement and the remainder comprised messengers, keepers of the bank's
godowns or warehouses and (at the larger branches) bank guards. Of
the clerical staff, the head clerks of the branches were especially influential appointments. They were responsible for the book-keeping work of
each branch and they also played an essential part in the training and
management of the local staff. Unfortunately the total number of the
bank's local staff was not recorded until the 1960s but in this early
phase the total can be estimated at about 3000, including approximately 2000 clerical staff. In practice the bank's role as a local employer
was even larger, as these totals exclude the domestic staff at the houses
of managers and other Eastern staff.

The bank's European staff were recruited into the London office,
where they remained for anything between a year and five years before
being sent to their first post in the East. In the first 20 years of its life
the Mercantile sent 88 new assistants out from London. In 72 of these
cases the names of clerks' previous employers are recorded and no less
than 61 per cent of the intake had previously worked in Scottish banks.
The Mercantile continued the tradition of the Chartered Mercantile in
recruiting young Scots, not only because of the superior training given
to bank clerks in Scotland but also because the preference remained
part of the instincts and culture of the bank.

In the posting of its staff, the Mercantile continued the practice of
sending new clerks to the East whenever and wherever they were needed,
according to the opportunities arising from the promotion and relocation of those higher up the order of seniority. The bank did try to move
assistants between the branches so that they could obtain a good all-
round knowledge of the bank's operations but, as William Robilliard
wrote to George Murray in Singapore in 1905, 'with our small staff
that is not as easy to arrange as it is to recommend'.[33] The Mercantile
also followed the old bank's tendency to associate particular managers
with specific branches, an approach which produced managers who
were familiar with local conditions, knowledgeable about the credit-

worthiness of their customers and able to cultivate long-term business contacts and relationships.

This tradition meant that after 1900 some managers became entrenched in particular positions, reducing the geographical mobility of the staff and the opportunities for promotion. The bank experienced a glut of resignations in the early years of the twentieth century, showing that the hopes of aspiring managers were being thwarted. For example, John Moir was made a manager of the bank in 1894 and he was manager at Bombay between 1895 and 1900. However, after returning from furlough in 1901 he was not reappointed to Bombay, where James Murdoch was now established as manager, but sent to Singapore for a year, then to Calcutta for a year and then back to Bombay for a year. All the senior positions were now filled by established staff and Moir was being used as a relief manager. In December 1902 Moir resigned from the bank to take up a post elsewhere.

Even if the career patterns of the bank's staff were similar to those of their predecessors, a significant increase in manpower was a further factor in reinforcing the Mercantile's presence as an Eastern bank. By 1913 the Eastern staff of the bank had grown to around sixty – double what it had been 20 years earlier. Much of the increase was obviously accounted for by the opening of new branches and agencies; the Calcutta branch staff, as a result of the acquisition of the Bank of Calcutta, had doubled in size, necessitating the creation of the new post of sub-manager in 1907. All the other branches had supplemented their staff by one or two new members, except for Shanghai which still only employed one sub-agent.

At the top of the bank James Campbell's retirement as chief manager in March 1913 was clearly a landmark in the new Mercantile's history. The board accepted his resignation with effusive regret. The directors also awarded him an annual pension of £1500 in recognition of the 'self-denial he for so long displayed'; he had accepted only two salary increases in 20 years, having been appointed at £1500 per annum and ending his career with a salary of £2500. Percy Mould was appointed in his place, at a salary of £2000, and James Steuart stepped up to second in command as London manager.

Campbell's departure was also a milestone in the longer view of the bank's development. As the first and only import into the senior executive role, he had identified himself completely with the rehabilitation of the bank and had taken a personal lead in shaping business practice, staff appointments and the complex facilities needed for customers of the Mercantile. He had overseen the early survival of the fragile new bank of the mid-1890s. He had then found a route towards growth and expansion in the more prosperous conditions after the turn of the century – a recovery which was subtle rather than spectacular, strengthening the scope of the bank's business without channelling its resources into high risks.

By 1913 the Mercantile Bank had restored a distinct identity in the East and in the London banking community. That identity was partly achieved through the seniority and experience of Campbell and his managers. It was also obtained through the standing of the bank's directors, shareholders and customers, as in the case of prominent Eastern figures such as Yule and the Sassoons. Not least, in the London market there was now a visible signal of the bank's recovery. The Threadneedle Street office which had served as an inexpensive headquarters since 1896 had become inadequate for a thriving overseas bank, certainly in comparison with the London offices of the Chartered Bank and the Hongkong Bank. The directors began their search for a new home in 1911 and, in February 1913, they acquired the site for 13–16 Gracechurch Street and 11 Bell Yard for £113 000.[34] The new head office on that site, designed by William Wallace, was completed in February 1914 at a building cost of some £45 000. Comprising 16 800 square feet in six floors and two basement floors, the Gracechurch Street property was large enough for the bank to let the top four floors; its tenants included the Malacca Rubber Company, one of the bank's own customers.

The new building, whose façade featured the stone-carved shields of London, India, Burma, Ceylon, Malaya and China, was greeted by the *London and China Express* as 'striking evidence to the growing prosperity and importance of the Mercantile'.[35] The bank's immediate neighbour was the new London office of the Hongkong Bank, and other Gracechurch Street residents included familiar City names such as the Colonial Bank, the Metropolitan Bank of England and Wales, and the National Provident Institution. In this setting and in this company the Mercantile Bank of India was now solidly placed in the ranks of British overseas banks.

CHAPTER THREE

Resurgence, 1913–23

Over the ten years from 1913, the records of board meetings of the Mercantile Bank of India do not offer explanation of or debate over the progress of the bank. Anyone reading the minutes of those meetings could be forgiven for asking whether there was any kind of political trouble in that period or whether there was any significant change in the fortunes of the bank itself. The directors' minutes scarcely make any reference to the Great War; neither do they hint that the size of the bank, in balance-sheet terms, all but trebled between 1914 and 1920. The board had by this time adopted a highly formal, almost taciturn style of recording their decisions. This chapter attempts to decipher these decisions, to explain the bank's remarkable growth and to assess the impact of the First World War on its business.

In the surviving records of the Mercantile's board meetings, the earliest reference to the outbreak of war on 4 August 1914 was an almost casual reference on 11 August to pay allowances to staff 'on duty with the Territorial Force'. Even though none of the bank's branches was in a theatre of war, other references to the conflict are rare. In December 1914, for instance, the directors appointed the Siam Forest Company as the bank's agents in Bangkok as the previous agents, Windsor and Co., were a German firm. The detention of cargoes on the German steamers *Moravia* and *Ambra* by the new Italian allies in November 1915 was an exceptional reference to the unprecedented dislocation of shipping around the world. Even the wartime regulations affecting banking, including the extensive Trading with the Enemy legislation, were barely mentioned in the mainstream records of the bank.

In reality the Mercantile and the other Eastern banks faced severe disruption of their traditional business from the outset of the war. As the political crisis in Europe deepened, so London office wired an increasing number of warnings to the branches. On 27 July 1914 branches were told that 'in view of political troubles' they were to act cautiously and leave the forward market alone.[1] The following day they were informed that bills on foreign banks or firms could no longer be discounted in London. On 29 July the order went out to stop operating in exchange business, to curtail advances and to keep a strong cash position.[2]

Information about the realities of the situation was slow in getting through. On 6 August Calcutta branch was still unaware that war had broken out; their only communication with Europe was via the line to Suez which they reported was 'much congested'.³ All branches attempted to keep positions as liquid as possible in case of panic withdrawals. The Mercantile's Karachi branch reported that its current accounts had been heavily drawn on and Calcutta's withdrawals amounted to around Rs 4 million from a total of around Rs 12 million on deposit in the branch. The Bank of Bengal was quick to offer assistance in case of trouble but the National Bank of India was the only exchange bank in India to suffer any serious loss of deposits.

In London the discount market was virtually at a standstill. A moratorium was in place and on 21 August 1914 London office explained to the branches that the Bank of England was the only place where bills could be discounted.⁴ The situation was eased, however, when the Bank of England announced that it would discount all bills accepted before 4 August, even those of German banks, under guarantee of the government. On 4 September a further package of measures was introduced to help breathe life into the markets and, as a result, London office advised branches that they might resume buying ready or near bills on London accepting houses.⁵ The discount market gradually returned to something resembling its former vigour, and by the end of the year Percy Mould, chief manager, was able to report to the Eastern branches that 'the position now under all the circumstances is wonderfully good'.⁶

Although the bank was able to cope with the financial exigencies caused by the war, further problems arose with the haemorrhage of staff to join the forces. On 1 August ten of the London office junior staff resigned, and by the end of the year a further nine had left the service. By 1915, 40 from a total of 67 of the London staff were on active service. In July of that year Mould wrote to the branches that 'owing to the heavy demand for young men for the war, we have not a single member of our foreign staff left in London'.⁷ From the Eastern staff four men left their posts to return home to fight. James Mitchell, formerly accountant at Calcutta, died in fighting in Mesopotamia in January 1915; James Horne, assistant at Calcutta, joined the army in December 1914; Walter Steuart, assistant at Karachi, resigned to join the army in September 1915 and Robert Mckenzie from Howrah followed suit in November 1916. In addition deaths, retirements and the inability to replace men with London-trained juniors left the Eastern staff short-handed. On the announcement of conscription in December 1915 at least one member of staff from each Eastern office applied to resign and join the forces. Mould strenuously encouraged their managers to lay before them the position of the bank, the importance to the war effort of the continuance of trade and commerce, and that, in leaving an already short-staffed branch, they would be placing intolerable burdens on their colleagues. His appeal worked: the staff remained.

The bank's Eastern and local staff endured exhausting conditions. The increase in business allied with the lack of staff meant more work and longer hours. With the withdrawal of troops from the Empire to fight on the Western Front, bank staff were also required for duty in the volunteer forces; an inspector's report on Calcutta branch in 1918, for instance, stated 'owing to military duty this office is never actually fully staffed'.[8] The dearth of relief staff available from London prevented existing staff from going on leave and in December 1915 the board decided that 'until Peace is declared' all furlough would be stopped except under urgent medical certificate.[9] Senior managers, who at this stage in their careers would be expecting to complete tours of duty of four or five years, found themselves serving for anything upwards of six years at a stretch.

In London the acute shortage of men in head office was overcome by recruiting those men too young for conscription or medically unfit for the forces. 'Lady clerks' also joined the staff on a temporary basis, as at other domestic and overseas banks. Because the bank promised those who joined the forces that their jobs would be held open for them, many of the new female staff were discharged with the return of men from the war. However, by 1919 ten women remained on the staff (including the Willson and Constable sisters) and their status was modified from temporary to permanent staff.

After the initial dislocation and shock of wartime conditions, the Mercantile found itself in a world of new opportunities. The commodity exports in the bank's traditional markets now became priority trades for Britain, its Empire and its Allies. The war brought the advantage of indirect protection to many economies in Asia. Imports of manufactured goods from Europe were substituted by the products of indigenous businesses, and export businesses revelled in the lack of competitors and the increasing prices of commodities. In India, textile mills began to provide goods for the home market, and the jute export industry found its order books growing, especially with the use of its products in the manufacture of sandbags. D. H. Buchanan, writing of the Calcutta jute industry in 1934, doubted 'if any group of factories in the world paid such handsome profits between 1915 and 1929'.[10] The Indian steel and cement industries also owed their origins during the war to the lack of competitors in their respective markets.

The bank also benefited from this increase in trade, especially at its Indian branches. However, the wartime boom also brought problems in its wake. The imbalance in trade – the surplus of exports to Europe over imports – meant that branches were becoming oversupplied with bills denominated in sterling and were needing to pay out large amounts of rupees to local exporters. Additionally, as the exchange rate of the rupee was rapidly changing in response to the rising price (and hoarding) of silver, these sterling balances were depreciating. In 1917 the Indian government acknowledged that the exchange banks were being placed in an untenable position and that the situation might arise whereby goods of strategic importance could not be exported because of the difficulty of finance. The government agreed to guarantee the exchange banks against losses and depreciation arising from their surplus of sterling bills. The guarantee took the form of an undertaking to sell 'Councils' to the banks at the end of the war at the exchange rate prevailing at the time of the guarantee: Councils were rupee bills sold in London by the Indian government and bought in sterling by the exchange banks. This government guarantee effectively cushioned the exchange banks from any loss they incurred by holding large amounts of sterling in India as the exchange rate turned in favour of the rupee. In April 1917 London advised branches that 'India, Burmah and Ceylon branches are now at liberty to buy sterling regardless of amount of their general position'.[11]

As the pattern of trade moved in favour of the Eastern banks, the Mercantile's board and management also sought sources of new business. Percy Mould, who had succeeded Campbell as chief manager in March 1913, played the leading role in this search. Aged 45 when he took the senior post, Mould had been with the bank throughout his career, and had held appointments in the Mercantile's foremost branches. His longest and most influential service had been at Calcutta, where he had been accountant (1896–1902) and manager (1903–12). Towards the end of his tenure at Calcutta he was also commissioned by the board to carry out rigorous tours of inspection of the other Eastern branches. As to his outlook and skills, he was one of life's natural inspectors. His letters and instructions show him to have been meticulous, conscientious and impatient with failures. Contemporary accounts of his personality have not survived, but clearly his attention to detail, combined with his long practical experience of the workings of the bank, contributed to one of the most successful periods in the Mercantile's history.

A key event in Mould's career was his first-hand supervision of the acquisition of the Bank of Calcutta in 1906. The personal and business success of the operation no doubt influenced him in favour of strengthening the Mercantile through further acquisitions. There were other pressures in that direction. In this period the urge towards amalgamations and acquisitions was being felt throughout British banking. The second great wave of amalgamations among the domestic banks in

England and Wales had begun in 1909 and, in the years immediately before the Great War, these mergers had included the union of the London and County with the London and Westminster in 1909 and the acquisition of the Metropolitan by the Midland in 1913. For the directors and shareholders of the overseas banks, many of whom had interests and even directorships in the home banks, the prevailing mood in favour of amalgamations could not be ignored. This was a period in which there were few (if any) boardrooms in British banks which neither had embarked on merger negotiations nor were contemplating their own next move in the acquisitions market.

In February 1915 James Murdoch, the bank's inspector on tour in India, was already writing to Mould about the possibility of acquiring the Delhi and London Bank. This concern had been founded as early as 1844, and by 1913 it had six branches in India and had accumulated assets of £2.3 million. On 3 March Murdoch wired that 'the business referred to has gone off' and the negotiations were abandoned.[12] A year later the Delhi Bank's business was bought by and divided between the Alliance Bank of Simla and Boulton Brothers of London (both of which were to fail in 1923 as a result of frauds at Boulton Brothers).[13]

At the time of the sale of the Delhi Bank in 1914, gossip in Calcutta suggested that Boultons were too small to be acting on their own account and that they were buying on behalf of one of the British clearing banks. The Mercantile's manager in Calcutta suggested to Mould that the Midland, which had recently recruited a director with interests in India, was involved.[14] The rumour was erroneous but it was a signal that overseas bankers were aware and even anxious that the large domestic banks should be acquiring or setting up subsidiaries for overseas business. The formation of Lloyds Bank France in 1911 and Westminster Foreign Bank in 1913 were other examples of these incursions and the trend was likely to have encouraged Mould and his directors to look for alliances of their own.

Mould's negotiations with the Bank of Mauritius in 1916 were altogether more successful. This island bank had been promoted in 1894 to take over the Mauritius business of the failed New Oriental Bank Corporation (a brief history of the Bank of Mauritius appears in Appendix Seven). Its assets in 1916 were approximately £800 000, but its profitability had steadily improved over the previous 20 years to a level of over £15 000 net profits per annum. The bank's headquarters were in George Yard, off Lombard Street in London, but the business of the bank was specific to the island.

The principal ingredient in the Bank of Mauritius's business was the finance of the island's sugar crop and the export route to Britain and

Europe; there were also close trade and shipping links with India. Similarly the affairs of the bank were dominated by sugar export firms. Lord Stanmore, formerly governor of Mauritius between 1871 and 1874, was a prime mover in the promotion of the bank and was its chairman from 1894 until his death in 1912. His co-directors in London and Mauritius were all closely linked to the sugar trade. Initially the bank had been known locally as 'la banque anglaise' in view of these connections but since 1908 it had sought closer links with the French community – for example by recruiting Pierre Adam of Adam and Co. to the board and by opening a branch at Mahé in the Seychelles in 1911.

In 1909 the Royal Commission investigating the financial position of the island had commended the operations of the Bank of Mauritius. However, the Commission also deplored the fact that the Eastern exchange banks were not represented in the colony. The bank's directors were also concerned about the narrow base of the bank's business. Lord Stanmore, who succeeded his father on the board in 1912, argued in 1916 that the bank's resources were 'employed exclusively in Mauritius, a colony subject to hurricanes and dependent for its well being on but one staple industry'.[15] If the island suffered a setback, or if the threat of new competition materialized, then 'the effect on our business would be far more serious than in the case of a larger institution with a wider field of operations'.[16] The day-to-day management of the bank was also a worrisome issue. F. P. Murray, secretary of the bank since its foundation in 1894 and managing director since 1910, died in post in April 1915.

For the Mercantile, the assets and earnings of the Bank of Mauritius made it a natural long-term opportunity. Its trade connections were compatible with the bank's customer base on the sub-continent. The Mercantile and the other Eastern banks had previously found it difficult to compete for business between India and the island, largely because the Mauritius banks had operated through their own agents in India. Acquisition would bring Mauritius into direct and profitable contact with the Mercantile's branches, a clear advantage for the bank over its competitors. In the shorter term there was also the certainty that the island's economy would be sustained by the British government's purchases of almost the entire crystal-sugar crop during the war.

On the strength of these mutual advantages, in 1916 the two banks agreed to the Mercantile's acquisition of the business and goodwill of the Bank of Mauritius. The terms were a cash payment of £234 536, an offer which was accepted by the eleven principal shareholders of the island bank in February 1916.[17] The Mercantile covered this cost from the surplus assets of the Bank of Mauritius which also covered compensation to the Mauritius directors for loss of office and the legal costs of the acquisition. All but one of the Mauritius bank's staff transferred to the Mercantile, while its local board was invited to continue as an advisory committee. In addition P. R. Chalmers, a director of the Bank of Mauritius since 1912, joined the Mercantile board. In the aftermath of this agreement, Percy Mould urged the Mercantile's branch managers to 'at once get in communication with the new office for all information they can get as to names of firms doing business from their ports to Mauritius and ... in short do everything they can to foster business between themselves and Mauritius'. The call was heard and understood, and almost immediately the new Mauritius branch was making a distinctive contribution to the bank's business and profitability (see below, page 49).

Although the acquisition in Mauritius was paid for without needing to raise additional capital, by the later years of the war the Mercantile's capital structure was becoming outdated. The 1918 balance sheet showed that the paid-up capital of £562 500 comprised only 3.7 per cent of total liabilities, barely half the figure of 6.9 per cent current in 1913. Clearly the ratio of capital to total assets needed to be adjusted to the sustained increase in the value of the balance sheet. In addition the Mercantile's board could not ignore the yawning gap between paid-up capital and the market value of the bank (reckoned at £1.58 million in 1918). The bank's main competitors were in a similar position. While the shareholders' funds (principally the capital and reserves) of the Mercantile Bank amounted to £1 262 500 or 8.25 per cent of the balance sheet, the equivalent figures for the Chartered and National Bank of India were 6.9 per cent and 7.8 per cent respectively. The Hongkong Bank, with 11.8 per cent of its liabilities represented by shareholders' funds, had a markedly higher capital ratio.

The bank adjusted its capital structure in two stages. In January 1919 paid-up capital was increased to £750 000 by the issue of a further 15 000 A shares (the class of £25 shares, created in 1892, of which £12 10s. 0d. was paid up). Then in April 1920 the board created a new class of 300 000 C shares of £5 fully paid. The issue of 60 000 of these shares lifted the bank's total paid-up capital to £1 050 000 and also left a comfortable margin for introducing new capital in future. Large and regular payments into reserves throughout the war years had created published reserves of £750 000 by the end of 1919, increasing to £1 100 000 in the following year. In parallel to these payments, undisclosed inner reserves had increased steadily to over £260 000 by 1918 and then jumped rapidly to £869 000 during the post-war boom of 1919–20.

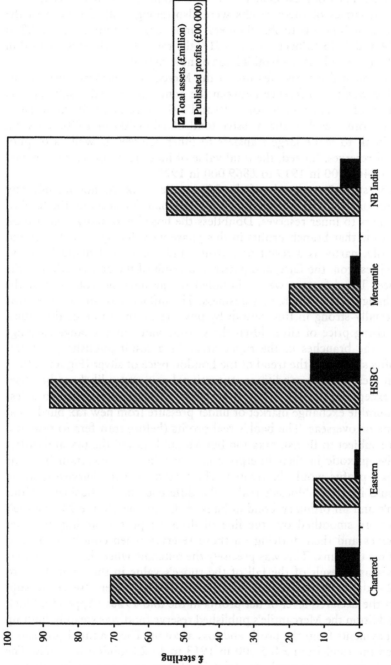

3.1 Eastern banks: total assets and published profits, 1920

Legend:
- Total assets (£million)
- Published profits (£00 000)

Y-axis: £ sterling

X-axis categories: Chartered, Eastern, HSBC, Mercantile, NB India

National Bank of New Zealand and all the other British overseas banks.[19] The dynamics of these results were also telling, with the ratio of the Mercantile's profits to shareholders' funds surging from less than 9.0 in 1914 and 1915 to over 13.0 in 1917; the ratio then fell back to 11.0 in 1920 as a result of the bank's issue of new capital.

The most distinctive feature of the Mercantile's performance in this period was the difference between the bank's published results and its 'real' profits. The returns for 1919 and 1920 were especially impressive. Real profits reached the massive total of £666 000 in 1920, allowing the bank to make large transfers to inner reserves as well as to published reserves. Indeed, the total value of inner reserves nearly doubled from £463 000 in 1919 to £869 000 in 1920.

The surviving records of the Mercantile Bank do not include any policy or technical statements on the rationale for deciding the level of transfers to inner reserves. Doubtless the board and management took the view that branch profits in this phase were highly exceptional and volatile, partly as a result of wartime and post-war demand for commodities from the East, and partly as a result of the appreciation of the rupee. These factors were additional to the intrinsic volatility of the exchange side of the bank's business. The influence of silver prices was especially strong in this period: by pushing up the value of the rupee, the rising price of silver lifted the sterling value of exchange earnings from the branches in the rupee area. As a result published and real profits shadowed the trend of the London price of silver (Figure 3.2).

In these market conditions, exceptional gains were likely to be offset by exceptional losses in the short term, perhaps in reaction to a less favourable exchange market or under pressure from new tax burdens at home or overseas. The bank's real profits (before transfers to reserves) were subject to British taxation but Mould believed the tax authorities to be quixotic in their interpretations and he was uncertain how the bank's profits would be treated. The Inland Revenue Surveyor, wrote Mould in 1918, 'doesn't realise the difference in the business of our Bank and an ordinary London bank'.[20] Consequently the Mercantile's directors smoothed out the line of declared profits, adding to inner reserves and then drawing on those reserves when conditions turned against the bank. This was precisely the outcome when, hit by exchange losses as a result of the fall of the rupee's value in the years 1922 to 1924, the bank was able to transfer funds from inner reserves to support the declared level of net profits in the mid 1920s (Appendix One). In addition the Mercantile's published reserve fund was steadily built up by payments from the profit and loss account. These annual provisions lifted the fund from £465 000 in 1913 to £1.25 million by 1923. The bank's directors also published details of their payments to the Officers'

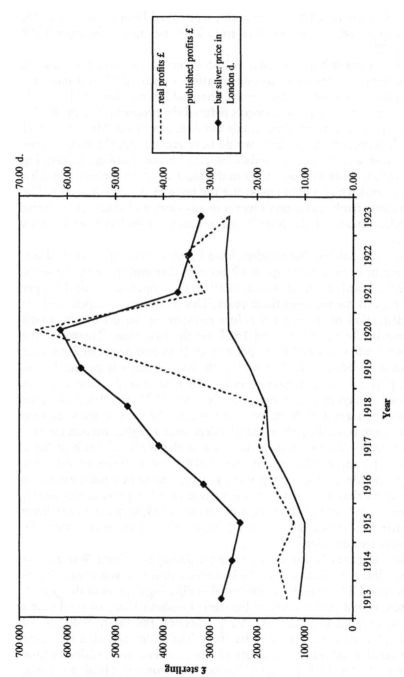

3.2   Mercantile Bank: published profits, real profits and bar silver price in London, 1913–23

Fund. Contributions to this account, which had been created in 1906, quadrupled from £5000 in 1916 to £20 000 per annum between 1919 and 1923.

Where records have survived, British domestic and overseas banks in the inter-war years were making transfers to published and inner reserves before publishing their results. Shareholders may have had grounds for complaint, in that the transfers reduced the proportion of the bank's profits passed to them. Conversely the directors of the Mercantile and their banking contemporaries would have argued that the process protected their shareholders by stabilizing year-on-year earnings, by creating reserves for more arduous times in the future, and by removing sudden fluctuations which might jeopardize the price of the bank's shares. The Mercantile Bank was a small world in any case, and shareholders were doubtless aware of the board's conservatism in declaring each year's results.

The Mercantile's shareholders were by now enjoying a marked improvement in their earnings. A 10 per cent dividend on both classes of share was paid for the first time in 1915, in comparison with the 8 per cent paid in the previous three years. This more than compensated for the deduction of income tax before payment of the dividends, which applied in the second half of 1915 for the first time. Thereafter the dividend rate was lifted to 12 per cent in 1916 and a special 2 per cent bonus was added in 1917. By 1919 the Mercantile was paying 14 per cent, plus a 2 per cent bonus, and in the next year the new C shares received a payment of 8 per cent. Between 1921 and 1923 all three classes of shares were being paid 16 per cent. Admittedly some Eastern banks were rewarding their shareholders with a higher percentage rate of dividend – 20 per cent in the cases of the National Bank of India from 1917 and the Chartered from 1918 – but in terms of value for money the Mercantile's shares were now proving to be a more attractive investment than overseas banks operating in other parts of the world. Between 1914 and 1920 average dividends, dividend payouts per share and the yield from the shares all improved in comparison with the previous two decades.[21]

The Mercantile's impressive progress during the Great War and its extraordinary profitability in the immediate post-war years was diverse in character. The branches contributed in differing degrees to the growth in volume and profitability of business. London's share of total assets shrank to 30.2 per cent by 1920, reflecting the relative decline of sterling balances against rupee balances. The senior branches increased their relative shares of the assets of the branches, with Calcutta now responsible for 27.9 per cent, followed by Bombay (16.6 per cent), Singapore (9.7 per cent) and Colombo (8.0 per cent).

The branches' contributions to earnings did not follow such a stable pattern. In such a volatile period for trade and exchange, there were almost freakishly large net profits at Calcutta in 1919 (£311 803 or 41 per cent of the branch net profits) and at Colombo in 1920 (£219 885 or 30 per cent of the total). On the reverse side of these figures, heavy losses were incurred at Colombo in 1919 (£108 194). The Shanghai branch, which had been upgraded from a sub-agency to a full branch in 1915, suffered persistent losses, reaching as much as £154 108 in 1921. Table 3.1 shows net profits of the principal overseas branches between 1918 and 1922, a span which includes the last year of war and the post-war boom and slump. In these exceptionally unstable conditions Calcutta was significantly the largest source of earnings, followed by Bombay, the new branch in Mauritius, Singapore and Colombo. These results emphasise that the pre-war boom in Ceylon could not be sustained. They also suggest that the branches at Madras and Hong Kong had moved out of the first rank of the bank's profit centres.

The striking growth of the Mercantile's business and profitability in the war and post-war years could not be achieved solely by the volume of demand in the bank's traditional markets. The character of its day-to-day dealings was also bound to alter. Shifts in the rankings of the branches, particularly the strengthening of Calcutta and the entry of Mauritius, changed the profile of the business. The bank also took a forward step in its international capability by establishing its own New York office in 1919. Previously the Bank of Montreal had acted as the Mercantile's agent in the city but the vital importance of the New York foreign exchange market, together with the payment needs of the bank's merchant customers, persuaded the directors to apply for a banking licence in New York in September 1919. The office became a familiar (though not especially profitable) adjunct to the branch network for the next 40 years.

At the customer level there were also changes of emphasis. Before the war the Mercantile's board and management were increasingly willing to take on new and diversified risks (see above, pages 31–4). In the post-war period that trend was followed on and developed, giving the bank a wider range of business partners and a wider reach in international trade. Evidence of the bank's confirmed credits again helps to identify its customers and to discover the nature of its risks.[22] These credits were granted to a trading house or individual so that a named third party (usually an exporter) could draw upon the trading house or individual up to an agreed limit for a specified period. In 1920 the Mercantile granted 256 such credits with a total value of £1 774 031 – appreciably more than the 185 credits valued at £951 748 ten years earlier. The average level of credits of £7485 was well above the

Table 3.1 Mercantile Bank: net profits of selected branches, 1918–22

Date	Bombay	Calcutta	Colombo	Singapore	Mauritius	Total branch profits
1918	40 482	86 218	20 545	22 159	34 393	310 238
1919	162 342	311 803	–108 194	61 366	8 078	760 670
1920	2 479	115 546	219 885	101 325	91 443	732 086
1921	87 134	48 570	7 861	16 400	87 561	354 609
1922	–9 700	–3 084	–2 563	–10 923	44 995	223 069
Total	282 737	559 053	137 534	190 327	266 470	2 380 672
Per cent of total	19	23.5	5.8	8	11.2	

equivalent of £5145 in 1910. Such facilities could be as great as £100 000 (for raw jute from Calcutta) or as apparently trivial as £230 (for gum waste from Madras).

A small number of trading houses dominated this aspect of the business. Thornett and Fehr obtained no less than 49 confirmed credits in 1920, mainly to finance the exports of its own Singapore subsidiary and of Hayley and Kenny of Colombo. The firm had been founded by Henry Fehr on his arrival in London from Zurich in 1857. Renamed Thornett and Fehr in 1904, it emerged as a leading name at the Baltic Exchange and in the commodity markets in the early years of the century.[23] C. A. and H. Nichols, who were granted 20 credits that year, were also major customers but with a wider range of trading links. This firm of commission merchants had been established by Charles Dufoucet in 1874 and had been a Mercantile customer before the war. By 1920 it was using the bank's credits for coconut exports from Colombo, soya from Hong Kong, and *nux vomica* (tree seeds) with mixed cargoes from Madras. The Mercantile's other regular customers for credits included T. Middleton and Co., with 18 credits (all in favour of C. S. C. Kumarasamy, a chettiar bank in Madras); Charles Weis and Co. Ltd, with 13 credits; the Ceylon Land and Produce Co. Ltd (12 credits, all for Ceylon tea exporters); and McKerrow Brothers Ltd, with 10 credits.

Even though some of the names were new, these customers as a *type* were in the tradition which had prevailed before the war. The British trading house, based in the City of London and with regular business partners in the East, was at the heart of these transactions. Yet there were recognizable newcomers to the list of the Mercantile's customers. London merchant banks, which had not turned to the Mercantile before the First World War, were applying for credits by 1920. William Brandt and Sons and Kleinwort Sons and Co. obtained finance of this kind, while in September 1920 C. J. Hambro and Son was granted the exceptionally large credit of £350 000 for exports of copra from Singapore and Penang to Aarhus in Denmark.

This new business reflected the merchant banks' enforced diversification when their traditional activities were reduced or suspended during the war. Although it has not been possible to analyse credits in every year, there is evidence that their links with the Mercantile multiplied after 1920. By 1923 the names of Lazard, Huth, Schroder and Seligman appeared amongst the bank's credits. International merchant banks also moved into this territory: in 1922 and 1923 Goldman Sachs, in particular, and Chabrieres Morel and Co. featured in most lists of credits approved at the weekly meetings of the Mercantile's directors.

The customer base also widened at the distant end of these credits, where firms or individuals could draw upon the bank's principal customers. Before the Great War the clear majority of these credits were granted in favour of British exporters, whereas by 1920 at least 107 credits (42 per cent of the total) was in favour of local non-European traders. The chettiar firm of C. S. C. Kumarasamy of Madras, appearing in eighteen transactions, was the most prominent example. Others included M. K. Govinderaju and Co., another Madras chettiar; Nalam Lakshmikantham of Madras, exporting nuts and divi-divi (seeds for tanning and dyeing); and Soorajinull Nagarimull, shipping jute and hemp from Calcutta.

In these cases the Mercantile and its London customers were responding to overseas markets which were increasingly in local hands. Furthermore, the records of confirmed credits suggest that by 1920 British traders were taking a diminishing share of the business. In addition to the multiplication of local exporters, expatriate European firms were also in greater evidence. Xavier Brothers, a Portuguese firm in Hong Kong, featured in thirteen cases, mostly for cargoes of soya. G. R. de Zoysa and Co., exporting mainly coconuts from Colombo, featured eleven times. Firms such as Brunnschweiler and Co. and E. M. Breithaupt of Madras or J. S. Vereschagin of Colombo self-evidently were not from the traditional groups of British traders.

The expanding role of local and international traders in this period was underlined in other types of lending. In Mauritius, for instance, discount limits were regularly granted to local or French concerns such as S. Noorani, A. R. Oosman and Forget Suzer and Co. In Shanghai, the local branch of Tata Sons and Co., the prominent Indian house with offices in China and Japan, turned to the Mercantile in July 1919 for a new limit of Rs 50 million for its bills on Bombay.

Alongside these changes in type of customer, the bank was willing to finance a wider range of commodities and trade routes. This trend had been apparent before the Great War, but ten years later the dominance of exports from the sub-continent had reduced further from 83 per cent to 76 per cent of confirmed credits. As to commodities, the type of trade was specified in four-fifths of the credits recorded in 1920. Traditional Eastern trades were well represented, including (in order of frequency) rubber from Singapore and Colombo, usually exported to New York or London; jute from Calcutta; hides and skins, mainly from Madras; desiccated coconuts from Colombo; and soya from Hong Kong. Tea exports rarely featured in the credits in this period, although the Mercantile remained closely and regularly in support of the tea estates through advances and discount facilities.

These long-standing trades were now joined by exports of commodities for new industrial uses such as high-value copra from Singapore and Penang, mica from Giridih in the Ganges valley, and shellac from

Madras. The bank's credits were also used in unexpected ways, including the shipment of egg yolk from Shanghai; kamala dye from Lahore; rice exported from Hong Kong to Peru; milk sent from Bombay to the United States; and a shipment of £13 000 worth of sheepskins from Amritsar to the United States.

The Mercantile's board and management did not take these risks lightly. It was characteristic of the bank in these post-war years that it required more security for its credits. Whereas 44 per cent of its confirmed credits had been 'open' (that is, unsecured) in 1910, a decade later that proportion had shrunk to a mere 9 per cent. The remainder of credits required the security of shipping and insurance documents, mainly on a DP (Documents against Payment) basis. Additionally, many of these carried the condition that they would be available 'only if satisfied with drawers'. Similarly, the period allowed for credit was shortened, with terms of credit halving from an average of 8.4 months in 1910 to 4.1 months ten years later. In its management of risks, the bank was in this way strengthening its security requirements as its lending became more diverse and untried.

The expansion of the Mercantile's business and earnings, together with the changing character of its customers and products, was not purely the achievement of the directors and senior management. It also represented the adjustment of the Mercantile's staff and local managers to wartime and post-war conditions, reflecting their adaptability to the trading opportunities of the expanding and volatile markets in the East. In this process the recruitment, training and retention of staff was a special and continuing concern.

In the immediate aftermath of the war the bank's personnel priority was to relieve those members of the Eastern staff who had endured long stints of service. In January 1919, for example, the board received simultaneously five applications for leave from Calcutta and 'several' from Colombo. In order to achieve its aim, the bank needed to change its policy towards training its London juniors. Previously juniors had been expected to spend between three and five years in London, learning the business of the bank. Now there was no time for such an apprenticeship. Of the twelve individuals who joined the London office in 1919, four were sent East almost immediately and another five followed in the subsequent year. In 1920 thirteen new recruits swelled the ranks in Gracechurch Street, and again four of these were sent to their first overseas posting the same year. Although this policy may have alleviated the pressing need to allow existing members of staff to take leave, its legacy was to leave the bank with a generation of undertrained staff at precisely the moment when the bank's resources were ample for business expansion. 'The majority of the junior officers at our branches', the bank's inspector fretted in 1922, 'are not so well trained from a business point of view as formerly ... they undoubtedly suffer in several instances from the lack of the London office training.'[24]

The lack of time spent in the head office of the bank disadvantaged officers in more ways than just formal training. The period spent in the London office with other juniors was valuable for creating a bank ethos and allowing friendships to be formed which would endure throughout a career. Starting salaries depended on age and experience: in 1913 a seventeen-year-old with little experience was paid £40 and by 1923 this had risen to £80. In comparison, junior staff at a domestic clearing bank could only expect about half of these sums. Juniors were encouraged to take part in team sports and in 1920 a proposal was put to the board to buy a sports ground for the bank. The board declined, arguing that the small numbers of staff did not warrant the expense, but in 1921 it was agreed to share the ground of London Assurance at New Eltham. This socialization process of creating a cadre of Mercantile bankers was helped by the presence in the London office of ex-members of the Eastern staff.[25] Mould and Steuart had had long and varied careers in the East, but on a lower and more approachable scale were men who had once worked in the East but who had returned to the home staff, usually for reasons of health. These men were able to prepare the juniors for the realities of life overseas.

Once overseas, a junior banker found his social standing very different to that experienced as a London clerk. All routine and clerical work at branches was undertaken by the local 'native staff'. A new arrival from London could suddenly find himself as the head of a department and would be shown how to perform his job by his local staff, many of whom remained with the bank in the same post for many years. Unfortunately, the surviving records of the bank do not reveal the names or salaries of the local staff, nor do they give any indication of the numbers employed in this period. The most important member of the local staff was the compradore (in China) or the shroff (in India). These positions were filled by men of good local standing with a thorough knowledge of the business and the businesses of the locality. They had the responsibility for guaranteeing and garnering local business and, additionally, were in charge of the cash department. The shroff at the Calcutta branch of the bank had his salary increased to Rs 600 a month in 1919, at a time when the branch manager was paid Rs 2000 and a junior assistant received Rs 400. Local staff could not automatically expect any gratuity or pension on their retirement. Staff who had worked for the bank for exceptionally long periods of time, however, were often granted pensions. The matter was decided by the local manager in the first instance, and if he thought the case a deserving one he would recommend it to the board. On the retirement of the Rangoon shroff in 1921, a gratuity of Rs 500 was granted but the board decided that a pension was not justified. In contrast, in 1923 Poran Chunder Dutta of Calcutta was given a pension of Rs 70 per month after 30 years' service as a clerk, and Chan Kwan Chee was granted a monthly pension of $20 after 35 years as a clerk at Hong Kong branch.

The pay and conditions of British juniors in the East excited great interest in the banking industry in the post-war period. At home the profession was suddenly overcrowded with bankers returning from war service, temporary staff wishing to stay in banking, and ex-servicemen seeking new careers. Many bankers looked east for new opportunities, and their curiosity was no doubt fuelled by proposals that the new Imperial Bank of India, which was formed in 1921 to bring together the three presidency banks, would open a further 100 branches throughout the sub-continent. A correspondent to the Institute of Bankers, writing from Calcutta early in 1920, reckoned that the cost of living for 'a single young man in Calcutta or Bombay' at Rs 505 per month; he warned against 'exaggerated expectations of a life affording ample opportunities in money and leisure for the more expensive forms of sport and amusement'. On the other hand a correspondent from southern India, arguing that the monthly costs need not exceed Rs 231, sang the praises of up-country stations where 'though life is quiet, living is cheap, and as a bungalow and other allowances are provided, a normal man will find himself relatively affluent'.[26]

In the case of the Mercantile, pay in the East and at home was dominated in this period by the level of 'war allowances' and other supplements granted by the directors. In 1917 the staff were rewarded for their loyalty and diligence (and compensated for the effects of inflation) with a more generous scale of salaries. A special letter of July 1917 set out the new scales of pay and told the staff that 'in view of the lengthening service of assistants and accountants and the fact that the Chartered and National banks have recently increased their scale of salaries ... the Directors have considered it advisable to revise the scale in force'.[27] In addition the directors approved the payment of war allowances, including 20 per cent of salaries for Eastern staff, female staff and unmarried staff; 20 per cent cost of living allowances for local native staff (in October 1919); and 30 per cent for married men at London office earning less than £300 a year (in January 1919). These allowances became a regular feature of Mercantile salaries after the war, and it was not until January 1924 that these additions – by then at a standard 20 per cent – were consolidated into 'substantive salary' awards.

The bank's board, in common with other bank managements, was also prepared to distribute profits in the form of bonuses to the staff. A bonus of 10 per cent of salaries became an annual fixture in the war years, but in March 1920 an extra 10 per cent was awarded 'owing to the exceptionally good and prosperous year the Bank has enjoyed'. The board was also more attentive to pensions. Since the pension fund had been formalized in 1906, each case of retirement had been treated on its merits. In 1917, however, the directors appointed A. G. Hemming FIA, actuary of London Assurance, to carry out a valuation and to establish a scale of pensions.[28] The directors set themselves a target of contributing 15 per cent of salaries of foreign staff and 5 per cent of home salaries to the pension fund.

These salaries and supplements left the Mercantile's foreign staff relatively well placed in their local banking communities. In return, the obligations of their appointments were greater and more varied than for equivalent posts in domestic banking. The British members of staff overseas were expected to behave in a manner that would throw a good light on the bank at all times. They were also expected to mix with the commercial and business men of the area, and court popularity with the brokers to ensure that the bank was offered a fair share of any business. Staff reports always remarked on the conduct of individual members of staff, and in 1915 the whole staff of Calcutta branch were criticized because not one of them belonged to the Bengal Club. The inspector stated that it was not so much that this was causing them to lose business, but that it was 'more a question of social standing'.[29]

Ultimately the prospects for the Mercantile's staff were enmeshed with the fortunes of the bank itself. Here, although the volume and earnings of the bank had grown at a remarkable rate since 1913, the physical network of Mercantile offices had barely altered in the decade since then. The new Mauritius branch re-employed the staff of the Bank of Mauritius, at least in the first instance; the New York office was essentially a one-man band; and in 1920 the board had shelved the possibility of a new office at Hankow in China.

It was not until 1923 that the Mercantile made a concerted effort to extend its branch network. That initiative, described in Chapter Four, was developed when James Steuart was already acting as chief manager. For Percy Mould had been taken ill early in 1923 and in May he was granted six months' leave on full pay to recuperate. He had already shown signs of frailty, as Steuart had deputized for him for long periods in 1919 and 1920, and sadly he did not survive his sick leave in 1923. His death was reported to the board in November. The directors, in awe of the 37 years which Mould had given to the bank, simply referred to the 'affectionate regard' in which he was held throughout the staff. As reticent here as they were in the minutes of their meetings, the directors might also have added recognition of Mould's personal contribution to the resurgence of the bank. Latterly he had worked closely with Steuart, but the guidance of the bank through the war years and the management of the huge increase in wartime and post-war business were essentially his own achievements.

CHAPTER FOUR

Resilience, 1923–35

Business and economic prospects deteriorated dramatically between the mid-1920s and the mid-1930s. After the slump of 1929, few phases of market development have been so weighed down with negative factors: labour unrest, profound monetary disturbance, and a worldwide depression in production and prices created a prolonged crisis of confidence in trade. The world of international banking was neither immune to the crisis nor well placed in dealing with its consequences. British overseas banking certainly suffered. The Anglo-South American Bank, for example, was close to collapse in 1931, was then rescued by inter-bank co-operation and was eventually sold to the Bank of London and South America; the Anglo-International Bank was severely battered in 1931 and was quietly put into liquidation in 1933.[1]

The Mercantile's career in the 1920s and 1930s, through all these adversities, showed endurance and enterprise. Total assets continued to build up during the mid-1920s, reaching nearly £19 million in 1928. The Depression briefly reduced the balance sheet total to only £14.7 million in 1931 and, in common with banks throughout the overseas sector, the Mercantile cut its dividend. From 1931 the dividend on all classes of shares was reduced from 16 to 12 per cent and these rates were maintained for the rest of the decade. The bank's total assets soon recovered, however, and by 1935 the balance sheet total had reached £17 million.

This solid performance was conducted by James Steuart, chief manager from 1923 to 1935, and James Crichton, London manager from 1925 to 1935. Steuart was one of only three remaining staff who had been recruited by the old Chartered Mercantile (he had joined in 1889 and went East in 1891). He had spent much of his Eastern service in Colombo, serving in six different appointments there with a total of over ten years on station between 1891 and 1912. He also had experience in Calcutta, Bombay, Madras, Singapore and Rangoon, but his most influential posting was as London manager and in effect Mould's deputy between 1913 and 1923. Crichton's Eastern service had also been dominated by appointments at branches in the 'rupee circle'. Apart from two years in Penang and Hong Kong, his postings were all on the subcontinent, including five appointments and nearly nine years in Bombay.

The promotion of Steuart and Crichton in London ensured close continuity in the management of the bank. At board level continuity was not so certain. In the mid-1920s the bank lost Sir Robert Black, who after 22 years as a director died in 1925; Lord Carmichael, who also died in 1925; and Henry Melvill Simons, who after nineteen years on the board died in the following year. The death of Sir David Yule in 1928 was perhaps the most obvious of the losses. Joining the board on the acquisition of the Bank of Calcutta in 1906, he had been a director for 22 years. Through his interests in the Yule group of companies, he personified the bank's connections with long-standing British merchant houses in India. Described by John Ryrie as a man of 'wide interests and ripe experience', Yule had also held an impressive hand of directorships at Midland Bank, Royal Exchange Assurance and Vickers.[2]

These losses removed two-thirds of the board membership which had ruled the bank between 1918 and 1923 (Figure 4.1). Of that membership only John Ryrie (from the East India merchants, Arbuthnot, Ewart & Co., who had become a director in 1908) and P. R. Chalmers, who had joined in 1916 as part of the Bank of Mauritius acquisition, remained on the board. As replacements for the losses, the Mercantile's directors and shareholders chose a blend of traditional links with the East and new recruits from the banking élite of the City of London. J. O. Robinson, a director between 1926 and 1931, was a partner in Spencer and Co. of Madras; W. H. Shelford, a director from 1926 to 1937, was a partner in Paterson, Simons and Co. of Singapore. Charles Jocelyn Hambro, in contrast, was selected from one of the City's leading dynasties of merchant bankers. 'For some time', Ryrie told the shareholders in 1924, 'we have been on the look-out for a young director who was actively engaged in the City and could bring business to the bank.'[3] Hambro, only 27 when he joined the Mercantile's board in 1924, was already a director of Hambros Bank and he was soon to join the court of directors of the Bank of England at the remarkably early age of 30. His other directorships included Cable and Wireless and Union Corporation.[4]

Sir Thomas Catto, elected to the Mercantile's board after Yule's death in 1928, combined City pedigree with a strong Eastern connection. In 1919 Catto had been appointed chairman and managing director of Andrew Yule and Co., at the suggestion of Vivian Smith of Morgan Grenfell (which then controlled the Yule empire). He had quickly become the confidant and business ally of Sir David Yule. Their ventures – sometimes a far cry from Calcutta – included the purchase of the *Daily Chronicle* from David Lloyd George in 1926. Catto also carried political weight, having been a member of Lord Inchcape's Indian Government Retrenchment Commission in 1922–23. He was liberal in his approach to Indian affairs, advocating dominion status rather than the imperial *status quo* which was still widely supported by many of his City and Westminster contemporaries.[5]

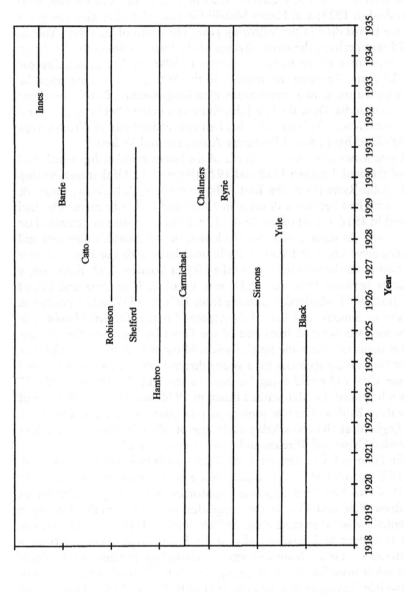

4.1 Mercantile Bank: board service, 1918–35

Hambro and Catto were later joined on the board by Sir Charles Barrie and Sir Charles Innes. Barrie, a director between 1930 and 1940, was also on the board of the London and North Eastern Railway, Phoenix Assurance and Cable and Wireless. Innes was a more political choice. He had spent most of his career in the Indian Civil Service, becoming under-secretary to the Indian government from 1907 to 1910. He was subsequently a member of the governor-general's Council (1921–27) and served as governor of Burma from 1927 to 1932. The old Chartered Mercantile Bank had recruited directors of this type: Sir Frederick Halliday, C. J. Erskine and Sir William Grey in the 1860s and 1870s were examples.[6] The Mercantile had followed suit with the appointment of Lord Carmichael in 1917. The migration of senior civil servants to City boardrooms was not infrequent in the inter-war period. In the Mercantile's case, Innes was chosen for his direct knowledge of the bank's markets. His political experience was also valued at a time when the bank's directors and managers were anticipating major change in India – including the probable creation of a reserve bank – and in the bank's other traditional territories.

These recruits to the board gave more balance and breadth to the interests of the bank. The long period of Black and Yule's pre-eminence, successful as it had been, had represented a relatively narrow business constituency. The new directors brought an entry to a wider community and also added a greater measure of prestige and the weight of the City and Whitehall establishment to the Mercantile's affairs. The senior directors – no doubt with Steuart's help – were shrewd in their choices as the newcomers proved to be working directors rather than figureheads.

The continuity of management and the quality of the board gave direction to the bank's performance in the 1920s and 1930s. The directors' approach was to protect the Mercantile's business in its traditional but turbulent markets and to follow its customers to new or developing markets. While the Mercantile may not have been large enough to pioneer new banking products or services, it had sufficient resources and skills to adapt its business links and representation. This applied especially to the management of the bank's branches.

Under Steuart's management the volume of business and earnings at the principal branches followed a consistent pattern. London office remained the largest business, holding 36.3 per cent of the Mercantile's assets in 1927 and 39.7 per cent in 1935, and generating as much as 53 per cent of the net profits of the branches in 1935. Its agency in Edinburgh, which had been opened in 1863 and was latterly under the management of R. & E. Scott, was closed in 1927, but by then the agency's contribution to the London business had dwindled away. In the darkest days of the Depression, London's earnings contributed all but £856 of branch net profits of £173 294 in 1930, while in the following year the London net profits of £155 000 were matched against overseas losses of £110 000. Even so, the business and earnings of the London branch were on behalf of the overseas branches and the comparison of these branches' results is a more helpful guide to the fortunes of the bank.

Lending activity at all the Mercantile's principal overseas branches (with the exception of Colombo) consistently exceeded their levels of deposits between the mid-1920s and the mid-1930s. Bombay and Calcutta reversed their traditional rankings in the same period, with Bombay's share of the total assets of the overseas branches rising from 19.0 to 26.1 per cent between 1927 and 1935. Calcutta's share fell by comparable proportions from 24.5 to 20.2 per cent. Bombay office suffered from the depression in the cotton industry which lasted from 1923 until the mid-1930s. The industry was hard hit by increased competition from Japan and the US, and was also racked by labour troubles. These problems had a sharp impact on the business of the branch, which was unprofitable in most years until 1932 but then produced sharp increases in earnings in the mid-1930s. Its net profits of £43 033 in 1935 were equivalent to one-fifth of all branch net profits in that year. The earnings of the Calcutta office were similarly dependent on the fortunes of the jute industry, which experienced fat years between 1922 and 1928 but then fell on lean times as overproduction and a drop in demand led prices to plummet. The net profits of Calcutta branch dropped as a result and the office posted a loss in 1931 (see Figure 4.2).

Singapore, with as much as 18.4 per cent of assets of the overseas branches in 1927, and Colombo held station as the next largest in the branch rankings. These two branches together contributed over one quarter of the bank's net branch profits in 1928 and 1929 but were then badly hit by the Depression. In 1930 net losses at Singapore (£41 418) and Penang (£20 789) were barely covered by the net earnings of all the bank's overseas branches put together. The other exceptional fluctuations in Steuart's period of office were new signs of profitability at Hong Kong (in 1929–31, in the depths of the slump), Shanghai (in 1933 and 1934), and Madras office's loss of £27 259 in 1929. This 'unfortunate business at Madras', as Ryrie described it, was the result of a major and costly fraud on the valuation of groundnut stocks. The Madras affair eventually cost the bank over £100 000.[7]

Outside this group of principal branches, the Mercantile's branch network had been virtually static since the acquisition of the Bank of Mauritius in 1916. Only the New York office, opened in 1919, had

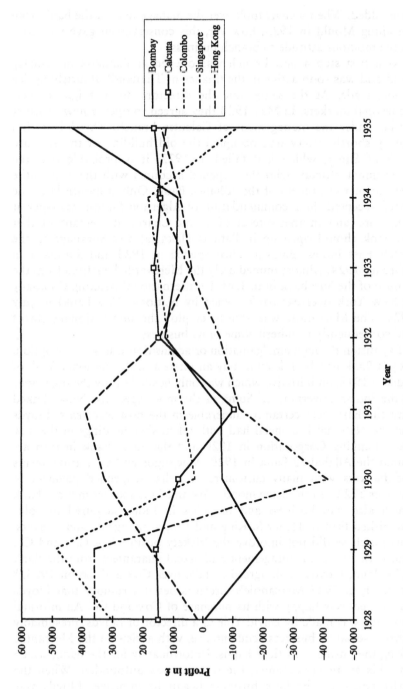

4.2 Mercantile Bank: net profits of principal overseas branches, 1928–35

been added. When Steuart took over the management of the bank from
the ailing Mould in 1923, however, this conservatism gave way to a
more ambitious attitude to branch business.

As a first step a new branch was opened at Bangkok in January
1923 and was soon active in the finance of Thailand's flourishing rice
export trade. At the same time the directors did not ignore their
traditional markets. In May 1923 they agreed to open a new office at
Simla, under the management of Calcutta branch. This hill-station
agency shortly afterwards occupied the old building of the Alliance
Bank of Simla, which had failed in 1922; it is probable that the
government officials who then opened accounts with the Mercantile
were former customers of the Alliance Bank. Only a month later the
board accepted the recommendation of Algernon Linton, manager at
Singapore (and another veteran of the old Chartered Mercantile), that
the bank should open up in Batavia (Jakarta) and Surabaya in the
Dutch East Indies. Batavia office opened in 1923 and Surabaya in
February 1924. Almost immediately the Mercantile benefited from the
closure of the Surabaya branch of the International Banking Company
(a New York overseas bank owned by National City Bank) in July
1924. The Mercantile was able to employ the International's shroff
and consequently to inherit some of its business.

Expansion through amalgamation or acquisition was another option.
Lloyds Bank had been keen to buy an interest in the National Bank of
India in 1918, an initiative which was only headed off by the objections
of the Indian government.[8] Some of the more specialist banks linked
with the East were certainly vulnerable in the post-war years. Lloyds
and the National Provincial had both taken shareholdings in the new
P&O Banking Corporation in 1920 and the P&O Bank in turn acquired the Allahabad Bank in 1920. Macgrigor and Co., army agents
and bankers with many customers in India, suspended payment in
October 1922.[9] In the same month Cox and Co., another military bank
which also had business and branches in India, acquired the old-
established firm of Henry S. King and Co., army agents and bankers.
This purchase did not improve the 'rickety position' of Cox and Co.
and, with strong encouragement and actual guarantees from the Bank
of England, Lloyds Bank agreed to take over Cox and Co. in 1923.[10]
However, in 1927 Mercantile's directors heard a rumour that Lloyds
was not entirely happy with its purchase of Cox and Co. An informal
approach was made by David Yule to a director of Lloyds, presumably
either a social or business acquaintance, with a view to the Mercantile
taking the business off their hands. Unfortunately for the bank, which
saw this as an opportunity, the rumour was unfounded. When the
performance of the Cox business began to improve, Lloyds was

certainly not disposed to sell, and its 'temporary intrusion' in India was to continue until 1960.[11]

This willingness to take on short-term opportunities evolved in the late 1920s to become a more deliberate strategy of expansion. The most active front in that expansion was the Federated Malay States, where the huge growth in the rubber industry since 1909 was now accompanied by a renewed surge in tin mining. Tin, rubber and railways plainly influenced the bank's initiatives in Malaya, but the views of local British advisers and an anxiety over the intentions of other British banks were also familiar themes. Indeed, one of the Mercantile's first references to new branches in this period included a report that the manager of another British bank had 'got drunk in the Tumpat Club & announced to all and sundry that the object of his visit was to inspect the possibilities of [Kuala] Krai as a branch'.[12] The Mercantile's expansion plans concentrated on the east coast of Malaya, as this was virgin territory for banks and the Mercantile could gain the advantage of being the first competitor in the area. One east coast manager wrote back to London in 1935 'on no account can you allow the Chartered and Hong Kong to get ahead of you in that part of the coast'.[13] The Chartered Bank and the Hongkong Bank had gained on the Mercantile on the west coast by opening branches in Ipoh, for instance, in 1912 and 1910 respectively.

The Mercantile, already represented by branches at Singapore, Penang, Kuala Lumpur and Kota Bharu, opened its first new Malayan agency at Kuantan on the east coast in 1926. This office was directly linked with the tin industry, as its principal function was to provide cash payments for wages at the up-country Pahang Consolidated Tin Mine. The new agency, in its remote site on the east coast, also had the advantage that Frederick Stocks, the accountant in charge in the first two years, was a fluent Malay speaker. In the wake of this initiative, in the summer of 1927 Steuart instructed Linton at Singapore and Ronald Cromartie (on inspection in the East) to investigate the possibilities for new agencies in the states of Kelantan, Trengganu and Pahang. Cromartie was told that the bank 'should not be forestalled in opening an agency by another bank, which may damage the business we have already built up in Kota Bharu'.[14] In the teeth of the autumn monsoon, Cromartie set off on an up-country tour to consult government officials and potential customers. He soon secured the agreement of the British adviser in Kelantan that the Mercantile would be given first option of opening in the state. Cromartie also persuaded the board to establish an office at Ipoh. 'HAVE YOU CONSIDERED OPENING IPOH: LIKELY TO BE AS IMPORTANT AS KUALA LUMPUR', Cromartie telegraphed to Steuart in November 1927.[15] Ipoh's tin industry was then flourishing and the fast-growing town was about to become the new state capital of Perak. The Mercantile's office, which began business in 1928 under the management of Penang branch, faced the competition of its old rivals the Hongkong and Chartered banks.

The investigation of other potential sites continued throughout 1928 and 1929. Robert Kennedy, acting manager at Penang in 1928, stressed the urgency of expansion. He argued that Penang branch was handicapped by the lack of up-country offices and, as a result, practically all tin and rubber company accounts were kept with the Chartered ('who run 12 ledgers') and the Hongkong Bank ('4 ledgers'). A year later Kennedy – by then manager at Singapore – had won the argument and was operating on the basis that 'It is apparently the policy of the Bank to expand in Malaya as opportunity offers.'[16]

The locations under consideration included Kampar, which was favoured by Kennedy, and Trengganu, where the bank eventually opened an agency in 1936. The decisive issue was the extension of the Federated Malay States (FMS) Railways along the east coast to connect with Kelantan and the Siamese Railways to Bangkok. The FMS Railways' managers were dissatisfied with the existing arrangements with the Mercantile's office at Kota Bharu 'which necessitated money being brought across the river at Kota Bharu'.[17] They also threatened to take payments business to the Chartered Bank which, along with the Oversea Chinese Bank, was rumoured to be setting up in Kelantan.

In response the Mercantile opened full-time agencies at Kuala Lipis and Kuala Krai in the autumn of 1929, a process which was speeded up by the agreements which Cromartie had obtained earlier from the Kelantan authorities. The Kuala Lipis agency also benefited from the expansion of the rubber estates of the Compagnie de Selangor but the Kuala Krai office was solely dependent upon railway business. Kuala Krai was predicted to be the main centre of the east coast railway but, when the FMS Railways changed their plans, the agency was closed in 1931. As a whole, nevertheless, the initiatives in Malaya strengthened the spread and capacity of the bank's business (see Figure 4.3). The 1920s and early 1930s saw a marked increase in business volumes at the Malayan branches. Total assets at Kuala Lumpur and Penang increased by 58 and 81 per cent between 1920 and 1935. By then the new branch at Ipoh was also well established and was already comparable in the scale of its business with branches such as Bangkok.

The opening of the up-country offices in Malaya showed that at this stage Steuart and his directors took a positive stance on expansion and competition. London continued to push these new opportunities even when the bank's local managers and government advisers differed with London over the location of new offices. Steuart was also prepared to look much further afield. In May 1927 James Crichton, London manager, wrote to all managers in the East and sought their views on the

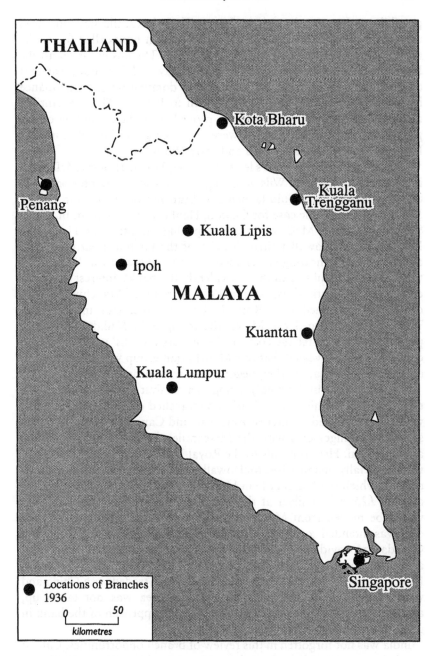

4.3   Locations of branches of the Mercantile Bank in Malaya, *c.* 1936

possibility of a new branch in Japan. The Mercantile had not been represented in Japan since 1885,[18] and Crichton now called for statistics on each branch's recent trade with Japan. The answer from all the Eastern offices, with the exception of Bombay and Rangoon, was that the small volume of trade and the apparent domination of trade finance by the Japanese banks ruled out a return to Japan.[19] The Mercantile's managers in Bombay and Rangoon proved to be better judges of the prospects, as Japanese textiles were to make great inroads into the Indian market in the late 1920s and early 1930s.

In their replies to Crichton's letter regarding Japan, Thomas McDowall in Shanghai and Norval Wilson in Singapore made the counter-proposal that the Mercantile should launch new branches or agencies in China. McDowall argued the case for Canton, Hankow and Tientsin. In return Steuart consulted McDowall about opening an office at Harbin in Manchuria. McDowall visited this city of the far north early in 1929 and, after a very thorough assessment, concluded that it was 'inevitable' that the bank would open there. Evidently the bank's interest in northern China was noticed as, later in 1929, a group of Manchurian 'high officials' approached John Ross, McDowall's successor in Shanghai. This delegation urged the Mercantile to open in Mukden and even promised to guarantee the costs of the first six months' working. When consular advice revealed that this Manchurian group was attempting to corner the soya bean market, negotiations were promptly halted.[20]

McDowall was undoubtedly acting as a catalyst for new initiatives in this period. After his visit to Harbin he travelled on to North America, where he attempted to interest American and Canadian banks in correspondent arrangements with the Mercantile's branches in Hong Kong and Shanghai. His proposals to the Royal Bank of Canada in Montreal were especially imaginative. McDowall proposed an ingenious arrangement in which the Mercantile in Hong Kong would make the Royal an offer of £25 000 in silver at the end of each day's business; this offer would be moved from Montreal to Vancouver on the same day. The deal was intended to use the time differences between Hong Kong and Canada to provide the Royal Bank with much finer rates than were available from banks which quoted rates less frequently. The Royal Bank's branches in Cuba, Panama and Lima also traded with China and would benefit from this daily service. The idea was not taken up, although it was a signal of the more expansive approach of the bank in general and McDowall in particular.

India was not forgotten in this review of branch opportunities. Calicut was being considered as a branch location as early as August 1927, and in 1928 the bank looked at the proposals for a new east coast port at Vizagapatnam. Steuart – against advice given by Cromartie while on a local inspection tour – reserved a site on the reclaimed land at 'Vizag' and the possibility of a new office continued to be under review when the port was eventually opened in 1933. Alleppey, on the far south-west coast, was also mooted as a potential site. In June 1930 Steuart suggested that William Cruden, manager in Madras, 'might take a gun down to Alleppey and shoot at snipe and find out what is going on in that district'.[21] The idea was not as casual as it seemed, as Cruden's fact-finding visit later led to proposals for a branch at nearby Cochin.

Although these investigations did not produce additions to the branch network in the short term, they prepared the ground for future initiatives. The consideration of new branches in Japan and China, together with the reinforcements in Malaya, was also evidence of a more progressive, outward-looking management. This readiness to expand into new markets gave an assertive and confident message to customers, staff and shareholders – and perhaps even to the bank's own directors.

Did the performance of the new branches justify this confidence? It is worth looking in more detail at the prosperity of the new branches themselves and the bank's attitude towards them. In exchange banking new branches were usually established for one of two reasons: either they acted as deposit-taking branches to funnel funds to the larger parent branches which were short of local resources (the sub-branches in Ceylon, for example) or they were intended to respond to and take advantage of a growing export or import business (for instance, Rangoon branch's share in the financing of rice exports from Burma).

The Mercantile Bank's new sub-branches were established for a combination of these reasons. The sub-branches on the east coast of Malaya were partly to provide funds and contacts for Singapore and partly speculative in that the bank was hoping that the extension of the FMS Railways and the expansion of the rubber estates of the region would provide exchange and bill business. Yet in the short term the sub-branches barely paid their way. By 1935 Kuala Lipis office had been open for six years and had never made a profit. The then manager estimated that although the branch gave the bank Rs 2.5 lakhs in resources, they were really paying a rate of interest of about 5 per cent for this money.[22] This was not necessarily the fault of the bank – the area was in the process of development and the volume of business was not yet large enough to generate any meaningful surplus. Moreover, profitable business such as granting loans and overdrafts was hampered by practical difficulties. The most usual security offered for the granting of credit in this part of the world was property, and the Mercantile was wary of locking up its funds in this way. Even if the bank had been willing to advance against land, in many cases satisfactory deeds did not exist and land registries were only just being opened. The managers of both Kuala Lipis and Singapore wrote to head office in 1935, pleading the case for moving the agency to Raub, which was more centrally placed within the state of Pahang and which would attract more estate accounts. London did not agree (although an agency at Raub was eventually opened in 1961), and the Kuala Lipis office continued to make losses.

The new Simla branch also suffered from the lack of business opportunities: the branch only made a profit in one half-year between its opening in 1923 and 1935. Apart from the private accounts of government and military officers, the only important business of the area was the financing of potatoes which were grown there and transported throughout India. In 1929 London decided that the business of the branch did not warrant the expenditure on a senior officer as agent. The Calcutta manager was told that in future he should send an assistant there of three to five years' standing. In 1934 the future of the office hung in the balance, but in the event the branch was reprieved.

The story was similar at the sub-branches at Batavia (Jakarta) and Surabaya. These were established largely to finance the import of rice from Burma and Siam and the export of sugar from the Dutch East Indies, trades for which the bank already financed the other side of the business. However, Surabaya branch made a loss every year from its opening in 1924. In 1927, John Ross, one of the more energetic managers of the bank, was posted to Surabaya. He immediately attempted to forge an alliance with Fraser, Eaton and Co., export agents with a large business in India and China and branches throughout Java. Ross suggested that the Mercantile and Fraser, Eaton should work together. Fraser, Eaton would provide the godowns and the expertise and the Mercantile would provide the trade finance. This alliance was intended to meet competition from the Dutch banks which were refusing to advance against goods held in the godowns of Fraser, Eaton in order to capture the business for themselves. However, by 1929 business had still not improved and the new manager, John Ferrier, wrote to London, 'life here is an awful struggle'.[23] In addition to the competition from the Dutch banks such as the Java Bank, the Mercantile also had to contend with the Chartered (established in Surabaya in 1877) and the Hongkong Bank (established in 1896). Both Surabaya and Batavia (Jakarta) were to be closed in 1933 during the Depression. Steuart, reviewing the episode in November 1932, told the Dutch colonial department that 'As late-comers to [Java] we had no chance of building up a satisfactory business before the economic storm broke ... it would have taken a large economic profit to compensate for the actual losses incurred on the Island.'[24]

The opening of new branches led to expansion of staff numbers. Between the wars the total number of the bank's staff grew to between

1200 and 1500 employees (excluding domestic staff at bank houses and flats). In 1923 the Mercantile employed about 75 men on the Eastern staff and by 1935 this total had swelled to nearer 90. Recruitment policies, however, still remained *ad hoc*, with the bank following several methods according to the urgency with which staff were needed. The usual and age-old method was to accept suitable candidates who had been recommended to them by persons with connections in the East, ex-members of staff or directors. For instance Robson Thomas, joining in 1925, was introduced by an old family friend who had been the Mercantile's manager in Calcutta; Charles Pow, joining in the same year, had an entrée through his uncle who was a friend of Steuart, the chief manager. The following year James Shirreff was secured employment by Benjamin White, the silver expert at the merchant bankers Samuel Montagu and Co., who claimed to have placed over 100 young men in positions in the City.[25]

This method was augmented in the mid-1920s when the bank realized that all the men recruited and sent east immediately after the Great War were now becoming due for their first spell of furlough, and there were not enough juniors in London to replace them. The bank placed an advertisement in *The Times* in 1924 ('Wanted by an Eastern Bank'), offering a salary of £540 for a post in the East and requiring candidates to have passed Part One of the Institute of Bankers' examination.[26] This minimum qualification ensured that those who applied for the positions would have a modicum of banking experience and could therefore be sent to the East much earlier than a raw recruit. This was also the argument that was used to recruit young bankers from Scottish banks. In 1926 Crichton, Steuart's second in command in London, wrote to John Ross and Eric Paton who were then on leave in Scotland: 'We are short of men on the Eastern staff in London who are old enough or experienced enough for our purpose. If you should come across likely men in any of the Scotch Banks who with a few months in head office would suit our purpose we shall be glad if you would let us know.'[27]

In the period of Steuart's management the Mercantile began to stipulate that London juniors should pass Part One of the Institute of Bankers' examinations before they were sent east. Until then, although new recruits to the London office had been encouraged to study in the evenings to take these exams, this training had not been compulsory. In the 1930s this attitude altered. Increasing numbers of home and overseas banks were expecting their staff to obtain Institute qualifications and in the early 1930s there were over 15 000 candidates for the Institute's examinations (approximately one-tenth of the banking workforce) each year.[28] The London management of the Mercantile none the less remained acutely aware that qualifications were not the only indication of what would make a successful Eastern banker. They had their own image of a suitable candidate in terms of education, background and character. Crichton, in his efforts to recruit young Scots bankers in 1926, argued that 'The matter is somewhat urgent but we shall take only men who are completely suitable. There is no use in sending out men of the wrong type.'[29] One member of staff who joined in 1926 remembered that he was initially rejected because he had not attended a public school, but the intercessions of his sponsor eventually won him a place.[30]

The career prospects of juniors joining under Steuart's managership were probably better than those of their predecessors. The new agencies gave assistants the chance to prove themselves able and responsible. Those juniors who were lucky enough to be in Calcutta branch between 1929 and 1936 also benefited from the training they received from the manager, Ronald Cromartie. Cromartie held exchange classes in the 'chummery' (the mess where the junior members of staff lived), where he taught the assistants the rudiments of exchange working and took them through various transactions showing how to calculate a final rate of exchange. This kind of training within the bank was rare; in general it was expected that a newcomer would pick up the work on the job.

At the strategic level the Mercantile's experiments with its branch network showed that Steuart and his board were willing to follow their customers into new or altered markets. This ability to adapt was also evident in the changing character of the bank's customer base. The internationalization of the bank's business, which had been signalled in the immediate post-war period (see above, page 52) now gathered pace. In 1930 or 1931 the bank compiled a list of firms in India and the East 'in whose favour we open credits from time to time'.[31] British trading houses with networks of overseas branches feature strongly, as for example Ralli Brothers ('various places, India'),[32] Andrew Yule and Co., Harrisons and Crosfield, and the Sassoon companies. The list also had an international scope by including long-standing traders such as the East Asiatic Company ('All Branches and Agencies'), Volkart Brothers, and Speidel and Co. at Hankow, Newchang, Shanghai and Hong Kong. Likewise Japanese traders were prominent. Of the 84 firms listed, fourteen were in Kobe, Nagoya, Yokohama or Tokyo; the Bombay offices of Nippon Menkwa Kabushiki and Gosho Kabushiki Kaisha were separately listed. These linkages facilitated the growing trade in Japanese textiles. The Mercantile also named firms which were based along the trade routes to the East at locations where the bank had no branches or agents – six firms were noted at Djibouti in French Somaliland, for instance, with others at Aden and Cairo.

The evolution of the bank's customer base was also reflected in its granting of confirmed credits. In 1927 – the last full year in which the records of these credits are available – the directors granted 269 confirmed credits with a total value of £1 108 492.[33] While this was a larger *number* of credits, the average facility of £4121 was at a lower level than in 1910 (£5145) or in the boom year of 1920 (£7485). The Mercantile's willingness to provide very small credits contributed to this trend. In 1927 credits were granted for as little as £30 (for the export of mattress fibre from Colombo) and another 25 credits of less than £100 were agreed during the year. At the other end of the spectrum, the bank continued to finance deals as large as £100 000 for jute exported from Calcutta by Birla Brothers Ltd, one of the leading entrants to the jute industry since the First World War.[34]

The localization of export deals was the most striking feature of this business in the late 1920s. This feature had already emerged in the immediate post-war years (see above, page 52), but by 1927 a clear majority of credits was granted in favour of local, non-European exporters. The exact number cannot be verified as the origins of all names in the list are not always obvious. At the very least, however, 149 credits or 55.4 per cent of the total in 1927 were in favour of local exporters. This was a marked change in the composition of the Mercantile's business, which British exporters had dominated before the First World War and had still held the majority share in 1920. Prominent examples of local exporters in 1927 included Chananmull Kanmull Lodha, exporting jute from Calcutta (18 credits); Yue Lee Yuen, shipping baskets, mats and other goods from Hong Kong (18 credits); Heeralall Agurwall and Co., exporting jute from Calcutta; and S. G. C. Munirathnam, trading hides and divi-divi (seeds for dyes) from Madras. British exporters such as C. S. Mitchell and Co. and Shand and Co. were now a dwindling group at the Eastern end of trade financed by the bank.

The principals in this business were import companies and firms which needed finance for specified contracts with exporters. These importers, as in the Mercantile's earlier history, were mostly London-based trading houses and agencies operating from the warren of offices in the area of Eastcheap, Great Tower Street, Mark Lane and Mincing Lane (where the regular tea auctions were held). Yet the pattern of demand continued to shift. The London and overseas merchant banks which had turned to the Mercantile in the post-war years had vanished from the list of credits by 1927. The suddenness of their appearance and disappearance suggests that their experiments as importers were limited short-term responses to the conditions and opportunities of the post-war boom.

The case of the merchant banks showed that trade finance was a fluid market for overseas banks such as the Mercantile. The customer base was certainly not static. Thornett and Fehr, whose Singapore trade had dominated the demand for credits in 1920, no longer applied to the Mercantile in 1927. Conversely two major firms – C. A. & H. Nichols, commission merchants, with 44 confirmed credits (16 per cent of the total number) in 1927, and Bastone and Firminger, old-established 'colonial brokers' with 36 credits – had been customers of the bank before the First World War. The other principal customers were recent applicants. They included Hall and Partners (33 credits), Allan and Roseberry (20 credits) and H. B. Sleeman and Co. (14 credits). Of this group Allan and Roseberry, jute brokers of Eastcheap, had been incorporated as recently as 1923, but by 1927 they were operating on by far the largest scale of all applicants for the bank's confirmed credits. Their credits, exclusively for the export of jute from Calcutta, amounted to £490 000 in 1927. This level of business averaged £24 500 per credit and dwarfed the demand from merchant firms such as Hall and Partners (£73 980 at an average of £2242 per credit) or Nichols (£17 150 at £390). The only customers who needed a higher level of credit were the East Indian Produce Company (with two credits of £100 000 and £50 000 for Calcutta jute) and Rowe White and Co. (with three tea credits totalling £110 000).

While the identity of principal customers may have been changing in the later 1920s, the commodities and trade routes financed by the bank did not vary dramatically. The sub-continent's share of the business was 77 per cent in 1927, a similar level to 1920 (see page 52). Jute from Calcutta, still enjoying boom conditions, was the largest single trade receiving credits in this period (in 53 cases). Other fibres (mostly from Colombo and mostly mattress fibre), rubber, hides (especially from Madras), and tea followed in importance. Facilities for Calcutta were also much higher in value than for other export centres. Confirmed credits for Calcutta amounted to £735 428 in 1927 at an average of £10 977 per credit. This was a marked contrast to Colombo where, although the bank agreed a larger number of credits, the year's total of £149 795 and the average credit of £1971 were only a fraction of the levels required for Calcutta.

Outside the sub-continent no credits were provided – and perhaps not requested – for exports from Singapore. Other Eastern ports were now prominent in the bank's confirmed credits. At Hong Kong all 19 credits were for mixed exports by Yue Lee Yuen; at Shanghai 18 credits were provided for shipments of tea, hen albumen and, in one case, 'leopard cat robes'; and at Rangoon the bank financed exports of rice (for Samuel Dobree and Son) and rubber (for Harries and Son). The bank was also providing credits as far afield as Surabaya, Tsingtao and Tientsin. New or unusual risks included wolfram ore from Penang, cuttlefish and lizard skins from Calcutta, and wood oil from Hong Kong.

The Mercantile's management ensured that this diversity, and the greater 'localization' of export business, did not entail any increase in risk to the bank. DP (Documents against Payment, or the presentation of bills of lading by the shipper to the bank) was the favoured form of security in 1927, when it was provided in 90 per cent of credits. The terms of credit continued to shorten to an average of 2.8 months for drafts and only 2.6 months for the duration of the credits. Open or unsecured credits, which had been so prominent in the business before the First World War, were allowed in only four cases in 1927. Clearly the bank's directors and managers were anxious to reduce the period of their exposure to credit risk and to strengthen the level of security required from customers.

The impact of the Depression on this pattern of business cannot be assessed with any precision, as the directors did not record their decisions on confirmed credits after 1928. Yet it is certain that the bank faced and then overcame disruption throughout its traditional markets. The commodity trades had already entered a period of unprecedented turmoil in the late 1920s. Bombay's cloth exports were in steep decline from 1926, contributing to a decline in the price index of Indian exports from 233 in 1925 to 177 in 1930 and only 128 by 1935. Malayan rubber and tin prices, which had boomed in the mid-1920s, fell sharply in 1927 and 1928 and then created a glut which depressed markets (especially in the US) could not reduce.[35] Sugar prices were also in decline, damaging the prospects for the bank in Mauritius and Java.

These trends were affecting the bank's business and the earnings of its branches even before the stock market crashes in the autumn of 1929. The slump itself damaged all the bank's markets, but the situation in India was of paramount concern. In late 1929 news of the financial crash, followed by the Indian National Congress's declaration of a campaign of agitation against British rule, put pressure on the rupee and encouraged a flight of capital from India.[36] In 1930 and early 1931 the Indian government responded by restricting the money supply, but its efforts to obtain a special credit from the British government produced only a promise of 'financial support under suitable conditions'.[37] The outflow of capital and the pressure on the rupee resumed in the summer of 1931 and the position was only relieved by the British government's decision to take sterling off the gold standard in September that year. London had unilaterally decided to link the rupee to sterling in coming off the gold standard – an action which created deep anger in the Indian government.

In the short term the decision did not lead to the dislocation which might have been expected. The banks and stock exchanges closed between 21 and 24 September but, although the exchange banks discussed 'the possibility of a general run on the banks',[38] assurances by the Imperial Bank and the Indian government produced a quiet reopening of the banks and exchanges on 25 September. In the longer run the departure from the gold standard led, fortuitously, to a gradual return to stability. Indian export prices had suffered and continued to suffer a steep decline: from late 1931 the effective depreciation of both sterling and the rupee led to a surge in exports of gold, fuelled partly by 'distress' sales of Indian landlords and moneylenders selling hoarded gold.[39] Indian industry, in contrast, was actually less damaged than in the recession of the early 1920s. By 1935–36 output was substantially ahead of its level ten years earlier in all sectors except jute and woollens.[40]

The heaviest impact on the Mercantile was seen in its results for 1931. Both in London and India the bank had incurred exchange losses after the suspension of the gold standard, while its investments had suffered as a result of the depreciation of the bank's British and Indian securities. The board and management were by no means sure of the duration of the crisis. Robert Edlundh, their representative in New York, had told them that confidence in the market remained extremely fragile. 'In the highest financial and governmental circles there is suppressed hysteria and panic accentuated by a dread of communistic activities if things do not improve ... the outlook could scarcely be worse.'[41] In preparing the 1931 results, the bank therefore took a pessimistic view of bad debts. The directors told shareholders that profits were insufficient to cover bad debts, and that £450 000 had been transferred from the published reserves to inner reserves. This transfer reduced published reserves to £1 050 000 (their lowest level since 1920). Provision for bad debts and the other losses was then made from the inner reserves; these provisions included £140 000 against exchange losses in Shanghai, Bangkok and Java as a result of the end of the gold standard.

John Ryrie, in the chair at the shareholders' meeting in March 1932, promised that the bank would 'go forward with courage and confidence, seared a little perhaps by the ordeal of last year, but richer by the experience'.[42] The shareholders themselves were not richer by the experience. In common with most domestic and overseas banks, the Mercantile cut its dividend. The reduction from 16 to 12 per cent between 1930 and 1933 was comparable to cuts by the Chartered (20 to 14 per cent) and the Eastern Bank (9 to 6 per cent). Although the directors succeeded in maintaining the annual payments of £15 000 to the staff pension fund, they agreed to cut their own fees and imposed cuts on staff salaries. In September 1931 Steuart had written to all the managers in the East with the solemn news that

> In view of the uncertain outlook and ... a deplorable falling off in business ... it is essential that expenses be reduced until conditions improve. In regard to the Eastern staff ... a reduction of 10% [on salaries] has to be made and the Board trust this will be received without complaining. All allowances to native staff in the East have to be discontinued with the exception of Hong Kong and Shanghai.[43]

This salary reduction remained in force until 1937.[44]

Throughout the most severe years of the Depression, the Mercantile's directors and managers were watching political developments as closely as they were keeping track of commodity prices and security values. The political scene in India was the principal worry. The campaign for independence led by the Swaraj Party repeatedly brought disruption and doubt into business life throughout the Depression years, and also influenced the Indian domestic markets against British products and services. An unnamed banker in Bombay, writing to the Eastern Exchange Banks' Association in September 1930, reported on the 'growing hostility to British and foreign institutions ... we are reaching a stage of political rancour'.[45] Rural unrest over the slump in wheat prices, which became a factor in Gandhi's 'salt march' in the spring of 1930, added to this hostility. There were also direct challenges to the exchange banks which were accused of prejudicial treatment of Indian business. Various proposals were suggested to curb their influence, including requiring them to be licensed and not permitting them to accept Indian deposits. These deposits were increasingly turning away from the exchange banks and towards the strengthening Indian banking sector. Traditionally, the exchange banks held a higher proportion of total deposits than Indian joint stock banks, but this position was reversed by 1935 when the Indian banks held Rs 897 million and the exchange banks only Rs 762 million. The total number of Indian-owned joint stock banks nearly trebled from only 54 in 1930 to 154 by 1939.[46]

The future structure of banking in India was a key part of the political debate. Any changes in the currency and banking regulations were of vital concern to exchange banks such as the Mercantile. The arguments for an Indian central or reserve bank were not new, but they gained new impetus in the late 1920s. In 1925 the government of India had appointed a royal commission to report on Indian currency and consider the stabilization of the rupee. Managing the currency in this way would require some kind of mechanism for supervision and regulation, implying the need for a central bank or monetary authority. In

1927 the government published three bills which were largely based on the recommendations of the report of the Royal Commission. The first of these sought to stabilize the rupee at 1s. 6d., the second set out the constitution of a reserve bank, and the third dealt with the future status of the Imperial Bank of India. This bank would suffer from the loss of government business to the proposed reserve bank, and so the former restrictions placed upon it (for example prohibiting it from dealing in foreign exchange) would be removed.

The Mercantile Bank's board was in favour of the first bill (which was later enacted as the 1927 Currency Act) and was resigned to accept the other two, but with modifications. In particular the bank took issue with the amount of reserves which the exchange banks would be required to keep permanently with the proposed reserve bank, a requirement which would obviously affect their liquidity. The bank was also anxious that competition in Indian banking, which was already at its height and was described by Ryrie as 'suicidal', would be exacerbated by the entrance of the Imperial Bank. The directors' concerns were shared with the other exchange banks and in 1927 the Eastern Exchange Banks Association presented their objections to various provisions of the Reserve Bank Bill. The bill was shelved but was eventually revived in 1933. The passage of this legislation brought the Reserve Bank of India into being in 1935, enabling it to take control of India's currency and credit. In effect the new central bank brought together the former functions of the Controller of Currency and the Imperial Bank of India. The Mercantile would have to adapt to the demands and requirements of the new regulatory regime.

When James Steuart retired as chief manager in 1935, the Mercantile had proved to be at least as durable as its competitors in withstanding the economic and political onslaught of the Depression years. Total assets of £17.2 million were only 6.5 per cent below the level of £18.4 million ten years earlier. In the same period, the balance sheet total of the Hongkong Bank had fallen by 18 per cent to £68.5 million, the Chartered's had been reduced by 16 per cent to £59.6 million, and the assets of the National Bank of India had been depleted by 14 per cent to £35.2 million. All three banks remained much larger enterprises, but they had felt the impact of the crisis more severely than the Mercantile Bank.

The Mercantile had also responded to the Depression years by adding an extra layer of security to its internal balance sheet. Charles Innes, as a newcomer to the board, wrote to his colleagues in 1934 and argued that the bank should significantly increase its transfers to inner reserves. Assuming that the published reserves were already substantial, 'these inner reserves strengthen the position of the bank for with them it has greater liberty of action'.[47] As the experience of the Depression had already shown, banks 'can make use of them without any fear of loss of credit or damage to prestige'. Innes pointed out that the Mercantile's published reserves were already stronger than those of any other British overseas bank except the Hongkong Bank (which 'was in a class by itself'). Innes also emphasized the importance of flexibility in the face of uncertainties and possible bad debts in India and Malaya: 'everything in my view points to the need for a policy of caution'. His arguments won round his colleagues, and from 1934 onwards more substantial additions were made to inner reserves. While the published reserves remained untouched at £1 075 000 between 1932 and 1947, the inner reserves were increased in the same period from £623 592 to £2.2 million. Innes was chairman for most of these years and it can be assumed that the increased additions to inside funds became orthodoxy within the bank.

The Mercantile's published profits had shrunk at an even faster rate than the reduction of the balance sheet during the Depression. The total of £152 082 in 1931 was more than £100 000 below published profits in 1928 and 1929. Again, other Eastern banks had suffered more damage. Hongkong Bank's published profits, for instance, were nearly halved to £78 700 in 1935. The Mercantile's share prices, dividends and yields also fared remarkably well. In 1935 the high-point prices of all three categories of the bank's shares were equal to or above their levels of ten years earlier. In comparison the high-point prices of shares of the Hongkong Bank, National Bank of India and, in particular, the Chartered, were well below their 1925 standings.

Share prices do not always mirror the full view of a company's performance, but in the Mercantile's case the contrast with its competitors shows the true resilience of the bank's business. The volume and profitability of its activities survived the commercial and political upheavals throughout its principal markets. On a more personal level, Steuart, as the only survivor of the old Chartered Mercantile's torments in the early 1890s, could have taken great pride in this achievement. His skills in the management of crisis left his successors a position in Eastern banking which was as secure as any in the sector.

CHAPTER FIVE

Ready or not, 1935–47

For British overseas banks, the period between the mid-1930s and the late 1940s was dominated by wars, rumours of wars and political upheaval. Bankers were forced to think and plan in terms of contingencies rather than opportunities. The likelihood of conflict in Europe persisted throughout the 1930s, while the Sino-Japanese war in 1937 marked the shift of military danger on to a global stage. Even in the post-war period, conflict and revolution were more immediate concerns than peaceful reconstruction. The Mercantile Bank and many other British overseas banks faced uncertainty in all their markets in these years. The bank's readiness and its ability to adapt to sudden change were to be severely tested, not only in the expected conflict in Europe but also in the volatile and unknown context of a Pacific war.

The durability of the Mercantile's leadership was an essential factor in this period of prolonged crisis. In established bank tradition, the retirement of Steuart as chief manager in 1935 presaged continuity, not change. James Bain Crichton, his successor, was a Scot who had been with the bank since January 1901, going east in 1903. He had been manager at Hong Kong, Penang, Calcutta and Bombay before returning to Britain in 1925 as London manager. Just as Steuart had brought him home to be his right-hand man, so Crichton brought back from the East Eric Paton, formerly inspector of branches, and William Cruden, formerly Bombay manager, to complete the senior management team in head office.

Steuart did not sever his connection with the bank but took up a seat on the board. The Mercantile's board was also bolstered in 1935 by the addition of another professional banker, Sir Thomas Smith. Sir Thomas had begun his career with the Royal Bank of Scotland but had served with the Allahabad Bank in India between 1895 and 1935, becoming a director in 1929. He was also well acquainted with Indian business through his chairmanship of the Muir Mills in Cawnpore and was to be a permanent fixture on the board during Crichton's managership. During 1937 the board lost the service of C. Hambro (through resignation), J. M. Ryrie and W. Shelford (who both died in 1937). Hambro had acted as the bank's contact in the City world of merchant banking and was replaced by R. H. V. (Rufus) Smith, a partner in Morgan Grenfell. This appointment was almost certainly brought about by Lord Catto, who had owed his position as manager of the Yule companies to Smith's father, Vivian Smith, also a partner in Morgan Grenfell (see page 59). The other vacant seat was filled by Clifford Figg, chairman and director of a large number of Ceylon-based tea companies including Whittall & Co. Figg's other appointments included the deputy chairmanship of the International Tea Committee between 1933 and 1947.

Another important addition to the board in 1941, following the death of Lord Abertay (Sir Charles Barrie), was Sir John Hay, chairman and managing director of the agency house of Guthrie & Co. Guthries were concerned with the tin and rubber businesses of Malaya and Siam, and Hay brought the expertise in these areas and industries that had previously been provided by Ryrie and Shelford. Then when P. R. Chalmers died in September 1942 after 26 years as a director, there was no direct replacement for his special knowledge of Mauritius. Instead, by appointing Evelyn Bunbury, the board strengthened its Indian hand. Bunbury was formerly chairman of Forbes, Forbes, Campbell and Co. of Bombay, president of the Bombay local board of the Imperial Bank of India and (between 1935 and 1937) a director of the Bank of England. He was also a formidable presence in other areas of the Mercantile's activities, notably as chairman of the London Tin Corporation and of the Anglo-Oriental Mining Corporation between 1935 and 1937. Throughout these changes of membership, continuity and leadership of the board was provided by Sir Charles Innes, who served as chairman between 1937 and 1952.

The composition of the board continued to provide the bank with an information and intelligence resource in those countries where the Mercantile operated and in those trades and markets with which its prosperity was linked. However, the directors did not necessarily provide the bank with customers. For instance, many of Figg's tea companies banked with the Chartered Bank, as did Guthries. Surprisingly, although the National Bank of India had the largest share of tea bills in the London market,[1] many tea companies did not even bank with the British overseas banks. In 1935, from a total of 157 limited companies in the tea trade in India and Ceylon, 53 named the National Bank of India as their principal bank, 17 banked with the Mercantile and 13 with the Chartered. Of the remainder, no less than 43 companies preferred to keep their accounts with Scottish banks, a striking reminder of the origins and loyalties of many directors and managers in the tea trade.[2]

The latter half of the 1930s was a period of stuttering recovery. The worldwide depression of the first half of the decade and the consequent fall in demand for and prices of the commodities of India and the East had stimulated the introduction of restriction and quota schemes, theoretically to harmonize supply and demand. Tea, rubber and tin all required intervention of this kind. The International Tea Agreement, which attempted to restrict tea production in order to support its price, was concluded in 1933 and by 1937 Lord Catto was able to tell the bank's shareholders that prices were improving. Rubber had been badly hit during the Depression, with the price dropping to 2d. a pound (the price had reached 3s. per pound in 1925). Growers subsequently nego-tiated a scheme for the international regulation of rubber supplies which helped to restore the price. The tin industries of South-East Asia had suffered from the 40 per cent drop in consumption of tin during the Depression. In 1931 the first International Tin Agreement was con-cluded which regulated production on a 'pool' or quota basis. This helped to reduce surplus stocks, but the price of tin was still subject to price fluctuations. Price stability was all-important in those countries that were dependent on commodity exports for their wealth: tea, for example, made up 57 per cent of the total of Ceylon's exports in 1936.[3] Even when commodity prices began to rise from the doldrums of the early 1930s, a new recession in the United States served to dampen both demand and prices for the commodities of the East from 1937.

Far East trade was severely dislocated following the invasion of China by the Japanese in 1937. By 1938 the Japanese army had control over the commercial and industrial cities of eastern China and had closed the River Yangtze, China's most important inland trade artery, to foreign ships. Although Shanghai still retained its International Settlement, the city occupied a precarious and vulnerable position in the middle of Japanese-occupied territory. The Sino-Japanese war, the disruption of China's exports and the loss of the Chinese import markets had reper-cussions for the trades which the bank traditionally financed. For example, Japan's preoccupation with China had some favourable side-effects for the Indian cotton manufacturers. Indian exports of finished cotton to Japan and China, whose own cotton manufacture had been disrupted by the war, increased substantially. Conversely, Indian ex-porters of raw cotton who had previously been shipping their produce to mills in China and Japan now found themselves without customers.

The results of the bank's branches reflected these varying economic influences. Not only were the exporters of primary products experienc-ing lower prices and volumes and thus reducing sales of exchange by the bank for export purposes, but the worsening terms of trade meant that the local demand for imports also decreased. Ceylon's heavy reli-ance on tea and coconut products and the continued depression of their prices meant that Colombo branch, previously a high earner for the bank, fared badly and consistently made net losses from late 1935 until 1942. Bombay's profits fluctuated seasonally as the branch was heavily exposed to the vagaries of the cotton industry. Outside the sub-continent, Singapore branch's profits suffered in the crisis year of 1937 but otherwise contributed strongly to the bank's earnings. Similarly Shanghai branch dipped into the red in the latter part of 1937 due to the turbulence in trade caused by the invasion of the Japanese but then made exceptional profits in the late 1930s and in 1940–41. These profits significantly boosted the bank's overall position and contributed nearly half of the total of branch net profits in 1939 and 1940. By the late 1930s real and published annual profits had climbed slowly from the nadir of 1931; assets too experienced steady growth reaching just over £22 million by 1939 (see Figure 5.1).

The ascent of the Mercantile's Shanghai branch was sudden and spectacular. Lionel Blanks, senior assistant at Shanghai when he was first posted there in 1932, recalled that 'it was a small business' at that time. 'There was Indian cotton ... there was a general run of imports. There was the egg business [and] all the trinket business, all the novelties and souvenir markets ... firms like Gammon and people sending masses of stuff to India as well as jewellery and jade.' It was crucial, none the less, that the cosmopolitan character of Shanghai gave great potential for growth: 'they were the most money-minded communities [sic] you could find anywhere in the world ... in those days'.[4]

The profits generated by Shanghai branch in the late 1930s derived mainly from its foreign exchange business. The rates in Shanghai were exceptionally volatile because of the direct link between the tael and the price of silver. On the back of this market the city was able to support a large and active broking community. John 'Jackie' Huxter, the Mercantile's manager in Shanghai from 1937, had direct telephone lines from his desk to 30 or 40 brokers, and he undertook a huge and successful exchange business for the bank. His success can be attributed to a number of factors. He was more active and responsive to the exchange market than his competitors. The Hongkong Bank, for example, whose size and customer base allowed it a market-making position, took a decision in the morning on what rates it would quote that day. In comparison, Huxter would give a new quote at any time of day. Those who worked with Huxter credited his success in the exchange markets to his energy and to his information methods – he devised a system of elaborate information cards so that he knew at all times his position in every currency and his general position. Robson Thomas, the second accountant at the branch from November 1938, noted: 'He had a flair for it. He was on good terms with all the brokers ... Very little went past him. He would do things at lower rates to stop it going elsewhere. He was a very active operator.'[5]

Between 1938 and 1940 Huxter was able to generate impressive profits for the bank. In the half-year that ended in December 1939 Shanghai branch made over £160 000 in net profits, more than half

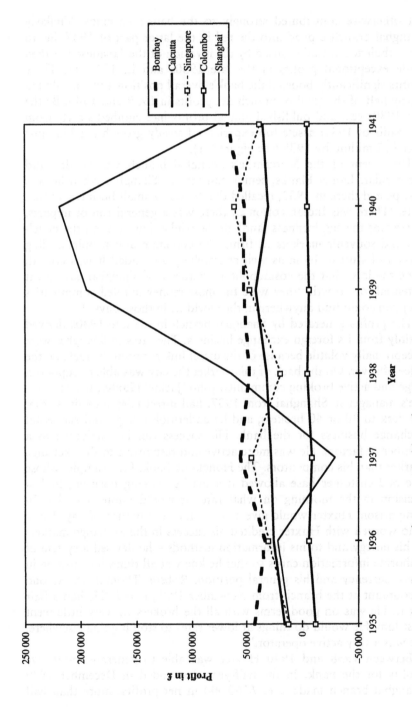

5.1 Mercantile Bank: net profits at principal branches, 1935–41

that of all the bank's branches and more than that posted by the Singapore, Calcutta, Bombay and London branches combined. His success and style of management, on the other hand, did not bring him great popularity. In 1941 he was so determined that the bank should acquire the Union Insurance building on the Bund that he repeatedly ignored the board's refusals and even persuaded the Foreign Office to put pressure on his own directors. The board again refused but the incident was characteristic of Huxter's ambitions for the bank. Blanks, in Shanghai office for a second time from 1938, reckoned that Huxter 'wanted to run it as the Mercantile Bank of India (Shanghai) Limited'.[6]

In the years immediately before the outbreak of the Second World War, other branches of the bank were more dependent for their earnings on the interest and commission from loans and overdrafts. An analysis of limits of the advances and overdrafts sanctioned by the board at the Bombay branch in 1938 demonstrates that the branch was heavily involved in financing the exports of cotton piece-goods.[7] In total, Rs 167 lakhs of advances and overdrafts were passed by the board. Of this, Rs 127 lakhs were advanced to cotton exporters on the security of their stocks in godowns or in course of shipment. Calcutta was similarly exposed to the fortunes of the jute and tea industries. In 1938 the board sanctioned a total of almost Rs 105 lakhs in advances at Calcutta. Of these just over half (Rs 53.5 lakhs) were advances to finance the export of jute. An additional Rs 15 lakhs consisted of loans to the tea industry. Nearly all of this money was lent on a yearly basis – the branch expected the loan to be repaid as the exporter realized the proceeds of his sale of a year's crop.

The vast majority of these customers at both branches were Indians, continuing the trend to localization of business over the previous two decades. Conditions on the loans varied between branch and between type of business. In Bombay, nearly all loans were secured by means of hypothecation of stocks of cotton which were stored in the bank's godown. Interest rates on the loans were typically at Reserve Bank rate. However, in Calcutta the interest rate charges were higher, usually ½ or 1 per cent over Reserve Bank rate, with a minimum of 4 per cent for jute exporters and 5 per cent for tea. Tea loans had the most stringent conditions attached to the security. Many companies were required to sell their tea through the agency firm of Thomas & Co., who would pay the proceeds of the sale direct to the bank.

Trade finance, the lifeblood of the bank's business, required stable and peaceful conditions for orderly processing and communications. War on a global scale immediately upended these requirements. At the Mercantile Bank, the outbreak of European war in September 1939 had three immediate effects on the bank. First, the young men in the

London office of military age were called up and the bank was forced to recall to head office members of the Eastern staff who were home on leave, and pensioners. They also took on a number of extra female staff and allowed them to remain at work after they had married. The shortage of staff in London was to prove an enduring problem throughout the war.

Second, the bank had advanced money to businesses on the security of goods under shipment. Some of these shipments were now fated not to reach their destinations and the bank was left with the problem of recovering the funds. This was such a complex task that a separate department to collect these debts and those owing from 'enemy' countries was set up in London under Robert Kennedy, previously the branch inspector.

Third, banking became subject to exchange controls and the Defence (Finance) Regulations (DFR) issued by the Treasury. The Mercantile's managers had already been warned in March 1939 that they should avoid the purchase of all bills against shipments to Europe, especially to Germany and Italy.[8] After the declaration of war, however, exchange operations could only be transacted through the Bank of England and – in order to maintain sterling reserves – imports into the United Kingdom of many goods were prohibited. On 22 September 1939 the general advice sent to all branches from head office stated that 'many of the regulations are not fully clear to ourselves and we are learning only by experience'.[9]

The outbreak of war did not find the bank unprepared. In August the board sanctioned the purchase of 'Courtlands', in Hurst Road, East Molesey, Surrey. This house would take over the functions of head office with a nucleus of staff if the Gracechurch Street office became 'untenable' as a result of air raids.[10] In the same month, Sir Thomas Smith had approached his old employers, the Royal Bank of Scotland, to obtain applicants for the bank who were already trained and so able to go east almost immediately, but who were over the army's age limits. As in the First World War, the Mercantile's senior managers anticipated serious disruption of communications (particularly by telegraph) with the overseas branches. It was recognized that managers would need 'to act on their own responsibility' when normally they would have referred to London. Managers in India, Ceylon and Burma were told to consult the managers in Bombay and/or Calcutta if their lines to London were cut, while managers in Malaya and Siam were advised to consult Singapore.[11]

The bank's business priority – again from the experience of the First World War – was to maintain as liquid a position as possible. Branch managers were told to examine all limits on unsecured advances and suspend, reduce or cancel those which they judged would place the bank at risk. 'During the present crisis', the branch managers were instructed, 'the first consideration is safety not profit and we expect officers to act on very conservative lines.'[12] Forward exchange operations were frowned upon and even Huxter in Shanghai was warned to curtail operations. In 1939 the bank transferred over £200 000 to inner reserves.

The warning to Huxter was well timed. The Japanese had been attempting to undermine the Chinese currency for much of the decade and in April 1939 a stabilization fund was established in Shanghai in order to support the *fapi*, as the Chinese currency was then called. An inter-bank agreement between the Hongkong Bank, the Chartered Bank and two Chinese banks established a fund of £10 million which was to be used to make foreign exchange available at a supported rate in the Shanghai market to finance the imports and exports of China. Each application for exchange was vetted to avoid flight of capital from China and to prevent it falling into Japanese hands. Huxter was 'a lone wolf'[13]whose exchange operations were perhaps too complicated, and too successful, for his own good; other bankers even suggested that he was assisting the Japanese through his dealings. He angrily denied such allegations but was forced to attend an interview in Hong Kong with a Bank of England official to explain himself. The result was official exoneration – 'the Mercantile Bank has not operated against the policy of HM Government'.[14] Huxter himself accused the other banks of denouncing him because they were outpaced by and envious of his exchange profits. The accounts of contemporaries in Shanghai certainly point to antipathy, at the very least, between Huxter and Henchman of the Hongkong Bank.

Back in London, the Mercantile was drawn into a closer and more active relationship with the Bank of England during the war than at any other time in its history. This situation prevailed throughout the banking sector, as the Bank of England was playing a key role in the application and enforcement of exchange controls and the DFR orders. The volume and quality of these operations in the war years cannot be overstated: the application of hundreds of these regulations and other orders throughout the banking industry between 1939 and 1945 was a huge achievement in supervision and – in the best sense of the word – bureaucracy.

In the Mercantile's case the relationship with the Bank of England was handled directly by Crichton and Paton through regular contact with John Fisher, an assistant adviser to the governors,[15] and other senior officials. In most cases the Mercantile was seeking rulings on the finance of specific cargoes. The bank needed to ensure that it was not in breach of either the DFR orders or the Trading with the Enemy legislation, which grew in scope as more and more countries fell into Axis hands in the first years of the war. Here the Bank of England 'did not wish to restrict irrationally the business of your non-sterling branches but we wish to prevent a drain on the national exchange resources'.[16] The Mercantile's business in New York was a particularly sensitive issue. Although Paton rather grandly insisted that 'my business in New York is confined to concerns of undoubted standing', the DFR orders were applied to the letter.[17] In particular, sterling securities could not be used as collateral for the Mercantile's overdraft facilities with the Bank of Montreal in New York. The Bank of England co-operated, however, by providing direct 'swap' facilities in New York for the Mercantile's sterling area branches. In 1942 the Bank of England also urged the Mercantile to move to London any balances held in New York on behalf of branches in occupied territory, as otherwise those balances would be seized by the American authorities.[18]

The exchange of political information was an essential part of the wartime relationship between the Bank of England and the Mercantile and the other Eastern banks. Crichton passed on portentous news when he told the bank on 2 December 1941 – five days before Pearl Harbor – that all the Japanese banks in New York except the Yokohama Specie Bank were about to close. In late January 1942, when the Japanese advance seemed inexorable, Fisher was urging the Eastern banks to destroy their government securities in Ceylon and Mauritius to prevent 'any possible seizure by the enemy'.[19] The Bank of England also gave discreet signals which were much more concerned with foreign policy initiatives than with banking business. In August 1942, for example, the Mercantile politely turned down a Bank suggestion that branches should be opened in Tibet.[20]

For the Mercantile's managers in the East, meanwhile, the outlook in 1940 and 1941 was increasingly ominous. Since March 1939 London office had warned them not to increase limits on any bills for Japanese firms.[21] The Japanese government was now requiring prior payment for all exports to Britain and the Empire; the British government responded in the autumn of 1940 by insisting on bankers' certificates of payment before permitting any dealings with Japanese firms.[22]

Events in the East moved quickly after the Japanese attack on Pearl Harbor in December 1941. Shanghai was the first branch to be affected. Robson Thomas, the second accountant at the branch, was telephoned during his morning bath by Huxter, the manager, who informed him that the Japanese had bombed Pearl Harbor. Thomas hurried to the office where he saw the American gunboat moored off the Bund flying the Japanese ensign (the British river gunboat had been sunk by the Japanese during the night): 'I knew bloody well then it was war. Then we just hung about in the office and eventually the Japanese turned up.'[23]

The bank remained open until 17 December, when it was ordered to close, and on 7 January 1942 the liquidation of all foreign banks was announced. Although the staff attended the office, Huxter was adamant in his refusal to co-operate with the liquidators. His attitude eventually resulted in him being ordered to stay out of the office from 31 January. However, the rest of staff decided to continue with their work. They had received instructions from the Foreign Office via the British Residents' Association to assist in the orderly administration of winding up; the staffs of the Hongkong Bank and Chartered were also assisting in the liquidation of their respective banks. Huxter was incensed that his staff had not followed his lead and wrote to head office complaining bitterly at his treatment and recommending dismissals. However, the Shanghai staff were now officially employees of the Japanese liquidators and Huxter had no further authority over them. The liquidation took around a year to complete and the Mercantile had only enough local funds to pay around 30 per cent of liabilities to depositors. Throughout the liquidation the staff had remained in their own houses but towards the end of 1942 both Huxter and Blanks were arrested and taken to the 'political' Haiphong Road camp. The remaining members of the Shanghai staff remained free until the spring of 1943 when they too were interned in the civilian Lunghwa camp.[24]

A similar pattern was followed in Hong Kong which surrendered to the Japanese on Christmas Day 1941. Of the Mercantile's four-man staff, three had been drafted into the territory's defence and were placed in the military camp at Sham Shui Poo; Barry Deane and Doug Hamilton were later transferred to Japan. The manager, Henry Hawkins, was required to assist in the liquidation of the bank before also being interned.

The theatre of war moved on quickly to Malaya.[25] The Japanese landed in Kota Bharu and South Thailand in early December, crossed the peninsula and began to drive down the west coast. The bank's staff was depleted to the bare minimum as volunteers were called up. Penang was heavily bombed and the branch there took a direct hit. Fortunately, there were no casualties as the staff were able to take shelter in the safe during the bombardment. The bank then moved into the house of the agent, Gerald Aste, before all the staff were evacuated on 16/17 December. Aste and colleagues were able to burn their remaining bank notes and bearer bonds, but the records of the bank were left behind in the confusion. As the Japanese advanced further down the west coast, so Ipoh came under threat and eventually the bank pulled out of the town. Consolidated statements and some of the records of the bank were taken down to Singapore by Samuel Hutchings, the agent, so that the accounts could be reconstructed.

On the east coast, the agent at Kuala Trengganu made a daring escape. Frederick 'Haji' Stocks, having concealed the bank's cash, was first hidden by Malay friends. Then, disguised as a Malay, he took a sampan up river into the interior. From there he travelled on foot over the central range of mountains and virgin forest to arrive at the bank's branch at Kuala Lumpur late in December. From there he proceeded to Singapore, with the remnants of the Kuala Lumpur staff.' Meanwhile the office staff at Kuala Lipis, where Ian MacFarlane was the bank's agent, beat a strategic retreat to Bentong. At this stage MacFarlane was able to take all the books with him and even managed to persuade the military to take the bank's safe to Bentong. All the spare cash from Kuala Lumpur was brought to Bentong and the whole labour force of the state, including all plantation workers and government employees, was paid before MacFarlane burnt all the records except the cash book and the general ledger (which he later handed over to Singapore branch).[26]

During the retreat through Malaya the bank had attempted to pay out to all customers who needed money to finance their own evacuations or to transfer their money abroad. The heavy volume of transactions needed to be recorded and branches were told to send copies of their records to Singapore and to New York. However, when some of the up-country agents arrived in Singapore without their books, which had understandably been lost at some point in their evacuation, they discovered that the copies sent to Singapore had never arrived. Their first task was to attempt to reconstruct their books. In addition, business in the Singapore office built up rapidly when up-country customers arrived needing to access their accounts, and the telegraph departments were working flat out in transferring funds. Inter-bank co-operation added a further but necessary burden to the branch's work in these desperate days. In particular the branch agreed to take over the deposits (amounting to Rs 50 lakhs) of the National City Bank office.[27] In the meantime the Singapore staff was depleted by losses to the volunteer forces who were mobilized on 1 December and pensioners were brought back to work to assist in the work of the office. Working conditions were made worse by the frequent air raids as the Japanese closed in on the island. By early February all the European officers and some of the clerical staff were living on the bank premises.

Banking business came to a standstill on Wednesday 11 February when the Colonial Treasurer issued orders to destroy all currency notes. On the morning of Friday 13 February the decision to evacuate the bank's key personnel was taken. These included John Ross, the

Singapore manager. Other senior members of the staff, including Stanley Stocks, James Ferguson, Gerald Aste, Samuel Hutchings and Colin Wardle, were granted exit permits. These officers (except Ferguson, whose fate is unknown) were evacuated on the same boat on the evening of 13 February.[28] The next day their boat was bombed and sunk by the Japanese, and Hutchings is presumed to have been killed during this attack. Eventually, Stocks, Aste and Wardle were able to escape across Sumatra to Padang from where the majority of refugees from the shipwreck were rescued. All three arrived together in Colombo on 9 March. Ross, however, after surviving seven hours in the water after the shipwreck, was one of the unfortunate few left behind at Padang where he was later captured. He spent the war interned on Sumatra. The staff remaining in Singapore and those who had joined the forces were either interned or assisted in the liquidation of the bank. At least four, Ian MacFarlane, Aubrey Curtis, Harry Maitland and John Gregoire, were later transferred to work on the Burma railway.

The fate of the local staff of the Eastern branches is not well documented. In July 1942 London office learned from the Foreign Office that three of the bank's Portuguese staff – Messrs Castro, Mattos and Elarte – were destitute in Macao. Permission was sought and obtained from the Bank of England for the Mercantile to send monthly allowances to them through a Portuguese bank. A similar arrangement was made for a Portuguese member of staff stranded in Hong Kong.[29] Some members of the local staff were employed by the Japanese liquidators, and some were forced to find other employment. In many areas the local staff were vital in supplying the interned bank officers with parcels of food.

From the spring of 1942 the earning power of the bank was greatly reduced and it was dependent for its survival on its branches in London, India, Ceylon and Mauritius. By the end of the year the bank had transferred a further amount of £102 381 to inner reserves and provisions to cover possible losses.[30] In their annual report for 1942 the directors announced that they were allocating £40 000 to contingencies account. Each year during the war the accounts showed an amount of £25 000 written off against freehold premises, a figure which was increased to £50 000 in the 1945 accounts when the full extent of damage to the bank's property in the East was apparent. The dividend was cut in 1941 to 9 per cent and this was further reduced in 1942 to 6 per cent; this payment was maintained until the end of the war. In common with the rest of the London-based banking system, the bank invested in British and Indian government securities to support the finance of the war and to guarantee an income – by 1943 around £15.5 million of its assets (51 per cent of the total) were in this form, compared with only £7.7 million in 1938. Profits inevitably dipped and in 1942 the bank was only able to post a £131 916 profit – £40 000 less than the previous year – and published profits hovered around this level for the remainder of the war.

The bank not only suffered from the loss of many of its branches. The character of its routine business was also greatly distorted. Export trades which the Mercantile traditionally financed – tea, cotton, jute, copra – were now subject to bulk purchasing orders of the British government. Moreover, the imports which the bank financed from England to the East were no longer available as manufacturing was turned over to producing items for wartime use. The fundamentals and the machinery of overseas trade were transformed as commercial bills of exchange were now scarce. Consequently the bank's wartime strategy was largely dictated by the role allotted to them by governments in London and overseas. In addition the inter-bank agreements of the Eastern Exchange Banks' Association prevented them from aggressively searching out new business.

In India many exporters found the war a time of prosperity with a guaranteed market and stable prices for their products. However, their earnings could not be spent on imports and the accumulation of capital in current and deposit accounts changed the nature of work in Indian branches of the bank. The outward and inward bills departments experienced a slackening in their work, but current accounts increased in activity. The amount and volume of transactions were also swollen by the presence in India of large numbers of servicemen from Britain and the Dominions. In Calcutta the amount of work on current accounts was 'really quite grim and soul destroying'.[31]

In all branches the most important problem facing the bank, after loss of income, was the lack of manpower. No new men were available to replace or relieve those who were in post when the war began, and all furlough was postponed until the end of the war. At the outbreak of war in 1939 the bank numbered 107 members on the Eastern staff. Of these, 20 were juniors in London, all of whom joined the forces; a further 16 had joined the forces in the East, and 35 were in captivity. This left a mere 36 to keep the bank's business in operation. For those interned or missing, the bank created a fund to accumulate furlough pay in their absence. The wives of the men interned were allowed to draw monthly allowances, the amounts of which were determined as a percentage of their husband's salary up to a maximum of £42 10s. a month. The wives were left alone by the bank and were only contacted if the bank received news of their husbands. Even then the news was sparse. Janie Stewart remembers a long silence after her husband Hamish was interned in Shanghai; when contact was eventually resumed, her husband was restricted to sending 25 word messages every four or five months.[32] Many of the wives, especially those with children, experienced some degree of financial hardship. Some were especially vulnerable and isolated, as escape from the Japanese had stranded them in Australia or South Africa and the danger of the seas, the shortage of shipping and the prospect of a bomb-blighted Britain forced them to remain where they were rather than return to friends and family.

The acute manpower problems the bank experienced during the war were leavened in India by the increasing role that the Indian staff began to play in the bank. In 1936 the bank had taken the first steps on the road to equality of position and opportunity for members of the local staff. The initial impetus seems to have come from Lord Catto, chairman of the bank. He recommended for a position within the bank a young man named P. S. Ramanatha Iyer. His candidate was well connected: his uncle was manager of the Calcutta Discount Co. (owned by D. Yule and Co.) and his great-uncle had at one time worked for the bank but had risen to a partnership in A. Yule and Co. Ramanatha Iyer himself held a degree from Madras University. He was thus overqualified and overconnected for a clerical job and the bank decided to employ him as an 'Indian assistant' at Madras branch. Crichton instructed Harold Graves, the Madras manager, to 'give him any help he needs in what may be at first a somewhat delicate position. You must also ask the European officers on your staff to treat him with proper consideration.'[33]

Good reports were received of Ramanatha's progress and in 1938 the bank decided to extend the scheme to Calcutta and Bombay branches. Crichton wrote to these managers explaining that for reasons of 'economy of administration' the bank was planning to introduce a new grade of Indian assistant 'to whom might be transferred certain of the duties at present carried out by European officers'. Suitable candidates for this rank were defined as 'well educated young men, preferably graduates, of good family and of steady and reliable character'.[34] As well as seeing this as a cost-cutting measure, the bank was also aware that similar schemes had recently been introduced at the Chartered Bank, the Imperial Bank of India and the Bank of India.

The upper reaches of this new rank were not clearly defined. The letter from Crichton stated that 'it is not proposed that an Indian Assistant should be placed in charge of any department'. However, later in the letter Crichton expands on the theme: 'If it [the scheme] develops satisfactorily it is to be hoped to extend it to other branches, and it may well be that some of the Indian Assistants may ... prove themselves capable of being entrusted with the full charge of a department.'[35] This ambiguity over the promotion prospects led the Bombay manager to reply that, as it stood, the post may not have been appealing enough to attract suitable candidates. Finer points of the conditions of service of the Indian assistants were also left unresolved for some time, for instance their leave allocation, signing authority and pay during the probationary period. These and other matters were to be settled during the next five years.

The first Indian assistants were doubtless in a delicate position, balanced as they were between the European assistants and the Indian clerical staff. Moreover, some of the existing Indian clerks were concerned that the new rank seemed to be open to external recruits but not to internal candidates. From the outset it was stipulated that Indian assistants should be addressed as 'Mr', and head office advised that all the European staff should 'do all that is possible to help the experiment and make it a success'.[36] One of the first Indian assistants in Calcutta recalled that he 'personally never had any difficulty with anybody'.[37]

The onset of war, the call-up of European staff under the age of 40, and the service of the others in the reserves hastened the transfer of responsibilities to Indian assistants. By 1940 the bank was granting powers of attorney to Indian assistants and in March 1942 junior and senior grades were introduced. The junior grade had a starting salary of Rs 180 per month, rising by increments of Rs 20 to Rs 300, and the pay scale for senior assistants began at Rs 320 and increased by Rs 15 to a maximum of Rs 500. No definitions were laid down as to the duties and tasks which each could perform, but it can be assumed that senior Indian assistants were by this time able to take charge of certain departments. A year later, in 1943, the bank announced that 'in future selected Indian Assistants should be eligible for promotion to the rank of Assistant Accountant', a grade which hitherto had been the exclusive preserve of European officers.[38] Assistant accountants would be paid the same basic salary irrespective of nationality. However, European staff would also be paid an 'overseas salary' of 25 per cent of their pay, thus continuing the effective pay differential. For instance, a European assistant accountant in Calcutta with one year's service received Rs 665 per month (if quarters were not provided) while his Indian counterpart received Rs 499. Additionally, married European members of staff received an extra allowance that was not extended to married Indians. The reasoning behind this difference was that married Europeans were likely to have children who would be sent home to be educated and/or a second household would have to be maintained back home. Notwithstanding these differences, an important rule had been set down: 'the general principle is that Indian assistant accountants should enjoy exactly the same status as their European counterparts and should receive exactly the same treatment'.[39] In November 1943 the first Indian assistant accountant was appointed at the bank's Calcutta branch – it was the same Mr Ramanatha Iyer who had been the first Indian assistant seven years earlier.

As the war drew towards its conclusion, so the bank began to make preparations for its return to Malaya. Stanley Stocks, Colin Wardle and Gerald Aste, who had served in Malaya before the Japanese occupation and who had escaped, were brought home from India and Colombo in late 1944 for special leave. During this leave they attended meetings at head office with Crichton and Paton to discuss the kinds of problems they might face on their return to Malaya and matters of procedure to be adopted during the reconstruction. The staff of the Rangoon branch, which had operated from New Delhi throughout the war, were told to prepare for their return. Events in Hong Kong and China were too confused and uncertain for the bank to plan far ahead, and it adopted a 'wait-and-see' policy in these areas. A special letter was prepared at head office and sent to all those members of staff who would be participating in the reopening of branches:

> When in due course you go back to territories which have been freed from the Japanese and in which the Bank formerly operated your main object will be to re-establish the Bank's business and to do this it is essential that you regain the confidence and goodwill of your constituents. Our wishes are that all constituents should be treated with the greatest possible consideration. By this, we do not imply, however, that Officers should adopt such an attitude of leniency when dealing with constituents' claims as to involve the Bank in losses ... It will be for Managers to deal with each situation as it arises. Tactful handling and great courtesy will be called for, but when necessity demands, firmness.[40]

The end of hostilities in the East in August 1945 did not signal an immediate return to normal conditions. Normality, as experienced before the war, would not be returning at all in some places. In 1943, Shanghai, for instance, had lost its 'extraterritorial' status which, since the 1840s, had allowed foreign trading communities to establish international settlements operating under their own jurisdiction. This would never return. The bank's most immediate priority was the safety and health of the staff who had been interned in occupied territory. Information was difficult to come by and news of the staff trickled back to London through a variety of sources, ranging from official notification to third-hand hearsay. Ralph Wyeth, who had previously been with the bank in Malaya, was part of the military force reoccupying the peninsula. He was able to inform London about the local staff whom he could trace in Kuala Lumpur, Singapore and Kota Bharu, and the state of the bank's offices there. Other news was telegrammed to head office by the internees themselves, as they were freed, by government channels and by family and friends. However, the news from the East was not always good, and it was not until the end of the war that the bank finally received confirmation that Hutchings and Ferguson had not survived the evacuation and occupation of Singapore.

By mid-September 1945 all the Mercantile's staff had been accounted for and news of their freedom was relayed to their anxiously waiting wives. The bank was especially pleased to have the first official news of John Ross, former manager of Singapore, who was freed from a prison camp in Sumatra. Ross wrote to head office in October 1945, his first communication for over three and a half years: 'Rip Van Winkle returns – a shadow of his former self.'[41] Sadly, soon after his release Ross discovered that his wife had been injured during the aerial bombardment of the evacuation ship from Singapore and had died shortly afterwards. Those staff who had been interned needed rest and time with their families. However, many heroically offered to stay on *in situ* to attend to the affairs of the bank until they could be relieved.

In Shanghai, the returning internees found the bank building undamaged, and Robson Thomas and Edward West, the former second accountant and senior assistant of the branch, were able to take possession of the bank house towards the end of August. The bank itself had been occupied by the Hwa Sing Commercial Bank, but many of the records that had survived were stored in a godown and jumbled together with the records of other overseas banks.[42] The records seemed to be plentiful and included the transactions undertaken during the liquidation under the Japanese. A skeleton staff under Thomas set about bringing back order to the branch. Jackie Huxter and Lionel Blanks, both of whom had been in Shanghai's 'political' camp, had been taken north to Peking towards the end of the war. After their release they left China to rejoin their families for a well-earned rest. Fred Thorougood was brought out of retirement to take temporary charge of the branch, which reopened on 10 December, until Huxter was able to return in the autumn of 1946.

In the immediate post-war period the situation in Shanghai was confused, due to the precipitate end to the war. Business in Shanghai continued despite the civil war in China and the rampant inflation in the city – between September 1945 and February 1947 prices rose thirtyfold.[43] The branch had problems supplying itself with Chinese national currency, and exchange business was closed to foreign banks until March 1946. On the resumption of exchange business, the branch found that the new requirements necessitated forms, licences and permits. Much of the work fell on the shoulders of the new accountant, Charles Pow. Pow remembered the winter of 1945/46 as 'miserable ... we had no heating and no booze, we used to make our own vodka'.[44]

On his return in late 1946, Huxter concentrated on trying to build up the finance of the export trade, as the bank already had a well-established import side. He was hampered by lack of staff: 'This is the grimmest situation I have ever faced. I used to think I could take it. Even current work is piling up on us now and I can't see daylight anywhere. How we are ever going to tackle the many problems which have been shelved I just don't know, except to keep on shelving them.'[45] Foreign business in Shanghai was now liable for Chinese taxation and in early 1947 Huxter wrote to London that there was a rumour that the bank would be taxed at 90 per cent on its profits in Shanghai. Huxter proposed that he should keep two sets of books so that money could be remitted to London and not be subject to taxation in China. Head office replied that the board would never sanction such a procedure.[46]

In Hong Kong, Henry Hawkins was released from Stanley prison camp on 30 August and he found that the bank office was intact. The building had been occupied by the Mitsui Busson Kaisha and the records and securities were safe. Donovan Benson, the pre-war manager, was able to return to Hong Kong in October, and the branch reopened in the same month. One of the most pressing problems in both Shanghai and Hong Kong was the lack of available US dollars for imports. The United States was benefiting from the release of the pent-up demand in the East for goods, as it was the only country able to supply consumer goods. Consequently, dollars were draining out of the East with no means of replenishing stocks of exchange and this situation became a factor in the operations of all the overseas banks in the Far East in the immediate post-war period.

In the Straits Settlements, Stocks arrived back in Singapore from London on 14 September 1945 and reported to head office: 'Premises good working condition with full equipment and furniture ... All essential records and liquidation accounts available ... our credit balance with liquidator Straits$ 25 lacs banana currency. Most securities on hand or accounted for ... Authorities urging early re-opening British Banks to relieve currency difficulties. Local staff fully reported.'[47] Stocks opened for business the next day. Wardle and Aste headed north into the peninsula to Kuala Lumpur and Penang. The situation in peninsular Malaya was chaotic and would remain so for some time. The country was under military administration but was suffering from the lack of any effective law and order agency: looting, thieving and banditry were rife. The lack of any imports, especially rice from Siam, had resulted in a rampant black market. Four months after the departure of the Japanese the country was still suffering from shortages in all areas, transport problems were severe, industry was unable to restart, and inflation was increasing. Civil unrest was endemic and strikes were commonplace. Against this background, the branches in Kuala Lumpur and Penang were reopened in late autumn 1945, and the agencies at Kuantan, Kota Bharu and Kuala Trengganu were reinstated during the first half of 1946.

In Singapore and Malaya the bank needed to wait for the leading companies in the rubber industry, as the branches' biggest customers, to reconstruct their own businesses. The industry needed large amounts of capital to restart, and expected the government to provide this in time through financing compensation claims. These claims arose from both war damage and from the scorched-earth policy adopted by the Japanese in their retreat through Malaya. In the days following the end of the war, factories had been looted and new machinery would need to be bought and installed before any exports could be available. The availability of synthetic rubber also meant that the rubber industry could not charge high prices in order to cover the cost of recovery. In the interval before the industry was in health again, the Mercantile's customers were therefore dependent on the bank for finance to tide them over. At the end of 1946 the bank agreed to participate in a scheme organized by the Malayan government to loan money to Malayan industries in order to help restart the economy. The Malayan government offered guarantees of repayment and the bank was involved to the extent of Straits $15 million.

In addition to these local difficulties and complexities, the bank's two most serious problems in the aftermath of the war were its lack of staff and the need to reconstruct the accounts of the occupied branches. The reconstruction process varied in difficulty between branches, depending on how many records had survived and how well transactions had been documented during the occupation period. Newly opened branches were furnished with the latest statements and returns as they had been compiled in London. Instructions were issued to accountants in charge of reoccupied branches that they were to open a set of 'new' books. As old transactions and balances were verified, they were to be transferred into the new books with a corresponding debit from the old books.[48] On the question of transactions passed during the liquidation, the bank was tied to the decisions of governments, and also tried to act in concert with the other exchange banks. In most cases, withdrawals of funds and liquidation of advances that occurred under Japanese rule were treated as legitimate transactions. Although this decision was not officially sanctioned for some time, the bank continued to operate on this understanding.

Immediately after the war there were many customers in newly liberated areas needing money urgently, and the bank advised its staff that each case should be judged on its individual merits. The bank also decided that local government, public bodies and 'first-class' European firms could be granted immediate overdrafts until final settlements on their old accounts were reached. The same could be granted to Chinese or local firms and European individuals who had evidence that they had had funds in their accounts. To these customers the bank could advance up to 60 per cent of what their credit balances seemed to be: 'generally speaking, the principle is that we wish to be fair to our constituents and to give them reasonable assistance. This, however, must be done in such a way as not to result in paying away the Bank's funds to those to whom they do not belong.'[49] Branches were particularly warned not to advance against local shares or bearer bonds which had been acquired improperly during the war (for instance documents taken from prisoners of war under duress).

The shortage of staff experienced in the war years was not eased by the prospect of peace. In all, thirteen members of the bank's Eastern staff had lost their lives during the war. The staff who had worked through the war needed well-earned furlough, but could not be relieved until the interned staff had recovered from their ordeal. Recruitment of new staff was impossible until 1946, and by the end of 1947 only nine new assistants had been recruited and sent out to their first postings. The position was exacerbated in September 1946 by a strike by bank clerks in Colombo. Two assistants, one each from Bombay and Madras, were lent to the branch and the staff wives and manager's sons were pressed into service as the strike dragged on. Throughout 1946 and 1947 the branches at Hong Kong, Shanghai and Bombay were clamouring for extra staff. Paton at head office wrote to Ronald Cromartie, by then in retirement, in July 1947: 'Insufficient staff for the Eastern branches is just about our biggest headache and furloughs are dreadfully delayed. [Arthur] Nicholson is on his way home after about ten years in the East.'[50] In the same month Paton wrote to Benson in Hong Kong and Huxter in Shanghai that, despite all their pleas, the bank was not able to send them more staff: 'if the only way out is to curtail your business, then much as you and we may regret it, your business will just have to be curtailed'.[51] Given the vitality of the post-war economy of Hong Kong and the fact that Benson was one of the most successful of the Mercantile's managers, this reining in of business in the colony prevented the Mercantile from emerging as a larger player in the banking community.

The shortage of manpower after the war also had implications for the local staff. The high demand in all areas for clerical staff meant that the local staff found themselves in a strong negotiating position. Coupled with wartime inflation and heightened political expectations, this resulted in a number of successful appeals by the local staff for better conditions and wages. Additionally, the local staff successfully called

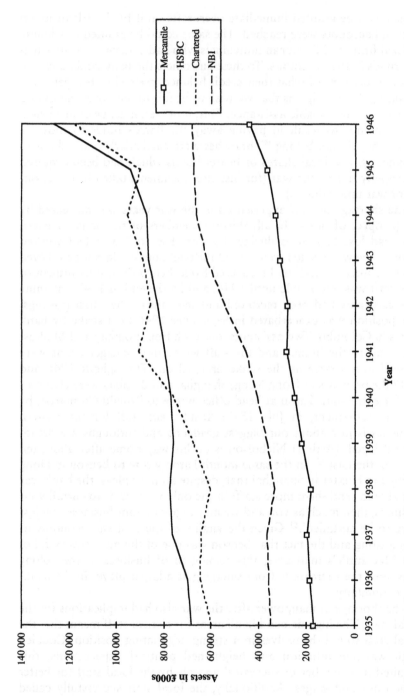

5.2 Eastern banks: total assets, 1935–46

for rehabilitation payments for those staff returning to work for the bank in the occupied branches. The local staff of Malayan branches were granted three months' rehabilitation payment in October 1945. Unfortunately, the board tended to respond to local staff demands as and when they were made rather than coming to a decision for all the local staff, as they had with the European officers. Subsequently, the Hong Kong local staff were not granted rehabilitation payments until July 1946, and those in Shanghai not until December 1946.

A series of strikes in Indian branches in the summer of 1946 led to new salary scales being agreed for clerical and auxiliary staff in India and concessions being granted, such as regularizing the amount of holiday allowed. In July an All-India Banking Union had been formed, and the bank was anxious to deter their staff from joining it and thus moving their demands from the practical to the political. Strikes in the police, mutinies in the navy and an escalation of communal violence in 1946 were sharp reminders that the bank needed to keep relations as harmonious as possible between all their staff. This awareness was to be an essential factor in the post-war history of the Mercantile.

On the eve of the independence of India and Pakistan in 1947, the Mercantile Bank of India was making an impressive recovery from the exigencies of war and the effects of the shut-down of many of the bank's Eastern branches. The total assets of the bank in 1946, at £44 million, were still appreciably below the balance-sheet totals of the Hongkong Bank (£128 million), Chartered (£118 million) and the National Bank of India (£69 million). Yet in the period since 1935, when Crichton had succeeded Steuart, the Mercantile's business had expanded at a greater and steadier rate than at any of these other banks.

Whereas the balance-sheet totals of the three other banks had increased by between 85 and 95 per cent, the Mercantile's business had grown by 156 per cent between 1935 and 1946 (Figure 5.2). Clearly the Hongkong Bank and Chartered suffered from the closure of a higher proportion of their branches in the East and their recovery was correspondingly slower. The comparison with the National Bank, which was only forced to close in Mandalay and Rangoon, is more telling. This relatively higher rate of gain by the Mercantile suggests that the bank had avoided the worst effects of the Pacific War but was also able to avoid damage from the uncertainties surrounding independence on the sub-continent. At the very least, the Mercantile Bank withstood the years of international crisis by adapting rapidly to sudden political and economic change. Although the bank had not been able to plan for these contingencies in a systematic way, the small and hard-pressed management team showed resourcefulness and flexibility in meeting the upheavals in its traditional markets.

CHAPTER SIX

Realignment, 1947–57

In the half-century after the reconstruction of 1893, the title Mercantile Bank of India accurately described the bank's activities and sphere of operations. Its business was the finance of trade and its principal theatre was the sub-continent. In the late 1940s and 1950s, however, the international positioning of the bank was more questionable. Could the focus of its business remain on India? Would political change in the sub-continent enhance or reduce opportunities for a British overseas bank? These were issues which affected not only the name but also the basic identity of the bank.

In a technical sense the partition of India in 1947 made the bank's title an anachronism. Whereas in 1893 'India' was the name for an empire, after 1947 it described only one of the independent states which emerged from the Indian Empire. Clearly the bank could not confine its business to modern India and abandon its long-standing interests in the new states of Pakistan, Ceylon and Burma. In a business context the alignment with the sub-continent was also shifting. Early in the century, after the acquisition of the Bank of Calcutta in 1906, the bank's Indian branches held 81 per cent of overseas (that is, non-London) assets in 1910. The equivalent shares in 1935 and 1947 were 66 per cent and 68 per cent respectively – a surprisingly low figure in the latter case in view of the 'wipe-out' of the bank's Far East business and the relatively strong economic position of India in the immediate post-war years. The earnings of the branches were even less dependent on the sub-continent. In 1947, for example, only 42 per cent of the total net profits of overseas branches came from India, Pakistan, Ceylon and Burma. This pattern of earnings raised the searching question of whether the bank, in the post-independence world, would either return to its specialization in Indian business or accelerate the diversification of its overseas markets.

The first and most obvious challenge to the Mercantile and its competitors was political upheaval. In the bank's traditional markets the old framework rapidly disintegrated in the post-war years. India gained independence in 1947, Burma and Ceylon followed in 1948 and other former empire territories won independence during the 1950s. Political reorganization followed hard on the heels of independence with the creation of Pakistan in 1947 and the Federated States of Malaya in 1957. Further east, the continuing civil war and subsequent communist victory in China effectively closed the country to European firms. The outcome in China also increased fears that countries such as Malaya, Burma and Indonesia (which had claimed independence from the Netherlands in 1947) would succumb to communism. Uncertainty over the future of the entire region of South-East Asia was already an international preoccupation of the post-war years.

Although the political empire had fragmented, many former imperial possessions retained strong economic links with Britain, not least through their membership of the sterling area. Sterling's relative weakness *vis-à-vis* the dollar in the post-war period made it imperative that the British government should impose tight control on the sterling area so as to prevent depletion of reserves. Subsequently, exchange controls and import restrictions were implemented in many of the countries where the bank operated, with immediate repercussions for their overseas trade. The bank was similarly affected by the fragmentation of customs rules and import–export restrictions, which could lead to odd distortions in the market. The General Agreement on Tariffs and Trade (GATT) of 1947 achieved a reduction in worldwide tariff levels but it did not remove the endemic use of import restrictions in the post-war setting. In the United Kingdom, for example, no less than 96 per cent of imports were affected by import controls in 1946, and this level was still as high as 65 per cent in 1952.[1] Restrictions and controls led to oddities in international trade. 'What is one to think', Sir Charles Innes wondered in his chairman's address to the Mercantile annual general meeting in 1952, 'of a world where, as recently happened, a steamer takes a cargo of Polish coal from a Baltic port to Chittagong and returns to a Scandinavian port with a cargo of Indian coal from Calcutta?'[2]

The bank's traditional role also became increasingly precarious as trade patterns shifted. Britain's trade with Europe grew at the expense of links with the former Empire, and British overseas foreign investment shifted away from former parts of the Empire to Western countries or to 'white' dominions such as South Africa and Canada. The niche that the bank had carved for itself 'seemed destined to confine [it] to an ever-dwindling market'.[3]

Moreover, the bank was now faced with new or more powerful competitors in its established markets. In particular, the National Bank of India presented a more formidable challenge after its acquisition of Grindlays Bank in 1948. Grindlays, with eleven branches on the subcontinent and total deposits of about £20 million at that time, had been a force in Indian banking since 1828. Since 1924 the business had been wholly owned – but never fully integrated – by the National Provincial Bank. In the post-war period this large London clearing bank welcomed the chance to move ownership to the National Bank of India, which was one of its own customers in London.[4] Elsewhere in the East,

American banks such as Chase and the National City Bank had taken an aggressive approach to overseas expansion since the end of the war. Inevitably local domestic banks in the countries where the bank operated were also becoming increasingly interested in capturing the business of British overseas banks.

In addition to these new factors in the business environment, the bank faced new regulatory regimes in many of its markets. Political independence brought the establishment of new central banks which attempted to control monetary conditions and regulate local banking systems, often with the help of appropriate legislation. For instance, the Pakistan Banking Companies Control Act of 1948 made it compulsory for overseas banks to retain in Pakistan not less than 20 per cent of the value of their time and demand liabilities in the form of cash, gold or approved securities. More onerously, the assets of the bank in Pakistan were to be not less than 70 per cent of the value of time and demand liabilities. Similar requirements came into force in India. Since 1935 the Mercantile had been required to keep 10 per cent of its deposits in cash and balances at the Reserve Bank of India. From 1951, under the Banking Companies Act of 1949, the Mercantile and other exchange banks were required to keep 20 per cent of their deposits with the Reserve Bank in the form of cash, gold or approved securities.[5] Although these requirements were largely being fulfilled by the bank as a matter of course, they created new work for the branches in filing returns and they also hampered the ability of the bank to lend between branches which – previously neighbours – were now in different countries. The new or enhanced regulations also included powers to grant banking licences for new branches: any plans for extending the branch network needed to take into account the attitude of the national authorities towards foreign bank expansion.

Political fragmentation also threw financial burdens on to multinational banks such as the Mercantile. Taxation levels and procedures varied greatly in the markets where the bank operated in the late 1940s and 1950s. In 1955 – to take a single year as an example – the Mercantile was liable for local taxes in eleven countries. The Inland Revenue in the United Kingdom was the bank's principal tax authority but there were also significant tax bills in India, Pakistan and Malaya in particular. The Mercantile was also liable for local tax in Burma, Ceylon, Hong Kong, Japan, Mauritius, Singapore and Thailand.[6]

In these circumstances the leadership of the bank required political astuteness as well as business vision. At board level, the alignment with the bank's traditional Indian markets and the preference for former officials in the Indian government appeared to be constant. The continuity of membership of the board was maintained throughout the post-war period, with a core of six directors serving throughout the years from 1948 to 1957 (Figure 6.1). This core group included James Crichton and Sir Kenneth Mealing, who both joined the board in 1945/46. Mealing had just retired from Andrew Yule and Co., long-standing customers of the bank, which he had joined in Calcutta in 1920 and where he had later served as director and chairman. Before his retirement from India he had also been a member of the Council of State for India and president of the Bengal Chamber of Commerce.

As in the inter-war years, the Mercantile board opted for a succession plan in which the special business or political interests of a departing director were replaced by equivalent expertise of a new director. Hence when Clifford Figg died in 1948, Robert Dunlop of Walter Duncan and Co. was elected in his place. Like Figg, 'Jumbo' Dunlop was appointed for his knowledge of the sub-continent in general and the tea trade in particular. Sir Thomas Smith, with his long, direct experience of Indian banking, retired in March 1951. He was replaced in 1952 by Sir Cyril Jones, who had been secretary of the Indian Finance Department between 1939 and 1947 and had then 'done important work of a financial nature for H.M. Government'.[7] The emphasis on continuity was even more obvious in the example of the Innes family. Sir Charles Innes had joined the board in 1933 after a distinguished career in the Indian Civil Service, and he served as the Mercantile's chairman from 1937 until his retirement in March 1952. He had been a formidable figure in the Mercantile's affairs during the war and in the immediate post-war years, providing 'wise counsel and unsparing devotion to his duties'. In the year after he stood down, his son (also Charles Innes) returned from India and was elected to the Mercantile board in April 1953. Latterly the junior Innes had been president of the Associated Chambers of Commerce of India.

The bank's preference for appropriate overseas experience was also maintained after the maximum number of directors was raised from eight to ten in March 1953. This increase was part of new articles of association adopted in response to the 1948 Companies Act, which had encouraged limited companies to broaden the responsibilities of non-executive directors. In the Mercantile's case one of the additional seats was filled by C. D. Miller, managing director of the Anglo-Thai Corporation (formerly the Anglo-Siam Corporation). Miller contributed business experience in India and Pakistan as well as in Thailand and Malaya. This board, under Sir Kenneth Mealing's chairmanship from 1952, provided valuable stability at a time when the bank's traditional markets were in such flux. It was not until Crichton and Rufus Smith retired in April 1958 (both after long service on the board and with Crichton by then in his late seventies) that the sequence was interrupted.

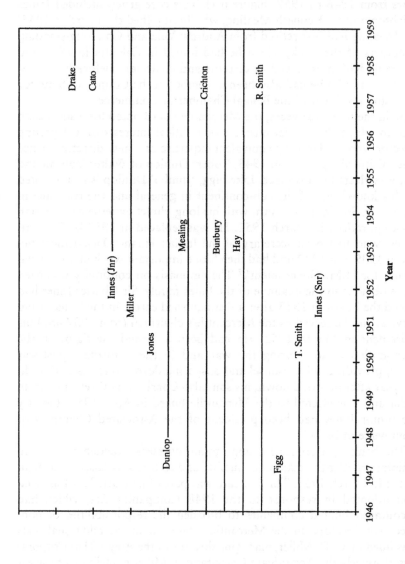

6.1 Mercantile Bank: board service, 1946–59

Continuity of management, initially with plentiful experience in India, was maintained in the same period. Although it was Eric Paton who took over the chief managership on Crichton's retirement in 1947, it was Crichton's obvious intention that he should eventually be succeeded by Robert Drake. Drake's first postings in the East at Bombay and Calcutta were both under the managership of Crichton and, when Crichton returned to England in 1925 to become London manager, he and Drake remained on close terms. Drake was agent in Delhi between 1930 and 1931 at the time that plans for the Reserve Bank of India were evolving, and he maintained a steady flow of letters to Crichton keeping him up to date with political developments in Delhi and opinions on the Reserve Bank Bill. Drake had additional managerial experience of the branches at Penang, Madras and Bombay, where he was manager during the war. After a fact-finding tour of the Indian branches of the bank in late 1946, he arrived in London in the spring of 1946 to take up a London managership. He became deputy chief manager in April 1947 on Crichton's retirement and then took over as chief manager in the spring of 1950.

Like Paton and Crichton, Drake had gained his experience and expertise mainly in India – in all he had spent only five years of his career out of the country. However, the importance of India to the bank was already diminishing as significant and increasing profits were being made at the branches further east, especially in Singapore and Hong Kong. Some of Drake's contemporaries felt that, through no fault of his own, he lacked an appreciation of these Far Eastern markets. It was important to have a manager in head office who could understand the business of these branches and the communities in which they operated. Henry Hawkins was appointed deputy chief manager in spring 1950 to fulfil this role. Hawkins had served in many of the bank's branches and had managerial experience in Singapore, Shanghai, Hong Kong and Bombay.

The Mercantile's board and management, with this strong pedigree in public service and in Indian business, needed to respond to a series of major political changes in the post-war era. Even if they could develop strategies for survival in the new political environment of the late 1940s and 1950s, growth and profitability were much less certain. In his study of British multinational banks, Jones points out that in the post-war years 'There was an increasing recognition that the banks needed size if they were to be taken seriously.'[8] At smaller banks such as the Mercantile, evidence was mounting to support this argument. Trends in the balance sheets of the major Eastern banks showed that the larger banks were achieving a proportionately higher rate of growth in these years. The Chartered Bank and the Hongkong Bank doubled their total assets between 1948 and the late 1950s, a period in which the Chartered distinguished itself by emerging as the largest of the peer group in 1955, even before its acquisition of the Eastern Bank in 1957. The Mercantile, the National Bank of India and the Eastern Bank meanwhile achieved a steadier rate of gain but added no more than about 50 per cent to their total assets in the same period (Figure 6.2); the National Bank of India, despite the acquisition of Grindlays in 1948, was still not growing at the same rate as the two largest Eastern banks. The difference in rates of growth was partly a reflection of business growth in the Far East (particularly Hong Kong) where the Chartered Bank and the Hongkong Bank were so strong; it was also a result of inhibitions to growth on the sub-continent (see below, page 116). Although the Mercantile was well represented in the Far East, its operations were not substantial enough to generate the gains marked up by its larger rivals.

The Mercantile's board and management were not blind to the risks of falling behind in the bank's rate of growth. They were ahead of some of their competitors, for example, in building up their bank's capital position. The British overseas banks had made little attempt to alter their capitalization since the 1920s, with the result that by the early 1950s their capital and published reserves were small and unimpressive in the international marketplace. The Chartered Bank was the first bank to make a correction when in 1953 it increased its paid-up capital from £3 million to £3.5 million. The Mercantile quickly followed in 1954 by adding £420 000 to its paid-up capital, giving a total £1.47 million. This outcome was achieved through a rights issue of new C shares to all classes of the bank's shareholders.

Simultaneously the bank attempted to simplify its capital. At the Mercantile's annual general meeting in March 1953, Colin Brodie, a shareholder, had commented adversely on the bank's 'unwieldy capital structure' and had suggested converting the shares into lower denominations.[9] Although the directors were not yet prepared to reduce the number of categories of the bank's shares, in July Drake advised shareholders that lower share denominations were now 'general current practice'. In September 1954 the A and B shares of £25 (£12 10s. paid) were split into five new A and B shares of £5 (£2 10s. paid) and the C shares were split into five new C shares of £1 fully paid (Table 6.1). The restructuring of capital gave the bank higher ratios of capital to deposits (2.5 per cent) and capital and reserves to deposits (5.5 per cent) than the National, Chartered and Hongkong Banks. In less than four years, however, the Mercantile was again forced to revise its capital to keep pace with planned expansion and modernization of the balance sheet (see below, pages 125–6).

The rearrangement of capital in 1954 provides a rare glimpse of the ownership of the bank in the post-war world.[10] The Mercantile's share

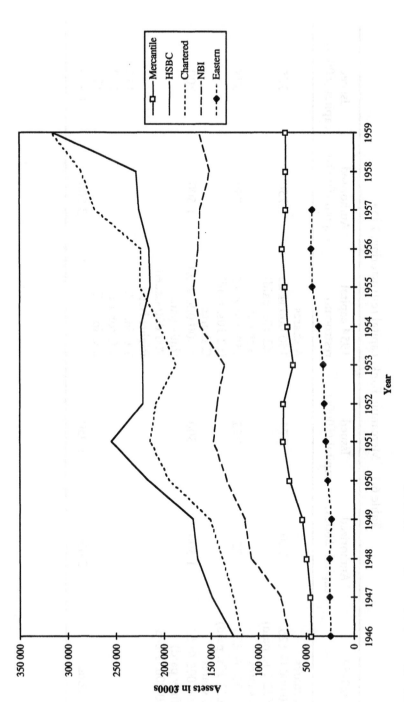

6.2 Eastern banks: total assets 1946–59

Table 6.1 Mercantile Bank, capital restructuring, 1954

1920–54	Authorized capital (£000s)	Issued capital (£000s)	1954 capital restructure	Authorised capital (£000s)	Issued capital (£000s)
A shares			**A shares**		
30 000 @ £25 (£12 10s. paid)	750	375	150 000 @ £5 (£2 10s. paid)	750	375
B shares			**B shares**		
30 000 @ £25 (£12 10s. paid)	750	375	150 000 @ £5 (£2 10s. paid)	750	375
C shares			**C shares**		
300 000 @ £5 (fully paid) 60 000 issued	1 500	300	1 500 000 @ £1 (fully paid) 300 000 issued	1 500	300
			Rights issue		
			1 C for 1 A		150
			1 C for 1 B		150
			2 C for 5 C		120
Total	3 000	1 050		3 000	1 470

register was dominated by British insurance companies.[11] Major share-holders in 1954 included Pearl Assurance, with 5.05 per cent of total capital value, Royal Insurance (3.57 per cent), Royal London Mutual (1.73 per cent) and Prudential (1.49 per cent). Nominee and trustee holdings were also prominent, with Midland Bank's trustee company holding 4.55 per cent of the total and Unit Trust Nominees holding another 4.48 per cent; the nominee companies of Lloyds Bank and Glyn's also retained substantial shares. This list of support reflected the investment world's confidence in the Mercantile as a solid performer and a reliable source of dividend earnings.

By 1954 the ownership of the Mercantile belonged almost exclusively to British-resident companies and individuals. The Eastern shareholders who had played such a significant role in the old Chartered Mercantile Bank had no parallel in the post-war share register. Only a tiny propor-tion of the bank's owners were resident overseas. A total of 67 shareholdings, representing only 3.6 per cent of the bank's .capital by value, were located outside the British Isles. Indian shareholders re-mained the largest group with 23 holdings, equivalent to 1.6 per cent of the whole, but there were also Mercantile shareholders in Singapore and Malaya, Hong Kong, South Africa and the other British dominions. European and American investors were negligible in number and held only 0.13 per cent of the total value. Overseas shareholders, moreover, were dwarfed by the large number of Scottish investors. The 1954 share register included 128 Scots holdings, equivalent to 8.6 per cent of the total capital of the bank. In reality the Scottish participation was even greater as this total excludes shareholders who gave addresses at Lon-don branches of Scottish banks. It also excludes residents of England and Wales who can be identified as Scots by their surnames or even by their addresses: the Scots-named owners of a house named 'Killiecrankie', for example, were surely not natives of Surrey.[12]

On the assets side of the balance sheet, the distortions created by wartime finance disappeared only slowly. In common with most British banks at home and overseas, the Mercantile was anxious to revert to a broad base of earnings. The war years had seen a massive accumulation of government investments as a result of official fund-raising and the diversion of conventional lending from banks to wartime government agencies. In 1946 the Mercantile's investments (mostly British and colo-nial government securities) amounted to £15.3 million, equivalent to 34.8 per cent of the bank's total assets. That level receded gradually as normal patterns of trade were resumed, allowing the Mercantile to switch assets from investments to trade finance and other lending. Even so, the bank's investments were still as high as £14.8 million (22.1 per cent of assets) in 1950. Thereafter they provided approximately one-quarter of the bank's assets throughout the 1950s, with temporary increases to match the rise in special deposits in 1952 and the fall in the value of government securities in 1955.

The handling of the bank's capital and investments, as part of the overall control of the balance sheet, remained the special responsibility of the board and management in London. The key element in the bank's size and performance, however, remained the earning potential of the overseas branches. It was here that the realignment of the bank towards new or expanding markets was most apparent.

The political and economic changes of the post-war world had the effect of opening new doors of opportunity for the bank while also shutting others. Indian independence and possible partition of the country forced the bank to examine its prospects in the sub-continent. In late 1945 Crichton had sent Drake on a tour of the Indian branches to learn the intentions of the bank's customers. In 1946 the board asked all the Indian managers to sound out their important clients as to their thoughts on the state of business in an independent India. Drake himself, and many of the Indian managers, were optimistic about the bank's prospects under a new government: 'honesty and probity will always attract business to them', Drake wrote to Crichton in 1946.[13] There were no suggestions regarding new ways of doing business or new opportunities, and the bank seemed to regard the transition to independent government as 'business as usual'.

The Mercantile's board and management nevertheless recognized that partition would result in profound disturbance for the economy of East Bengal and for the jute trade. The principal jute-growing areas would be located in the newly created state of Pakistan, separated from the major jute mills and from their traditional financiers and shippers in Calcutta. In July 1947 head office flew Lionel Blanks to Calcutta, and from there he travelled to Chittagong, Chandpur, Narayangunj and Dacca in order to report on the prospects of opening a branch in the area. Most important, he was to ascertain whether any of Calcutta branch's larger customers were thinking of opening branches or agencies in East Bengal, especially in Chittagong, and whether they would need and use the services of the bank. Blanks concluded in his report that 'the present does not appear a favourable time for us to open in Chittagong'. His reasons were that Pakistan had yet to build a jute mill; the harbour of Chittagong was still hardly developed; the Mercantile had little chance of attracting any big accounts; and there would be difficulties in finding both suitable accommodation and staff.[14] Head office and the board agreed with Blanks's conclusions and waited. Shortly afterwards the stimulus to establish a branch in Chittagong came when a Calcutta customer, Shaw Wallace & Co., decided to open an agency there in April 1948. Not only would their business in Chittagong go through the bank, but they also offered office accommodation in the building they were planning for their own agency. Chittagong branch began business in the summer of 1948. A further branch in East Pakistan, at Khulna, was opened in 1952.

In India itself, independence meant that the former political importance of Simla (as the seat of government during the hot months of the year) diminished and the bank's branch there was duly closed in 1951. It also became clear that it was essential to have an office in New Delhi, which was developing as both a capital city and business centre. Initial problems in finding suitable office accommodation were overcome by 1955, but then the initial application for a licence to operate in the city was rejected by the Reserve Bank. Subsequent negotiation led to the establishment of a branch in New Delhi in 1956.

Further east, the Chinese civil war and the victory of the communists also forced the board and London management to examine the prospects of Shanghai branch in a new political environment. Early hopes in the post-war world that Shanghai would regain its former pre-eminence in foreign trade soon dwindled. The communists took over the city in May 1949, and thereafter the bank's business shrank. At first the commercial community clung to the hope that the communists might wish to develop Shanghai's business and, until conditions stabilized, the British banks were content to keep their branches open. However, the branch was making no profit, and money to cover overheads such as taxes and staff wages had to be remitted directly to China from London. This was not a situation that could continue. By June 1952 all three Eastern exchange banks operating in the city (the Chartered, Mercantile and Hongkong banks) had decided to apply to the Financial Control Bureau to shut their offices. In all the subsequent negotiations the three banks attempted to act together. In Shanghai the three managers kept each other informed of the stages they had reached in their discussions with the relevant authorities, and in London the three banks acted in concert, especially in their dealings with the Foreign Office.[15]

For the staff in Shanghai it was an anxious time. J. B. 'Hamish' Stewart, who had already suffered captivity in Shanghai during the Second World War, took over the management of the branch in 1950. He was joined later in 1950 by Jack McSkimming. The foreign community in Shanghai slowly contracted around them and typical European haunts, such as the golf club, gradually closed or were requisitioned. At times the atmosphere was hostile towards foreigners in the city, especially during the Korean War when attention also turned to 'enemies within'. Foreigners were not permitted to leave China without exit permits. Such permits were not readily obtainable and were also much delayed, particularly for company managers who were effectively being held as hostages. In February 1953, Chinese inspectors began to investigate the bank's books. The officers made an inventory of all books and ledgers in the office and the staff were warned not to tamper with or conceal anything. Stewart wrote to Drake that the atmosphere in the office was extremely unpleasant and that it 'scarcely differs from that under the Japanese liquidator in 1942'.[16] The Shanghai branch found itself caught between the orders of head office and the orders of the Chinese authorities. For instance, in 1953 the bank's pre-liberation deposits were revalued and the bank was told to pay out to depositors who applied for their now vastly inflated sums. The branch did not have enough local resources to meet this estimated liability of around £15 000, but head office refused to remit funds from London to cover it. Stewart had to pay depositors piecemeal from recovered local loans.

The idea of an 'all-for-all' settlement – one in which the bank handed over all of its assets in China and responsibility for its liabilities – seems to have originated with Michael Turner, chief manager of the Hongkong Bank, in the summer of 1953.[17] All three British banks had begun negotiations on this basis by the beginning of 1954. The assets and liabilities of the bank would be taken over by a private company, Ta Hwa Enterprises, and the branch submitted its first offer to them in April 1954. Negotiations proved to be painstaking and prolonged. During the negotiation period the bank still needed to remit funds to cover overheads; by April 1954 the bank had brought £101 826 and US$38 300 into China since 1949. The situation was further complicated when Ta Hwa Enterprises stated that they would not accept a general 'all-for-all' principle. Instead they would take over all of the bank's assets in China but would only accept certain liabilities subject to negotiation and exact valuation. After detailed discussions, the agreement was finally signed on 28 February 1955.

At Shanghai one important issue was still not resolved. The branch's US dollar accounts had been frozen by the American authorities during the Korean War, and intense negotiation at the highest level had still not secured their release. The dollars amounted to some US$500 000 and were composed largely of margins deposited with the bank to cover letters of credit and the balance of the Bank of China's account. The Bank of China was insisting on their return and it was clear that the final closure of the branch and the safe return of the staff had now become a negotiating lever. The Foreign Office took the part of the bank and in July 1955 Jimmy Swales, the Mercantile's New York representative, flew to Washington to present in person an application to the United States Treasury for the release of the frozen dollars: 'requesting on our behalf their sympathetic consideration of our request on humane

1   James Campbell, chief manager of the Mercantile Bank from 1893 until
    1913. By courtesy of Mrs I. Campbell.

2   The staff of the Galle office of the Mercantile Bank in 1911.

3 The staff of Karachi branch in 1912, with A. Scott Smith as manager (seated, centre). By courtesy of Mr J. Wright.

4 $5 issued note of Shanghai branch of 1916, the first year in which the Mercantile issued notes in Shanghai.

5 The head office of the Mercantile Bank in Gracechurch Street, London, in
1914.

6 The staff of Delhi office, including the bank's agent K. Robertson (seated, fourth from right) and his family, in 1928.

7 The Mercantile Bank's Singapore office in about 1920.

8 The staff of Singapore branch, then numbering 91, with T. McDowall as manager (seated, centre), in 1935.

9 The Singapore manager's house at Chatsworth in about 1930.

10 'Jackie' Huxter, manager at Shanghai (right), with (left to right) Mrs Pow, anon., Charles Pow and Mrs Huxter in 1947. By courtesy of Mrs C. Pow.

11 The entrance to Shanghai branch during the Sino-Japanese war in 1937. By courtesy of Mr A. Bonbernard.

12   Kuala Trengganu office, on the east coast of Malaya, in 1940.

13   The staff of Kuala Trengganu office in 1957, with S. Muirhead (centre) as manager.

14 The new premises of Bombay office in 1950.

15 Robert Drake, chief manager from 1950 to 1958, and the Mercantile's managers in the 'rupee circle' in 1955. Standing from left: A. Cumming, G. Bamford, A. Bell, J. Beadon, D. Scott. Seated from left: H. Wyatt, R. Thomas, R. Drake, R. Graham, J. Shirreff. By courtesy of Mrs E. Shirreff.

16 The Calcutta officers of the Mercantile Bank in 1946. Standing, left to right:
A. Basu, J. Ray, A. Wood, A. Curtis, J. Ghose, W. McKerron, N. Paton
Smith, S. Singh Roy, S. Bhattacharya. Sitting, from left to right: A. Winslow,
E. West, G. Aste, A. Powles (manager), R. Bland, R. Murray, A. Bonbernard.
Front: D. Maitra (left), J. Mathur (right). By courtesy of Mr S. Singh Roy.

17 The Calcutta branch of the Mercantile Bank in the early 1950s.

18   Madras branch in about 1955.

19   The banking hall at Madras in about 1955.

20　Colin Wardle in Bombay in about 1947. 'Towkay' Wardle served as chief
manager of the Mercantile Bank from 1958 to 1962.

21　Sir Michael Turner, chief manager (1953–62) and chairman (1958–62) of
the Hongkong and Shanghai Banking Corporation.

22 Chittagong branch in 1954.

23 The mobile branch bank in Mauritius in 1962.

24 The staff of Bangkok branch during a visit by Sir Kenneth Mealing (centre), chairman of the bank, probably in 1955. By courtesy of Mr B. Bawden.

25 The current accounts department of Colombo branch in about 1955.

26 The football club in Hong Kong in 1947, with Donovan Benson, branch manager (seated third from left) and Lo Yuk Tong, compradore (seated third from right). By courtesy of Mr A. Bonbernard.

27 The headquarters of the Hongkong and Shanghai Banking Corporation, Hong Kong, in the early 1970s. The Mercantile's head office was located in this building from 1966 until 1984.

28 Ian Herridge (left) on his retirement as chairman of the Mercantile Bank in 1973, with Guy Sayer, chairman of the Hongkong Bank, on the right.

29 HK$100 note issued by the Mercantile Bank in Hong Kong in 1965.

grounds, our primary object being to obtain the release from China of our Shanghai manager'.[18] By this time the sole representative of the bank in the city was Douglas Smith, who had taken over from Stewart in September 1954: McSkimming had obtained his exit visa and left at the end of January 1955.

It was not until April 1956 that a final answer was received from Washington: the relevant accounts of the bank would not be unfrozen, but the bank would be permitted to pay 'free funds' to the Chinese on the safe arrival of Douglas Smith in Hong Kong. The 'free funds' that the Chinese would accept were in effect transferable sterling and on 19 June 1956 a cheque for £191 347 2s. 10d. was paid to the Banque Belge pour l'Étranger, which held the money on an escrow basis. On 9 July Smith arrived in Hong Kong and on the same day the Banque Belge duly paid over the amount to the Bank of China. As a bank official remarked, Smith had proved to be 'a very valuable young man'.[19] Since 1950 the bank had posted a total of £131 637 in losses at the Shanghai branch. The liquidation arrangements for the remnants of the business were not completed until 1959, when the Koon Sze Hoyin Bank was commissioned to deal with any remaining claims and to maintain the old Mercantile office records for at least five years.[20]

Although the bank had no representation in China after 1956, it was able to extend its coverage in the Far East by opening in Japan. SCAP (Supreme Commander, Allied Powers) did not hurry to reopen Japan's foreign trade, but in 1947 both the Hongkong Bank and the Chartered Bank were permitted to re-establish their offices in Tokyo.[21] Japan needed to import many capital goods for her reconstruction, and those shipments originating from the sterling area could only be arranged through British banks. Donovan Benson, the Mercantile's manager in Hong Kong, wrote to London management in 1948 that they should seriously consider opening in Japan: 'I feel this is the matter that must now be seriously considered if we are to retain our grip of all our business in the East.'[22] Once again, London sent Blanks out to investigate. After his trip in February 1949, he recommended that the bank should open in Japan and by July 1949 a branch was established in Tokyo. In a shrewd move, the bank also decided to open a branch in Osaka in the same year. This was the first foreign bank to open in the city and behind the decision lay a realistic appraisal of the bank's own business. Osaka was home to a large Indian business community, and the bank, with its reputation in the sub-continent, was well placed to provide banking services. The lack of competition and the high rates that could be obtained provided the bank with a very profitable branch in the first half of the 1950s. The Indian business community was initially concentrated in one building, the

Fukatake building in Semba, and the bank opened a 'liaison' office in the building in 1953.

The bank was constrained in extending its branch network elsewhere by two major factors. First, in the countries where the Mercantile operated, the banking authorities controlled the granting of licences for any new branches. In certain countries the expansion of foreign banks was not considered favourably. In the first half of the 1950s the bank applied to open in Ahmedabad and New Delhi in India and in Hyderabad and Lahore in Pakistan: all the applications were refused.[23] New Delhi branch was later permitted to open (see above, page 113) but the only other new branch which the bank was permitted to open in India in this period was at Gandhidham, in the Gulf of Kutch, in March 1958. The Indian government aimed to transform Gandhidham into a free port. Although that project was abandoned in the face of the costs of dredging the inlet, the new bank office was retained. The bank considered opening in Southern India in the late 1950s (as it had done 20 years earlier). Hamish Stewart, then manager in Bombay, was sent to investigate towns in the south as possible new sites, including Hyderabad and Bangalore. Permission to open was again refused.[24] A similar attitude prevailed in Ceylon after independence. MacFarlane, posted to the island in the late 1940s, recalled: 'We wanted to open more agencies, but by this time there was independence and there were limitations in what we could do.'[25] The bank managed to open a new agency in Pettah, in the Colombo bazaar area, in 1956 but any further expansion was not possible: domestic banks were competing for domestic funds and were unhappy about the extension of the foreign banks.

The second constraining factor was the Mercantile's perennial problem of staff shortages. In 1947, Drake replied tersely to a suggestion that the bank should extend its branch network in Malaya: 'no matter how keen the bank may be on extending its activities in the East, it would be impossible to do so as the European Staff is not sufficient for the number of branches we have already'.[26] This lack of staff was not for want of trying. Failing to find enough recruits in Britain, the bank took advantage of the holiday in Australia by a member of staff, Stanley Soul, and requested him to interview suitable candidates while he was there.[27] By 1950 the situation had still not eased. Drake complained to Wardle in Singapore, 'The staff position has never been so acute as it is today ... all the branches are crying out for assistants which they must have.'[28] In 1947 the European staff numbered 108; by 1959 this number had only risen to 126, whereas the number of branches and agencies had increased from 29 to 41.

As expansion in some of the bank's traditional markets was blocked, so new pastures were considered. The bank's chairman, Sir Kenneth

Mealing, circulated a memorandum to the board in June 1955 on the subject of the bank's future expansion. His note set out the stark choices that lay ahead for the bank:

> I suggest we face the fact that future extension of our business by the opening of new offices, is likely to be banned or obstructed in most of the territories in which we operate ... Moreover we must anticipate that, at least in some places, our business will decline either quantitatively or qualitively as favoured indigenous banking increases and as costs and local taxation increase. Unless we are prepared to make efforts to expand in other directions ... we may find difficulty in maintaining our position – let alone improving it.[29]

The board decided to explore the options that remained open to them by sending senior members of London management to areas of the world that they considered held potential for the bank.

This process was already under way. In 1950 Robson Thomas toured Kenya, Tanganyika and Uganda, investigating local conditions and analysing the scope for new branches. His last posting had been as sub-manager, Bombay, and it was the large business of this branch with East Africa that had prompted the expansion proposal. Thomas reached the conclusion that there was no profitable business to be had – the bank was interested in import and export finance and these services were already catered for by the existing institutions.[30] Drake visited the United States and Canada in 1953, attempting both to increase the bank's business with its correspondents on the other side of the Atlantic and to sound out prospects for a new branch. Drake was keen to open a branch in Canada but was reluctantly forced to conclude that there was very little chance of establishing a profitable business in such a mature market.[31] In March 1955 Walter Jowit (manager at Bombay) was sent to West Africa to investigate the business possibilities that existed in Nigeria and the Gold Coast. This business would be dependent on the bank obtaining a share of the business of the United African Company, a subsidiary of Lever Brothers, and the board decided against such a departure from the bank's traditional area of expertise which held no guarantee of profits.[32] The bank's management and board drew similar conclusions about prospective business in the Bahamas. In 1957 the bank was approached by the firm of Messrs Gordon, Grant & Co. to take over their merchant banking business in Trinidad and Tobago. 'Towkay' Wardle visited the islands *incognito* – an unlikely mission for such an outgoing personality – and his verdict was: 'I can see no prospects at all for a branch.'[33]

Despite these obstacles the bank did attempt to extend its operations in certain areas. Close to home, the bank opened a West End branch at

123 Pall Mall in 1956. In addition to the new branches overseas in Japan, East Pakistan and India, the bank also opened further offices in Malaya. Temerloh opened in 1956, followed by Seremban and Taiping early in 1959. The spur to activity here was the threat that the Chartered Bank was moving into the east coast, the area in which the Mercantile traditionally had a virtual monopoly of exchange banking. The location of the new offices in Malaya was decided in concert with the authorities, as local government business was often the mainstay of these small agencies. The manager of Kuala Lumpur was told in 1955, 'it is of paramount importance that the government should nominate the place at which we should open, for without government support ... the prospects of a sub-agency returning a profit are remote'.[34] Additionally, the business of Singapore and Bangkok branches was strong enough to demand extra local resources. The search for new deposits was continued by opening sub-branches at Rajawongse Road, Bangkok, in 1957 and Beach Road, Singapore, in August 1959. These new additions to the branch network found official favour and, because of the small nature of the operations, were relatively easy to staff.

In the 1950s the bank suffered not only from a shortage of staff but also from a continuous need to re-evaluate the terms and conditions of their local employees and local officers. By the mid-1950s, many Asian countries were putting foreign companies under pressure to employ Asian nationals in executive posts. The Mercantile Bank counted 20 Asian assistants and 19 Asian assistant accountants among the staff in 1955.[35] However, all of these were employed in India, Ceylon, Pakistan and Burma, while the informal ceiling on promotion meant that no Asian had been appointed to a position above that of assistant accountant. This issue of local executive staff was addressed by Sir Kenneth Mealing, the bank's chairman, in 1955. He proposed that a percentage of the executive staff of each country should consist of Asians; the percentage could be calculated by a formula that took into account the proportion of the bank's total profit derived from that country. His proposals were considered by the bank's London management, who 'were of the unanimous opinion that the time was not opportune for the implementation of the scheme.[36] They feared that such a scheme would destroy the British character of the bank that they believed was one of the features that attracted customers. However, they did agree to review the terms of service and to extend the employment of executive local officers to the other countries in which the bank operated. Greater prominence was also given to harmonizing training and procedures. Trainees from the Indian branches travelled to London for a spell in head office alongside trainees for the Eastern staff. In this way, and with the insistence that Asian officers would not necessarily serve in their home countries, the bank attempted to give all their officers a common induction and an international outlook.[37]

In addition to the ongoing debate about the pay, position and promotion prospects of the Asian executive staff, the post-war era was also marked by a series of disputes with the local staff and the bank clerks' unions. The problems were not confined to the Mercantile Bank; among the exchange banks India and Ceylon were especially prone to strikes of bank clerks. Many of the problems lay in the different conditions of service, pay and perquisites that existed at each branch, having evolved due to varying economic conditions and attitudes of the managers in charge. In India these differences were removed by the Sastri Award of 1955, a government measure which sought to lay down conditions of service and pay in detail for all the banks. However, the implementation of the award sparked off a wave of strikes in December 1955 and in the Mercantile's Calcutta office there were daily lunchtime demonstrations. These strikes seriously disrupted work, delaying the clearing process in particular. More important, they commandeered much time in negotiation – in Bombay office the number two accountant spent a large proportion of his working day on staff issues and interpretations of the conditions laid down by the Sastri Award. In Calcutta office, a dispute between an Asian executive and a member of the local staff (who was also the secretary of the employees' union) soured relations in the office for much of the early 1950s and required many hours of negotiation, in addition to the hours of work lost in impromptu strikes, walk-outs and lock-ins.

The exact numbers of the bank's local staff in the 1950s cannot be quantified, but the total may have approached 2000. The evidence from inspection reports shows that Penang – only a middle-ranking branch in terms of business – employed 97 local staff in 1957. In the same period Mr Ong, the Singapore compradore, employed 35 staff on his own account. This number included seven bill collectors and four storekeepers who supervised goods pledged to the bank in godowns around the city. As the branch itself would have employed local staff, the total number at Singapore was clearly much higher, probably in the region of 200.[38] Calcutta and Bombay branch employed around 350 local staff each, and by 1959 the time spent on staff issues prompted the inspector to suggest that the bank should appoint a European officer to handle all staff matters throughout India.[39]

The search for new branches, resources and profits shifted the emphasis of the bank's business from India. In the decade after independence the senior Indian branches still retained their place as the largest of the Mercantile's offices at least by volume of business. In 1956, for example, the assets of the Bombay branch slightly exceeded the Calcutta figure, while Colombo, Karachi, Madras and the new Chittagong branch all featured among the bank's ten largest branches (Figure 6.3). However, the Singapore branch was in a strong third place, with Hong Kong, Kuala Lumpur and Penang also contributing a significant share of business. The proportion of assets held in the sub-continent was declining. Whereas in 1947, 72 per cent of assets of the overseas branches were held there, by 1956 that proportion had fallen to only 42 per cent. The Malayan branches (16.9 per cent) and Hong Kong (4.5 per cent) had by then taken much larger shares of the bank's total business.

The bank's branches in the Far East also became its strongest performers in terms of earnings. The net profits at Hong Kong and Singapore surged ahead of the results of the traditional strongholds of Bombay and Calcutta and, in the three years from 1950 to 1952, these two Far Eastern branches earned total net profits of approximately four times as much as the two senior Indian branches (Figure 6.4). Singapore branch in particular, after its profits slumped in 1953–54, resumed its high level of earnings between 1955 and 1957.

The economic boom in both Singapore and Hong Kong was clearly more than a recovery phase. Hong Kong, the Mercantile's chairman argued in 1949, was 'a haven of law, order and stability in a very troubled part of the world ... the Colony continues to enjoy a great, if possibly hectic, prosperity'.[40] In the earlier 1950s the Korean War also benefited the business of the Far Eastern branches. Hong Kong and Singapore became vital for the distribution of food supplies, war materials and personnel for the United Nations forces. As a result the Mercantile's branches there took on large volumes of inter-branch business with each other and also with the bank's offices in Japan, Malaya and New York. This pattern, in contrast to the Mercantile's traditional reliance on the direct relationship between London and the branches, meant that London office took up a lower proportion of the bank's profits in the early 1950s. When the effects of wartime demand receded after 1953, Hong Kong and Singapore were able to sustain their dynamic growth. Hong Kong, where the population increased by four times to 2.5 million between 1945 and 1954,[41] benefited because the businessmen who arrived there from Shanghai brought with them their industrial traditions, dealing skills and even their machinery.

In the second rank of branches, there was also a distinct change in the balance of business and earnings in the 1950s. Branches on the sub-continent lost ground relatively to the offices in Malaya, Thailand and Japan. In Japan, the earnings of the new branch in Tokyo were modest but its sister branch in Osaka swiftly generated a large and profitable business. Against the background of the Korean War, the Japanese economy underwent a period of sudden growth coupled to price

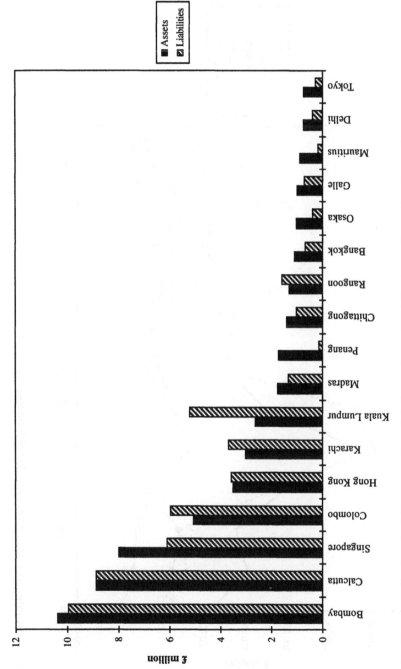

6.3   Mercantile Bank: principal overseas branch balance sheets, 1956 (by descending order of assets)

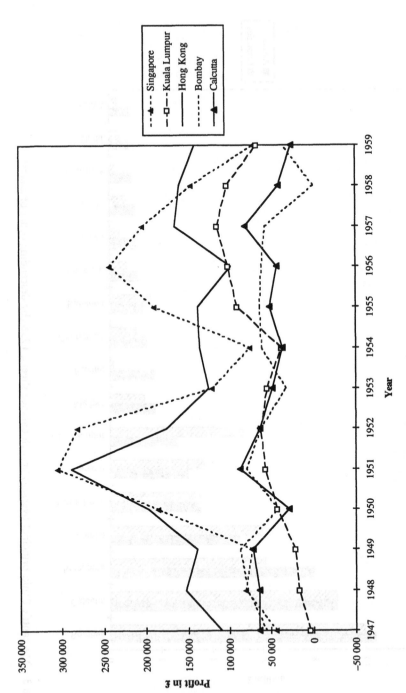

6.4 Mercantile Bank: net profits of selected branches, 1947–59

inflation (wholesale prices increased by 56 per cent between June 1950 and September 1951[42]). Elsewhere the older-established branches at Kuala Lumpur, Penang and Bangkok also enjoyed a period of strong growth. Annual net profits at Bangkok tripled to over £100 000 between 1949 and 1952 when Thailand was generating large surpluses from rice exports. The platform for Thailand's trade was also strengthened by loans of $25.4 million from the International Bank for Reconstruction and Development for irrigation and infrastructure projects.[43] At Kuala Lumpur in the same period branch profits tripled to £60 000, reflecting the wartime demand for tin and rubber at a time when Malaya was 'the principal dollar earner of the Sterling Area'.[44] These branch net earnings, which fell back as rubber prices halved and the Malayan emergency worsened in 1953, then surged to over £100 000 each year in the independence period from 1956 to 1958.

In addition to the favourable macro-economic climate and tax regimes in Singapore, Malaya and Hong Kong, some of the increased profitability at these branches can be attributed to personal factors. For instance, Hong Kong's post-war manager, Donovan Benson, was an expert on local business. Having managed the branch before the war, he was very friendly with Arthur Morse, the Hongkong Bank's chairman and chief manager between 1941 and 1953. Benson was well known and liked in the Hong Kong business community, evidenced by the great distinction of serving as chairman of the Hong Kong Jockey Club between 1953 and 1967.

Similarly, Singapore branch was managed by a series of energetic and effective managers including Colin Wardle and Charles Pow, both of whom later became chief managers of the Mercantile Bank. Singapore branch also gained market share by shifting its customer base. Traditionally, the Mercantile had won only a very small share of the business of the large European agency houses such as Harrisons and Crosfields, Bousteads, Patersons Simons, the Anglo-Thai Corporation, and Guthrie and Co. Rather than concentrating on increasing this side of the business, the branch sought to extend its business with Chinese and Indian constituents. When Drake sent Wardle back to Singapore after the war he gave him some simple instructions: 'European business is the same old story and that is why I suggested to you when you went to Singapore that you should go all out for Asiatic business.'[45] Among the largest customers at Singapore were Hardial and Gian Singh, two brothers who had a number of interests including import/export merchants and the management of a department store. In 1952 the branch had over Straits$ 15 million advanced to the brothers. Unfortunately, the restriction of imports to Indonesia in 1952 left the Singhs with large amounts of stock that had been destined for the Indonesian markets. The size of their debt to the branch caused some consternation among the board, and with monthly repayments set at Straits\$ 40 000, it would take some years for the branch to recover the funds. Other large Singapore customers included Aik Hoe, a Chinese rubber business, and Lam Soon Cannery, a coconut oil and products manufacturer and exporter. An inspection report of the Singapore branch in 1953 praised the office: 'the most heartening feature of the branch's advancement is their successful exploitation of avenues hitherto unexplored and the attraction of a larger share of Indian and Chinese business'.[46]

This view applied to many of the bank's branches during this time. The large European agency houses and multinationals often gave the lion's share of their business to the Hongkong Bank or the Chartered Bank, leaving the Mercantile to concentrate on smaller local businesses. This split of business also meant that the Mercantile was more likely to search out new forms of business. Bombay, for instance, had a very large inward bill business which derived from the many local importers of general goods who were customers of the bank. The branch also financed the large trade in raw cotton which was imported from the United States, Egypt and East Africa by local manufacturers. In the late 1950s the branch also dipped its toes into the business of industrial finance when it advanced some Rs 5 million to an old customer who was setting up the first nylon factory in India. This diversification of business was especially important after 1957 when further import restrictions came into force in India. In 1958 Harry Wyatt, during an inspection of the bank's branches, proposed that Bombay branch should set about 'an active reorientation of [its] investments' to replace the business lost due to the new import controls. The branch's funds, he suggested, could be profitably invested in local industry.

The extension of the branch network and the shifts in the customer base of some of its markets fuelled a steady growth of the Mercantile's balance sheet, even if that expansion could not compare with that of the Hongkong and Chartered Banks (Figure 6.2). In terms of total earnings, these developments generated outstanding results. Published profits climbed from £183 152 in 1947 to £331 243 in 1957, a record result which, after 35 years, eclipsed the previous highest levels in the boom years of 1920 to 1922. Real profits, however, moved into entirely new territory. Whereas the difference between published and undisclosed profits was previously measured in tens of thousands of pounds, in the 1950s the difference was ordinarily counted in hundreds of thousands of pounds. Hence in 1951 the actual result of £878 361 was more than four times the published figure and in the mid-1950s the difference was threefold. This vigorous performance enabled the bank to lift dividends on all classes of shares from 12 to 14 per cent from 1952 and, more importantly, to raise gross dividend payouts from £126 000 per annum in the late 1940s to £367 500 after the capital reorganization of 1957. This increase still allowed the bank to transfer the bulk of the additional earnings to inner reserves, greatly changing the shape of the internal balance sheet. Whereas in 1947 inner reserves of £2.2 million were twice the value of the quite separate published reserves, by 1953 the inner reserves of £4 365 152 had reached three times the level of the published equivalent. This pattern was unique among the British overseas banks. Where data are available the inner reserves of these banks were smaller or only slightly larger than their published reserves.[47]

The strength of the bank's earnings and inside funds provided a sturdy safety net, as Charles Innes had urged in the early 1930s. They were also a precious opportunity for new initiatives. By 1957, at the end of Drake's service as chief manager, the Mercantile's board and management recognized that a new perception of the bank was needed. The pattern of business, earnings, management and staff had altered substantially in the post-war period and the competitive threat of local and international banks had multiplied throughout the bank's markets. These factors were powerful arguments for a re-examination of the Mercantile's identity and fitness as an international bank.

At the top of the bank, Drake and his directors looked for ways of modernizing the public standing of the Mercantile. In May 1957 the board appointed a sub-committee (comprising the deputy chairman Sir Cyril Jones, E. J. Bunbury, J. B. Crichton and Sir Charles Innes) to consider changes to the name and the capital structure of the bank. As to capital, it was clear by then that the reorganization in 1954 had been only a half-way house. The issue of the additional C shares had increased the amount of issued capital, while the conversion of the A and B shares had followed the current corporate trend of reducing the denomination of shares. Yet this process had preserved the somewhat antiquated arrangement of three classes of shares with separate rights, in which the A and B shares still carried a large uncalled liability.

Jones's sub-committee, probably with the advice of Cooper Brothers as the bank's auditors, sought ways of reducing the classes of shares, equalizing the rights attached to all shares and eliminating the uncalled liability on the A and B shares. They also looked at the possibility of a major increase in total capital by making transfers from inner reserves (which then exceeded £3.2 million).[48] Their formula for this modernization was announced to shareholders on 17 July 1957. A two-stage conversion was proposed and then accepted by shareholders at an extraordinary general meeting on 25 November 1957. At the completion of the first and most complex stage, all three classes of shares were converted arithmetically into £1 ordinary shares, fully paid with no uncalled liability, and an additional 750 000 £1 ordinary shares were created. At the completion of the second (simultaneous) stage, an additional 1 million £1 ordinary shares were created and a rights issue of 1 for 1 ordinary share was made. This process, as shown in Table 6.2, raised the bank's total authorized capital from £3 million to £4 million – all in fully paid £1 ordinary shares – and doubled the paid-up capital to £2 940 000. These changes were to be financed by capitalizing £1 470 000 of published reserves and replacing these reserves exactly from inner reserves.

The restructuring of the Mercantile's capital, approved by the High Court in December 1957 and effective from 31 December, gave the bank a simpler and more robust financial position. The process gave a greater measure of transparency to the balance sheet (even though the proportions of the bank's published and inner reserves remained unusual in the sector). The rearrangement also signalled to the financial community that the Mercantile was preparing its position for the possibility of merger negotiations with other banks, either as the acquiring bank or as the object of a bid.[49]

The other task of Jones's sub-committee was less complex but still important for the future identity of the bank. Changes in name were being considered or adopted by a number of other overseas banks in the later 1950s. The underlying theme of these changes was the distancing of British banks from their regional origins or from any imperial connotations. The Chartered Bank of India, Australia and China, for example, adopted the shortened form of the Chartered Bank in 1956 and the Bank of British West Africa renamed itself the Bank of West Africa in 1957. The National Bank of India, which had acquired Grindlays in 1948, told its shareholders in March 1957 that it would take the title of National Overseas and Grindlays Bank; in the view of the bank's historian, there was 'a compelling case for a change which would bring the bank's name and title more into line with realities'.[50] The shortened form of National and Grindlays was adopted in 1959.

At the Mercantile, Jones's sub-committee was no doubt influenced by this rash of renaming. Their recommendation – the change from the Mercantile Bank of India Limited to the Mercantile Bank Limited – was not debated at any length at board level and there is no evidence that there were any other suggestions for a new name. Clearly by October 1957 the board had approved the change. The renaming was then agreed by the shareholders at the same extraordinary general meeting which assented to the capital restructuring on 25 November.

The change of name was not simply a matter of corporate fashion. The adoption of 'the Mercantile Bank' was also an attempt to reposition the bank in a wider international market. In the post-war years a

Table 6.2 Mercantile Bank: capital restructuring, 1957

1954–57	Authorized capital (£000s)	Issued capital (£000s)	1957 (completion of stage 1)	Authorized capital (£000s)	Issued capital (£000s)	1957 (completion of stage 2)	Authorized capital (£000s)	Issued capital (£000s)
A shares 150 000 @ £5 (£2 10s. paid)	750	375	Ordinary shares 375 000 @ £1 (fully paid)	375	375	Ordinary shares 375 000 @ £1 (fully paid)	375	375
B shares 150 000 @ £5 (£2 10s. paid)	750	375	Ordinary shares 375 000 @ £1 (fully paid)	375	375	Ordinary shares 375 000 @ £1 (fully paid)	375	375
C shares 1 500 000 @ £1 (fully paid) 720 000 issued	1 500	720	Ordinary shares 1 500 000 @ £1 (fully paid) 720 000 issued	1 500	720	Ordinary shares 1 500 000 @ £1 (fully paid) 720 000 issued	1 500	720
			Ordinary shares 750 000 @ £1 (authorized, not issued)	750	–	Ordinary shares 750 000 @ £1 (authorized)	750	–
						Ordinary shares 1 000 000 @ £1 (authorized)	1 000	–
						Rights issue 1 for 1 ordinary share issued		1 470
Total	3 000	1 470		3 000	1 470		4 000	2 940

decreasing proportion of the Mercantile's business and earnings derived from the sub-continent. The bank had reinforced its presence in the Far East (especially in the Malayan peninsula and in Japan) and it had flirted with the notion of opening in regions such as East Africa and the Caribbean. While the sub-continent remained the bank's principal overseas market, these initiatives reflected the Mercantile's willingness to modernize as an international rather than as a regional bank. In this way the change of name was more momentous than at first sight. It removed the direct and public identification with India which had been part of its inheritance since the foundation of the Chartered Mercantile Bank of London, India and China over a century earlier. It also signalled the Mercantile's entry on to a wider, more open and perhaps more exposed stage.

CHAPTER SEVEN

Reckoning, 1957–66

In the late 1950s, merger activity was creating a febrile mood in British business and in the wider community. Amalgamations and acquisitions were not new to the scene – historians have underestimated their importance in the inter-war period, for example – and the volume and market value of mergers would also reach significantly higher levels in the 1960s.[1] For the business world in the 1950s, however, merger activity was reviving significantly for the first time for more than 20 years. That activity also contained the heady new ingredient of the contested takeover, with one or more companies bidding for an unwilling target company. Although less than 20 per cent of mergers in British manufacturing industry were contested in the 1950s and 1960s, even the possibility of a disputed bid introduced a new awareness of threat and a concern for self-preservation.

The banking sector was also affected by this enthusiasm for acquisitions and amalgamations. In overseas banking, political change, the advance of nationalism and new local competition were additional spurs to the restructuring of banks. The exchange banks' share of business on the sub-continent, in particular, appeared to be in long-term decline: between 1952 and 1961, for instance, their share of deposits in India fell from 18 per cent to less than 13 per cent.[2] The realignments included the Chartered Bank's acquisition in 1957 of the Eastern Bank, whose share register was previously dominated by Barclays Bank and the Sassoon family. In the same year the Chartered Bank also purchased the Cyprus branches of the Ionian Bank, a bank which had been the focus of speculative share buying since the Second World War. Lloyds Bank sold its business in India, Pakistan and Burma (its 'temporary intrusion of the 1920s') to National and Grindlays in 1960.[3] Less publicly, between 1953 and 1956 there had also been a series of abortive merger negotiations involving Australasian banks and different combinations of the Chartered Bank, Ionian Bank and the British Bank of the Middle East.[4]

Business historians have frequently bemoaned the way in which the board minutes of many companies, particularly after the first quarter of the twentieth century, are unrevealing and even anodyne. The minutes of the Mercantile's directors are generally much more helpful, especially on the details of lending and other business issues, but in the summer of 1957 those board minutes briefly switched into a highly secretive mode. At the meeting of 11 June, the minutes recorded only a single item of business: 'A memorandum dated 6th June 1957 which Lord Bicester [formerly R. H. V. Smith] had received was duly considered. It was decided that the Board required further information and Lord Bicester was requested to obtain this information.'[5] This memorandum, which was mentioned in similarly opaque terms over the following weeks, was nothing less than an offer by the Hongkong and Shanghai Banking Corporation for the outright purchase of the Mercantile Bank.

The bid already had a long and complex ancestry. The offer was certainly not a sudden impulse on behalf of either the Hongkong Bank or the Mercantile's directors and advisers. The catalyst was George Marden's shareholding in the bank.

'Gem' Marden's career had begun with the Chinese Customs Service in Canton in 1913.[6] During the First World War he had served on the Western Front, won the Military Cross and then joined the young Royal Flying Corps. Returning to the Customs Service in Shanghai after the war, he developed shrewd expertise in the complex local and international trading practices of the treaty port. This knowledge was put to new use in 1925 when, with the brothers V. K. and V. J. Song, he formed G. E. Marden and Co. as a customs brokerage and transport firm. The new firm's first great coup was to provide transport for General Duncan's 'Shaforce', which was sent to defend the international settlements in China in 1927, and this success enabled Marden to convert the firm into a quoted company. In 1932 Marden and Co., the Shanghai Tug and Lighter Co. and the shippers Wheelock and Co. Limited were brought together under the Wheelock name but with Marden as the prime mover. This combination gained a strong position in Shanghai's international shipping industry while Marden himself became a prominent figure in the city's hectic business and social life; he was also an officer in the Shanghai Volunteer Corps.

Then, in the early stages of the Japanese occupation of Shanghai, Marden quarrelled with John Huxter, the Mercantile's mercurial manager in Shanghai. The cause of the dispute was Marden's suggestion that the British banks should jointly provide a cash float to enable the Shanghai merchant community to meet some of its outstanding demands. Huxter rejected the idea, partly because the Mercantile's cash resources were already stretched to the limit. Lionel Blanks, then serving as accountant under Huxter, remembered Marden's reaction: 'He was furious; as he walked out of the office he said "bloody impossible man! I'll buy this bloody bank one day!"' Thereafter Blanks and Edward West, then senior assistant, always wondered whether 'that was one of the seeds' of later interventions by Marden.[7]

Marden, although he was not to succeed in buying the bank, decisively influenced its future. He was repatriated by the Japanese in 1942 and the business, under the new name of Wheelock Marden and Co., continued and extended its shipping and trading interests in the United Kingdom. After the war Marden returned to the East and soon joined other British and Chinese trading houses in transplanting their operations from Shanghai to Hong Kong. There his entrepreneurial zest made Wheelock Marden one of the premier houses in trading, forwarding and shipping. He entered the property market and, well ahead of his time, commissioned the first study of a cross-harbour tunnel for Hong Kong. He was also at the centre of a long and celebrated dispute with the stockbroker Noel Croucher over the control of the old-established Hongkong and China Gas Co. – a feud which lasted throughout the 1950s.

Marden began to acquire Mercantile shares in 1953. He judged that the shares were good value; despite the Mercantile's 'local reputation for lack of enterprise', he believed that the bank would be attractive to other banks looking for a foothold in Eastern markets.[8] By 1954 he had bought the equivalent of 5 per cent of the bank's equity, although the Mercantile's board was not then aware of this holding as most of the purchases were made through nominee companies. When later that year he offered to sell his bloc of shares to the Hongkong Bank, Michael Turner, then chief manager, promptly turned him down. Turner, as King explains, 'would have been content to let the Mercantile stand as it was'.[9]

At the Mercantile's head office in London, Drake and his directors had become aware of unusual share buying through Hongkong and Shanghai Bank (Nominees) Limited in the early part of 1956. Parcels of Mercantile Bank shares were being bought even at a time when prices of these shares were falling – the Mercantile's shares fell by some 20 per cent in the six months to March 1956. Drake discovered from the stock market that the buying orders came from a buyer in Hong Kong rather than in London. At first he suspected that a rival bank or a syndicate was building up a position and he asked Sandy Donn, manager at the bank's Hong Kong branch, to investigate. Donn believed that an individual businessman was responsible and he narrowed down the list of candidates to three – including George Marden. Donn knew Marden through the Rotary Club in Hong Kong and, at a cocktail party on 4 April 1956, Marden confided to Donn that he already held 10 per cent of the bank's shares. Donn described the conversation to Drake:

> Over a year ago he [Marden] was offered a substantial number of shares and as he believed in the future of the Bank he took them up ... you can be sure he will buy anything on offer. This will continue until he has control of 25 per cent of our Issued Capital, or so he says.[10]

Drake was puzzled by the news. He had met Marden in the summer of 1955, when Marden had spoken bitterly of his treatment during the war both by Huxter and by the bank, and had sworn that he would never pass any business to the Mercantile. The fact that he had lost out by selling some of his bank shares immediately before the 1954 rights issue cannot have mellowed him in his attitude to the bank. Drake doubted whether Marden was interested for investment or income reasons and he wondered whether the real aim was a seat on the board.[11]

Marden, having been turned down by the Hongkong Bank, was no more successful when he attempted to sell his shares to the Bank of America. Instead, he framed a more ambitious plan. Supported by Samuel Montagu and Co., the old-established London merchant bank, in July 1956 he sought a controlling interest in the Mercantile. This control would be exercised by 'intervening in [the bank's] management for the purpose of making better use of its assets and business etc.'. Montagus left this alliance in October when it was rumoured in the London market that Marden and Montagus planned to split up and auction the Mercantile's business. Marden vehemently rebutted this suggestion when he spoke to Bank of England officials shortly afterwards.[12]

By the beginning of 1957, Marden's share of the Mercantile's capital had reached 14 per cent. He again contacted Turner and offered to sell his shares to the Hongkong Bank. For Turner and his colleagues, the issue was now much more pressing. If such a substantial share in the Mercantile fell into the hands of a major rival – an American bank, for example – it might provide an entry ticket to new competition with the Hongkong Bank throughout its Far Eastern markets. The Hongkong Bank could not ignore this threat and, at the very least, Marden's offer needed serious review.

As a first step Sir Edward Reid, a key member of the Hongkong Bank's London Committee, consulted Lord Cobbold, Governor of the Bank of England. Reid was senior partner in Barings, the merchant bank, and he was also a director of the Bank of England. Cobbold unequivocally encouraged the Hongkong Bank to take up the challenge. At a meeting on 8 January 1957 the Governor told Reid:

> Our concern was to see the Mercantile Bank strengthened and to avoid risks of its passing into disagreeable hands (or even disintegrating). I thought this important from the general British point of view ... we should therefore applaud a decision by [the Hongkong Bank] to take an active interest.

In response Reid assured Cobbold 'that in anything they planned for the Mercantile, they would keep in step with Lord Bicester', director of the Mercantile and also on the Court of the Bank of England.[13]

With this additional comfort, Turner visited London early in 1957 to consult with Reid and Lord Bicester. At a lunch at the Savoy Grill the three men discussed the options. These included the formation of a 'kongsi' or consortium to acquire Marden's shares: the shares would be placed in 'safe hands' so that they could not be used 'in a manner which might not necessarily be desirable for British Banking in the East'.[14] Bicester, however, would not contemplate an arrangement which would allow Marden the freedom to name his price. Turner concluded that Bicester 'obviously just wasn't keen'.[15]

As a result the Hongkong Bank reverted to the option of acquiring the shares itself, possibly leading to an amalgamation with the Mercantile. In March Turner obtained his directors' agreement to buy the Marden bloc 'if only to prevent the Mercantile being sold elsewhere'.[16] Over the next few weeks the ownership of the Marden shares was transferred to the Hongkong Bank, ending his direct involvement, and on 1 May Bicester told Cobbold that he had just heard that the Hongkong Bank 'has succeeded in buying out the piratical interest in the Mercantile'.[17] S. W. P. (Sam) Perry-Aldworth, the senior London manager of the Hongkong Bank, recalled that the Hongkong Bank had been driven to this position and that 'we ourselves originally had no intention of attempting an amalgamation'.[18]

The initial negotiations between the two banks were channelled through Lord Bicester. In addition to his directorship of the Mercantile, Bicester's directorship at the Bank of England made him the main contact point for the 'Old Lady' during the negotiations. At first, and perhaps for several weeks, Bicester seems to have kept the remainder of the Mercantile board in the dark as to his discussions with Turner. In late May or early June 1957, however, there was a heated meeting of the Mercantile board when the matter was introduced (but not minuted). At the same time, and probably as a result of the meeting, the Hongkong Bank was invited to submit its proposals to the Mercantile board meeting on 11 June.

In response, on 6 June 1957 Perry-Aldworth prepared a memorandum which put the Hongkong Bank side of the story and explained its intentions to the Mercantile board.[19] This note stated that the Hongkong Bank had come to an agreement with George Marden to purchase his shares in the Mercantile at above market price. The Hongkong Bank made clear its wish to acquire the Mercantile but, if an acquisition deal proved to be impossible, an option to resell the shares to Marden would be retained until 15 September 1957. The memorandum also stated that the Hongkong Bank intended to retain the Mercantile Bank as a separate entity but would prefer to transfer the Mercantile's head office to Hong Kong. The Mercantile's offices in the Far East would merge with those of the Hongkong Bank while the branches of the Hongkong Bank in India would be taken over by the Mercantile. The banks would retain separate boards but there would be overlap between the two; the separate London offices would also remain, dealing as they did with different trade areas and specialized groups of customers.

The Hongkong Bank envisaged that the amalgamation would be speedy. The Bank of England was also keen to see rapid progress. Lord Cobbold promised that he would 'keep an eye on any application by Hongkong and encourage Whitehall to deal with it as quickly as possible'.[20] However the Mercantile board, at least in the view of Turner and his directors, was being difficult.[21] Certainly some of the Mercantile directors were dissatisfied with the turn of events. Late in June Cobbold learned from Bicester that 'There is a good deal of unhappiness in the Mercantile board, some of whom regard this as a put-up job from [the Hongkong Bank] from the beginning. The question of valuation looks very difficult.'[22]

Valuation was made even more complex when rumours about an offer began to circulate and the price of the Mercantile shares began to rise. On 18 June, after a meeting between representatives of the two banks, the Mercantile agreed to hand over financial details to the auditors appointed by the Hongkong Bank, and in return the Hongkong Bank agreed to stop buying Mercantile shares.[23] The Mercantile's directors, by now preparing in earnest for negotiations, brought together a team of advisers to assess the Hongkong Bank's proposals. Their advisers included Mr Shearing and S. J. Pears of Cooper Brothers, the bank's accountants, and P. J. Terry of E. F. Turner and Sons, solicitors to the bank. With Cobbold's approval, they also called in Sir John Morison of Thomson McLintock, the leading firm of accountants, as a 'special adviser'. Morison was a veteran of reconstruction and merger negotiations since the heyday of Sir William McLintock in the late 1920s and 1930s, and he had played a prominent part in the complex rescue of the Royal Mail shipping group between 1931 and 1937.[24]

The auditors' review of the Mercantile's finances was completed rapidly and may have shown a stronger position than Turner and his colleagues had anticipated. On 2 July G. O. W. Stewart, Turner's deputy chief manager, gave his personal opinion that the Hongkong Bank should offer £4.5 million for the Mercantile: 'it is slightly higher than you wished to go but … I think the reserves disclosed are also greater than we might have expected'.[25] Within two weeks the offer had been finalized and on 15 July Sir Kenneth Mealing, the Mercantile Bank chairman, formally received the cash offer of £7 10s. 0d. per share, or three times the paid-up amount, on condition that it would be recommended to shareholders by the Mercantile directors.

The Mercantile valued itself at a higher price. The advice of Sir John Morison and S. J. Pears, who attended a special board meeting on 16 July, was emphatically against the proposal from Hong Kong and the directors duly decided that the offer 'could not be entertained'. Stewart and Perry-Aldworth were called into the meeting and were told that the Mercantile board could not recommend the offer to their shareholders. In return Stewart and Perry-Aldworth (on authority from Turner and the board in Hong Kong) announced that the Hongkong Bank's offer was withdrawn.[26] The Hongkong Bank's undertaking not to buy further shares lapsed at this point and the board in Hong Kong agreed to resume 'quiet' buying in the market.[27] On the following day the Mercantile declared an increase in the interim dividend from 7 per cent to 12.5 per cent. The directors also announced their intention to reorganize the capital of the bank (see above, pages 125–6). Both these measures increased the price that the Mercantile's shareholders would consider an attractive offer for their shares. Additionally the reorganization of the shares would slightly diminish the voting powers of the bloc held by the Hongkong Bank.

The withdrawal of the Hongkong Bank's offer left the Mercantile in the unenviable position of having a rejected suitor as its largest shareholder. Bicester admitted to Cobbold that 'a new chapter may some time be opened'.[28] On 20 September representatives of both banks met, including Mealing for the Mercantile and Perry-Aldworth and Turner for the Hongkong Bank. At this meeting, Perry-Aldworth recorded that 'Turner told them [the Mercantile directors] quite plainly that he thought they had been extremely foolish.'[29] He also told them that the Hongkong Bank was quite willing to sell them their shares back – but for a price. Turner would not accept less than £8 10s. 0d. per share for them. The items on the agenda were representation on the Mercantile's board and the proposed capital reorganization. The Hongkong Bank waived its right to be represented on the board but insisted that there should be close liasion at top level between managers in London, and sharing of information at branch level. This arrangement was to be given a trial period of a year. In the meantime the Mercantile directors pushed forward with the reorganization of the bank's capital structure.

Throughout the remainder of 1957 and in early 1958, the Hongkong Bank continued to pick up parcels of Mercantile shares, although their price continued to rise on the back of rumours of takeover offers. By February 1958, the Hongkong Bank began buying the shares in the name of Barings' nominees to avert speculation in the market. In April the bank decided to halt its purchases in the hope that the share price would fall. However, the Mercantile board may have been working through their brokers, Strauss Turnbull, to keep the price up to £1 10s. for each of the newly denominated shares.

The catalyst to further action was the arrival of the American bankers. In September 1958, David Rockefeller, president of the Chase Manhattan Bank, requested an interview with Mealing. A courteous discussion followed, in which the main theme was Chase's lack of representation 'between Tokyo and Beirut'.[30] Rockefeller also took pains to praise the quality of the Mercantile's management and staff.[31] A few days later John L. McCloy, chairman of Chase Manhattan, visited the Mercantile and explained that his bank intended to 'gatecrash the East in a big way'.[32] Clearly the Mercantile was being sounded out for a prospective partnership. There was a danger to the bank in refusal. The Mercantile maintained a lucrative correspondent bank relationship with Chase Manhattan and to reject their approach outright might also mean losing their business. Clearly it was necessary to inform the bank's largest shareholder of this new development, and a meeting was called for 6 October 1958. Perry-Aldworth – who recognized the possibility of a tripartite arrangement between Chase, the Hongkong Bank and the Mercantile – attended the meeting on behalf of the Hongkong Bank. When he reported back to Hong Kong, Turner's reply was characteristically prompt and to the point: 'I feel very strongly that [the Mercantile] board should reconsider the question of amalgamation with us less worse befall them.'[33] In the meantime the Bank of England was giving the Mercantile's directors hints and signals that the bank should remain British. This, and the Hongkong Bank's firm opposition as the largest shareholder, persuaded Mealing and his colleagues to end the discussions with Chase at the end of October.[34]

In the early autumn of 1958 the Mercantile's board remained wary of further negotiations with the Hongkong Bank, despite the Governor of the Bank of England's message that he 'was very keen to see larger units'.[35] Sir Edward Reid believed that Mealing was 'faced with a situation unlike any that he has ever experienced before and does not know what to do'.[36] Moreover, the Mercantile had other offers to consider. There was the chance of buying an unnamed Australian bank; a 'proposal of marriage' from the British Bank of the Middle East; and, with the knowledge of the Governor of the Bank of England, the notion of a three-way tie with the Hongkong Bank and the British Bank of the Middle East.[37] Although all three options were rejected, the Mercantile directors were determined not to give the Hongkong Bank the impression that they were enthusiastic about the proposed amalgamation.

It was not until 19 November that the Mercantile agreed to reopen discussions with the Hongkong Bank. The new contacts, which Reid described as 'very friendly',[38] brought much more rapid results. Within a matter of days, and amid a certain amount of press and market speculation, both boards of directors had agreed to make their engagement public. On 28 November a press release on behalf of the Mercantile's board announced that

> discussions are in progress with The Hongkong and Shanghai Banking Corporation with regard to a possible share exchange offer to be made by The Hongkong and Shanghai Banking Corporation for the whole share capital of the Mercantile Bank Limited. Shareholders will be informed in due course upon the outcome of such discussions.

The remainder of November and most of December 1958 were spent in negotiation over the price of the acquisition; the Mercantile's board was 'fully occupied with the Hongkong [Bank]' in these weeks.[39] The Hongkong Bank's initial position was to offer one of its own shares for 24 Mercantile shares or, if pressed, for 22 Mercantile shares. These Hongkong Bank shares would need to be new issues registered in London and a cash alternative would be available. But events were now moving in favour of the Mercantile shareholders. The bank's auditors argued that the Hongkong Bank's earnings were on a downward trend and that, in addition, the high denomination of the shares on offer would make them less marketable than Mercantile shares.[40] The Mercantile's directors were able to stand firm at a ratio of one Hongkong Bank share for 20 Mercantile shares, together with the alternative of a cash offer of £2 4s. 0d. per share ex-dividend. This formula also gave the Mercantile's shareholders a forecast increase of 20 per cent in their income from dividends. Perry-Aldworth, in the thick of the action, advised Turner that these ingredients should remove any remaining 'niggling objections': 'I am not yet round the bend, but very nearly!'[41] On 22 December this was the formal, outline offer tabled by the Hongkong Bank and the next day the Mercantile's board agreed to recommend the offer to their shareholders. The deal was all but done.

Without delay, on Christmas Eve 1958 the Mercantile Bank issued a circular to its shareholders confirming that an agreement for the exchange of shares and a cash alternative had been reached. The exact terms in full, agreed by the Mercantile board on 13 January, were then posted to shareholders on 23 January 1959. Advising shareholders that the offer was 'fair and reasonable', the directors explained that the Hongkong Bank would 'retain the identity' of the Mercantile. The news was quietly but well received both in London and Hong Kong, and Perry-Aldworth was especially pleased to report that 'they are all very pleased down there' at the Bank of England.[42] The Hongkong Bank's offer duly became unconditional on 16 February and was approved by shareholders of the Hongkong Bank on 18 February. By 3 March the

Mercantile's registrars had received forms of acceptance representing 94.3 per cent of the eligible shareholders, sufficient to allow the directors to sign and seal the share certificate which passed ownership to the Hongkong Bank.

In this final form the offer valued the Mercantile Bank at £6 394 500 (using the pre-offer market price of £43 10s. per share of the Hongkong Bank) or £6 468 000 (using the cash alternative of £2 4s. per share of the Mercantile Bank). In reality the purchase cost to the Hongkong Bank was rather less. King calculates that the actual cost was £5 969 804, comprising approximately £0.6 million in shares acquired beforehand, £0.9 million in payments for the cash alternative, and £4.3 million in new shares.[43] For this outlay the Hongkong Bank acquired a bank with £5 140 000 in capital and reserves (excluding £4 million of inner reserves) and total assets of £71 million. This result was relatively expensive in comparison with the Chartered's purchase of the Eastern Bank in 1957. Chartered had paid approximately £2 million for a bank with £2 500 000 in shareholders' funds (excluding inner reserves) and £44 million in total assets. On the other hand the Eastern Bank, whose earnings had proved vulnerable to bad debts in Bombay and Calcutta, was a very different proposition.[44] The business of the Mercantile Bank, in contrast, was in robust condition.

The acquisition of the Mercantile by the Hongkong Bank had been concluded relatively quickly after the protracted and prickly negotiations of 1957 and early 1958. What had made such a difference in bringing the Mercantile directors back into negotiations in November 1958? The Bank of England's preference for larger, British-owned units in overseas banking had become more explicit during the discussions. This official pressure was clearly a factor at board level in both London and Hong Kong. Second, the Chase Manhattan Bank's intervention also hurried the settlement, not least because the option of a strong North American partnership was a card which the Mercantile board probably could play only once. Third, changes to the tax treatment of the Hongkong Bank meant that the transfer of the Mercantile's headquarters from London to Hong Kong was no longer essential to a deal – a point which evidently won the approval of the Mercantile directors in the later stages of the negotiations.[45]

Perhaps the most telling factor in the change of mood was the change in the cast list of those most closely involved in the negotiations. Marden's controversial involvement had ended eighteen months earlier. The Hongkong Bank's negotiators had been reinforced in October 1958 by Sir Arthur Morse, who had been an outstanding chairman and chief manager of the bank between 1941 and 1953, and had been chairman of the London committee of directors since 1953. Morse brought a forceful presence to the team. On the Mercantile side Lord Bicester, whose handling of the original negotiations had dissatisfied some of his own co-directors as well as Turner in Hong Kong, retired from the Mercantile board in April 1958. At the same time the retirement of Crichton as a director and Drake, Crichton's protégé, as chief manager muted the voice of the old, independent Mercantile. Sir Kenneth Mealing, who took the main weight of the later negotiations, and C. R. 'Towkay' Wardle, who succeeded Drake as chief manager, certainly enjoyed a warmer and more outward-looking relationship with their opposite numbers at the Hongkong Bank.

The improved mood of the later negotiations was doubly valuable, for the demands of merger negotiations were very different from the skills which would be required for integrating the business of the two banks. In public the Mercantile maintained that a high level of independence would be preserved. The directors, in their circular to shareholders in January 1959, explained that

> It is intended that the change in control shall not affect the management, staff, relationship with constituents, or business progress of the Bank. The Head Office and Board will continue in London as hitherto, and the board believe that an association or merger of ownership such as this will strengthen the resources and provide opportunities for the progress of both banks.[46]

Likewise the Hongkong Bank told its shareholders that it wished 'to make it clear to the constituents and staff of the Mercantile Bank Limited that we have taken over this bank as a going concern and that we intend to keep it as a going concern'.[47] A similar message was given to the overseas banking authorities (the Reserve Bank of India in particular).[48] Even in the privacy of negotiations, the forward planning had gone no further than the transfer of certain offices between the two banks in their regions of special strength (see above, page 134). 'Dovetailing' the two businesses was the emollient phrase used by Turner.

Certainly there was no rapid progress towards integration. The Hongkong Bank had produced a successful outcome to a major bid which it had been reluctant to launch. Yet Turner, his directors and his managers were in new territory. Their bank, which was to become one of the outstanding exponents of bank amalgamations in the late twentieth century, had never before acquired a bank. It was the only significant organization in the sphere of British commercial or overseas banking which had never been involved in an amalgamation or alliance. Indeed, its only family members were its own nominee and trustee companies (both formed in 1941) and the Hongkong and Shanghai Banking Corporation of California, established as a subsidiary as recently as 1955. Distance from the scene of events also presented a serious challenge.

Negotiating a merger and then managing the consequences from the distance of Hong Kong placed great demands on Turner and his colleagues. As Turner recognized, 'the main problem is a London problem'.[49] For these different reasons there was caution, even uncertainty, at the top of the bank as to how to treat its new partner. That diffidence was increased by the Hongkong Bank's own indifferent banking performance in 1958 and the poor outlook in the Eastern and American economies in 1959 and 1960.[50]

Hence at board level change was kept to a minimum. At the Mercantile's annual general meeting in late March 1959, Sir Arthur Morse and Sam Perry-Aldworth were elected as directors of the Mercantile board representing the new owners. Perry-Aldworth attended his first board meeting on 7 April, when the directors dealt with an unprecedented volume of business. No doubt many decisions had been awaiting the conclusion of the deal but the long board meeting may also have been a deliberate demonstration of the onerous responsibilities of the Mercantile's directors. Wardle, at Morse's suggestion, became a director early in 1961 and it was agreed that he would be the channel for bringing the Hongkong Bank's concerns to meetings of the Mercantile board. It was a measure of the respect for Towkay Wardle which Morse and the Hongkong Bank team had built up in the later stages of the negotiations and in the first stages of integration.

Similarly, at management level, integration was not rushed forward. Wardle and his senior managers – Charles Pow as deputy chief manager and Walter Davies, John Elgar, Walter Jowit and Stewart Kirk as London managers – remained in place. The Mercantile's branch business also survived and flourished in this early and experimental stage of the new partnership. In the Federation of Malaya, where representation of the two banks overlapped, Turner agreed as soon as February 1959 that the Mercantile could complete its splendid new building in Kuala Lumpur.[51] The Mercantile's presence in the Federation's capital was long established and its business included Unilever's local account at that time. The Hongkong Bank also deferred to the Mercantile as to the opening of new offices in its continuing pursuit of new deposits. Seremban office opened as planned in March 1959, followed by Beach Road, Singapore, in August 1959. Over the next four years this programme of expansion was maintained purposefully in a wide range of Mercantile's Eastern markets (Table 7.1). Certainly some of the Mercantile's new branches were the offspring of plans which pre-dated the acquisition: the opening of Bentong agency in Pahang, for example, had been given board approval in 1957, four years before the branch became a reality. None the less this was the Mercantile's most ambitious programme of branch expansion since the early 1920s and it

Table 7.1 Mercantile Bank: branch openings and closures, 1959–66

Branch	Country	Status	Date opened	Date closed
Taiping	Malaya	Agency	January 1959	
Seremban	Malaya	Agency	March 1959	
Beach Road	Singapore	Agency	August 1959	
Madras, Sowcarpet	India	Agency	February 1960	
Raub	Malaya	Agency	January 1961	
Mentakab	Malaya	Agency	May 1961	
Bentong	Malaya	Agency	May 1961	
New York	USA	Representative office		April 1962
Curepipe	Mauritius	Sub-agency	April 1963	
Nagoya	Japan	Branch	May 1963	
Butterworth	Malaysia	Agency	December 1963	
Rangoon	Burma	Branch		March 1963
Tokyo	Japan	Branch		June 1963
Visakhapatnam	India	Agency	September 1964	
Bukit Panjang	Singapore	Agency	May 1965	
Osaka, Semba	Japan	Sub-agency		1965
Osaka	Japan	Branch		December 1966

gave a positive and expansive tone to the bank's business under its new ownership.

The attitude and treatment of the staff were important but sensitive issues in ensuring the success of the alliance. Even before the final stages of the negotiations, the Hongkong Bank team recognized that salaries and other rewards to Mercantile officers should be scaled up to match those of their new colleagues. Turner told Reid early in December 1958 that 'as far as possible I should like the emoluments of the staff of the Mercantile Bank to be similar to our own ... The foreign staff with different provident and pension rights and, in the case of the pre-war M.B. staff, early retiring rights, will have to be carefully considered.'[52]

These principles were converted into practice when, at Turner's instigation, the Mercantile's staff was admitted *en bloc* to the Hongkong Bank's pension scheme. This change immediately gave them superior pension terms and widows' benefits.[53] Salary scales were progressively harmonized from 1960, which helped the Mercantile staff to see the positive effects of a merger.

The attitude and morale of staff needed careful attention. Although improvements in pay and conditions were welcomed, anxieties about future prospects for Mercantile staff needed to be allayed. Some staff were worried that promotion opportunities could be curtailed; others were concerned that service in the Mercantile Bank would be restricted to the rupee circle while the branches in Hong Kong and Japan would pass to control of the Hongkong Bank.[54] Soon after the acquisition Wardle toured the Mercantile's branches, assuring staff that their salaries and conditions of service would benefit rather than suffer under the new ownership.[55] 'I think it is essential I should go out and explain matters to them in detail', Wardle wrote to Turner, 'and give the reassurance which some of them seem to need.'[56]

Most Mercantile staff welcomed Wardle's tidings. Their positive response was not purely an issue of improved staff conditions. It was also recognition that the business would benefit from increased lending powers and inter-bank co-operation. 'You needn't be afraid of big figures now', Wardle told officers during his visit to Pakistan.[57] This news was especially encouraging to the Mercantile's staff on the subcontinent. In the early stages after the acquisition the Hongkong Bank deferred to the Mercantile and acknowledged that, by sheer weight of business, the Mercantile's offices in Bombay, Calcutta, Madras and Colombo were the senior group offices. Mercantile managers also benefited from the Hongkong Bank's insistence that they should be given more responsibility in line with their own practices. The most notable outcome of this was the increase in a local manager's ability to make lending decisions without referral to London and the board: by October

1959 Mercantile branch managers had the power to grant advances of up to £5000 for new facilities and £7500 for renewals.[58] The sharing of information was at least as important as the new lending rules. In the autumn of 1962, for instance, a circular letter was sent to all branches of both the Mercantile and the Hongkong Banks. It instructed them that:

> Managers of both banks must work closely together and exchange information freely with each other. Each manager should periodically have a sight of the others' returns ... In many respects daily co-operation can be exercised on a common sense basis ... for example helping to tide over cash shortages and setting off exchange with each other ... In general each bank will make the fullest use of the other's services, while at the same time remaining responsible to its own head office.[59]

Sharing information obviously depended upon the personalities and attitudes of managers at local level. Overall, however, in these first years after the Mercantile was acquired by the Hongkong Bank, the bank was contributing to and benefiting from membership of the wider group. Its branch expansion, essential in the search for new funds, had accelerated in a way which the independent Mercantile might have baulked at. Its staff position had improved, the scope for lending appeared to have increased, and its systems and methods influenced procedures in the Hongkong Bank. Yet the Mercantile board and their officers needed to recognize that the Hongkong Bank would assert its senior position whenever there were genuine opportunities for rationalization.

Such opportunities soon occurred in the outlying parts of the Mercantile's network. In Bangkok, Thailand, the Hongkong and Mercantile Banks both had two branches. Early in 1960 Turner sounded out Wardle about the closure of the Mercantile's Rajawongse Road sub-agency. Wardle was able to postpone closure for some months but, when the office's results failed to improve, he recommended the closure proposal to his board in London. The Mercantile directors asked for 'compensation' for the closure in the form of a share of profits from the Hongkong Bank's Suapah Road agency (which was to take over the Rajawongse Road business). Turner felt that the incident showed the Mercantile directors' 'complete misunderstanding of the relationship between the banks'.[60] This was a management decision in the wider interests of the group and not a matter of debate at board level. In the event, however, the Rajawongse Road office remained open until the business was moved to a new Mercantile office in Asoke Lane, Bangkok, in 1970.

There were no such obstacles to integration in New York. The Mercantile's lease of its office at 37 Wall Street ended in April 1962 and neither the London nor the New York managers of the bank wished to renew the lease. John 'Jake' Saunders, Turner's successor as chairman and chief manager in Hong Kong, concluded that the Mercantile representative office should close at that time; James Shirreff, the representative, should move to the Hongkong Bank office at 80 Pine Street and should become a member of the Hongkong Bank staff.[61] At first Shirreff, one of the Mercantile's most senior officers, found himself marooned in a back office of the Pine Street building but he was to emerge from the reshuffle as the Hongkong Bank's New York manager in 1965.[62]

The Mercantile's New York presence had lasted continuously since 1919 but, because it was not required for general banking business, it had never been upgraded to branch status. Japan, in contrast, was home to two full branches of the bank at Tokyo and Osaka and a sub-office at Semba in Osaka. The Osaka connection was the more active of the two main branches, mainly through the large contingent of Indian businesses (see above, page 115). The Hongkong Bank was also represented in both cities. Pow, now chief manager, was proud to point out that the profitability of the Mercantile's offices compared very favourably with their neighbours' performance.[63] The most telling point in favour of rationalization, however, was the high value of the Mercantile's properties in both cities. With the main office at Osaka valued at over £400 000, the preservation of two group branches and the sub-office in the city would have been a conspicuous luxury. The Mercantile's local managers and their Japanese advisers urged the retention of the Tokyo presence, not least out of concern for the loyal Indian customers and the Japanese staff, who worked in a banking climate where branch closures or redundancies were rare indeed. The Mercantile in London and its parent bank in Hong Kong argued that the expense of maintaining so many full branches could not be justified now that Japan's own banks were providing such strong competition. As a result, in 1963 the Mercantile Bank closed its Tokyo office and sold its Osaka office; both properties were sold at handsome prices.[64] The Tokyo business was transferred to the Hongkong Bank branch while in Osaka the Mercantile office reopened in the Hongkong Bank's new building in the city. The Osaka office in turn was closed in 1966.

The Mercantile Bank did not entirely vanish from the Japanese scene. Property again played its part. The gains on the sale of the Tokyo and Osaka buildings would be subject to heavy local taxation, but this burden could be reduced if the group reinvested all or part of the gain in Japan. The opening of new offices in less costly markets was one option for using the proceeds of the property sales. The fast-growing city of Nagoya in central Japan was one such opportunity. When Saunders made initial enquiries about Nagoya, the Bank of Japan made it clear that – if asked for a new banking licence in Nagoya – it would prefer an application from the Mercantile rather than the Hongkong Bank on the grounds that the Tokyo and Osaka property gains had accrued to the Mercantile and not to its parent bank. The licence was duly granted to the Mercantile and the branch opened on 1 May 1963 under the management of Albert Furze; the former manager of the Hokuriku Bank in Nagoya was appointed as local adviser. Pow was particularly delighted with this outcome. 'The fact that the Hongkong Bank have accepted the situation about our opening in Nagoya means that our future in Japan is assured', he told W. G. Liddle, manager in Osaka: 'this is therefore very far from the beginning of the end of us.'[65]

In the immediate aftermath of the acquisition, even after the rationalization of these outlying branches, the Mercantile still showed an appreciable net gain in the number of its offices. In terms of performance, the gain from the new configuration of the bank was not so obvious. The volume of the Mercantile's business grew steadily in the late 1950s and early 1960s but this increase in total assets was far outpaced by the Chartered, National and Grindlays and the Hongkong Bank itself (Figure 7.1). Levels of real profits, after peaking at £780 000 in 1961, slid to a lower average level of £400 000 per annum between 1963 and 1965. In that latter period Hong Kong and Singapore branches headed the rankings of profits from the overseas offices. This performance was achieved despite the increasing volume of business at branches on the sub-continent such as Karachi, Colombo, and more especially at Bombay and Calcutta. Bombay branch was capable of higher but volatile earnings (as for example in 1961 and 1965), while profits from Calcutta branch were in steady decline.

There were pressing business reasons for this restricted growth and the relative decline of the senior Indian branches. A serious shortage of deposits, increasing competition from local banks, legislation hostile to foreign banks, and the growth in the bank's necessary expenses all curtailed the chances for expansion. The lack of ample deposits meant that the Mercantile was often forced to fall back on the inter-bank money market for its funds. This in turn limited the bank's income as there was only a small spread between the rates at which the bank could borrow and then lend out to customers. The lack of local funds was especially severe in India. In 1960, after the failure of the cotton crop and instability in the tea and jute industries, the bank was borrowing £8 million from its partners in the Hongkong Bank group to shore up its sources of funds.[66] Ordinarily the opening of new branches to garner local deposits would have been one solution to this shortage. The bank seriously attempted to follow this route, but its applications

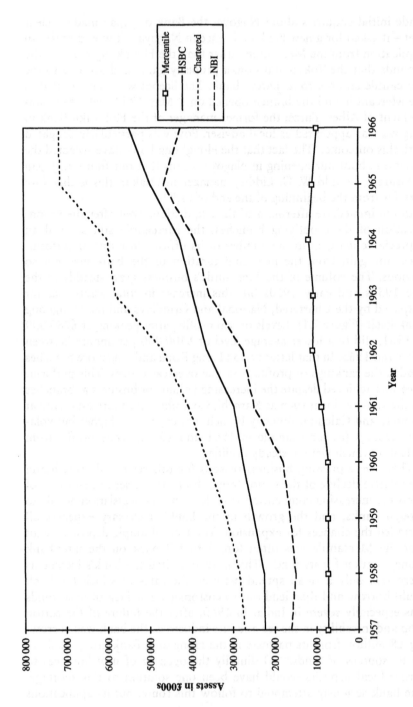

7.1 Eastern banks: total assets, 1957–66

to open in Bangalore, Hyderabad, Agra, Jaipur, Lahore and the suburbs of Bombay were all turned down by the Reserve Bank. In 1961 Wardle wrote mournfully to Turner: 'insofar as deposits were concerned ... the growth of the Exchange Banks in territories that have recently obtained political freedom may have reached their limits'.[67] In 1962, as the corollary of the shortage of deposits, the bank decided it was overlent and aimed to run down advances over the next two years by about £4.5 million. Three years later, however, the liquidity problem was still significant. Pow explained to Saunders in January 1965 that 'due to the local liquidity problems in India and Malaysia, I intend cutting employment back and therefore do not really expect to be able to increase income much beyond our anticipated increase in expenditure.' Some small relief had come when the Reserve Bank gave permission for the Mercantile to open an office in Visakhapatnam in 1964 – with approval in principle for further offices in Bombay and Calcutta in due course – but by then the emphasis had already switched to the reduction of lending and expenses.

Increases in expenditure clearly contributed to the restraint of the bank's profits. Much of the rise in charges derived from the increases in salaries and pensions to bring them into line with those of the Hongkong Bank. For instance, between 1960 and 1963 the bank's expenditure rose by £221 700 due to the increase in the wages bill, leave costs and contributions made to pensions and provident funds.[68] The large local staffs that the bank employed also placed a heavy cost in terms of local allowances. In India, in particular, the settlement of a long-running dispute over bonus payments for the period from 1956 to 1961 added to the bank's expenses; in 1965 the All-India Dearness Allowance imposed an additional £90 000 on running costs.[69] Pow also reckoned that the bank's charges at its Indian offices were 'twice as much as banks such as the Chartered and National Grindlays', and he recognized the need for internal economies: 'I have got to to do something drastic about reducing establishments', he announced to Saunders in 1964.[70] This was no easy task, given the strong resistance to reduction of local staff numbers, and a high degree of unionization. However, between 1962, when he took over as chief manager, and 1966 Pow managed to reduce the total staff of the bank from 3198 to 2863.[71] Numbers of expatriate officers in the East were reduced by seventeen in the same period. The reductions were achieved mainly by enforcing the normal retirement age (which had frequently been overrun) and by not replacing retirees.

Local banking competition, political change and the fiscal environment were also unfavourable in some of the Mercantile's markets. In Malaysia the bank had acted as banker to certain states; in Pahang, for example, the Mercantile manager at Kuantan was an *ex officio* member of the State Tenders Board. However, Malaysian banks were emerging as strong challengers in their domestic markets. In addition the Chartered Bank began to open further branches along the east coast of Malaysia where the Mercantile had held an advantage in exchange banking for many years. In response the bank needed to raise the rate it offered on its deposits to ensure the retention of funds, especially those of the state governments.

The most striking example of political constraints on the bank's performance was the nationalization of banks in Burma in 1963. Early that year General Ne Win, Chairman of the Revolutionary Council, announced a programme of nationalization throughout the country's economy. Almost immediately the entire business of the Mercantile branch was placed under the control of the People's Bank No. 5. 'We are left with nothing except a right to repatriation of our capital funds and compensation for our property', W. K. Dargie, the Rangoon manager, reported bleakly in March 1963.[72] It was a sudden and disappointing end to the Mercantile's long connection with Burma.

Fiscal change also inhibited the bank's performance in the early 1960s, most tellingly in Ceylon. The level of taxation of the bank's profits at its branches in Colombo, Galle, Kandy and Jaffna exceeded 70 per cent, rising to 82.25 per cent in 1964. In 1961 legislation was passed forbidding the opening of new accounts with foreign banks; severe import restrictions followed in 1963, greatly reducing the bank's exchange earnings; and from 1964 onwards the branches in Ceylon were not permitted to remit profits from the island. These were heavy blows as, historically, Colombo branch had been a large profit centre for the bank. Pow reluctantly concluded that the measures 'may mean that Ceylon will never again make a worthwhile contribution' to the bank's earnings, and he specifically cited the loss of remittances from Colombo office in 1964 as the reason for the bank's lowest published profit since 1956.[73]

These features of the business environment were only part of the restraint on the Mercantile's performance in the early 1960s. The bank's new role as a subsidiary company also strongly affected its earning capacity. The interests of the larger group – particularly in terms of earning power and tax treatment – now bore directly on the bank's balance sheet and profitability. An early example of this effect was the agreement by the Mercantile's directors in 1959 to place £4 million with the Hongkong Bank in Hong Kong at an interest rate of 1½ per cent. This represented 5.6 per cent of the Mercantile's total assets at that time; for comparison, the Mercantile's total cash in hand or with its bankers was then only £11 million, so that the decision was a large and immediate commitment. As the taxation of earning assets was lighter in Hong Kong, the transfer was designed to make more effective use of surplus funds and was clearly an advantage to the enlarged group.

In addition to this deposit, it had also been agreed that the bank's surplus profits (after tax) should be transferred to the Hongkong Bank, rather than to the Mercantile's own inner reserves. The Hongkong Bank, with its favourable tax environment, could then invest this money at increased profit to the group. This issue had been discussed and agreed upon as early as October 1959 by Mealing and Turner. Thereafter each March a 'service charge' or 'management fee' was paid to the Hongkong Bank, adjusted according to the level of profit for each year. The amounts transferred were substantial in comparison with the level of both published and actual profits in this early period under the new ownership (Table 7.2).

The transfer of these deposits and management fees to Hong Kong limited the Mercantile's scope for growth and profitability. It also ruled out the chances of enhancing its reserve position. A critic of the bank's earlier performance – George Marden, for example – could have pointed out that the tradition of building up healthy reserves had never generated significant growth and profitability. In the new circumstances, however, the restriction on the bank's reserves ensured that the Mercantile could not contemplate any sprint of growth under its new ownership.

The board and senior management of the Mercantile were certainly alive to the question of 'profits which might have been'. Each half-year in the early 1960s, Pow prepared for Saunders an analysis of 'notional profit'. These reports demonstrated the effects of the loss of interest on loans and deposits within the group, transfers of profits to inner

Table 7.2   Mercantile Bank: management fees transferred to Hongkong Bank, 1959–65

Year	Management charge (£)	Published profits (£)	Real profits (£)
1959	120 000	300 566	429 566
1960	275 000	326 103	612 103
1961	430 000	340 659	780 659
1962	120 000	325 685	461 685
1963	90 000	301 008	403 008
1964	40 000	260 087	376 431
1965	40 000	251 394	335 394

reserves, and other tax and interest gains to the parent group. The notional profits, together with the cost of the management charge, would have increased the real attributable profits by a significant margin and would have brought the rate of growth of published profits closer to the levels achieved by the other Eastern banks. These additions, based on Pow's 'what if' calculations, would have lifted the bank's real profits by £280 000 in 1964 and by approximately the same amount in 1965.[74]

In these ways the constraints on growth imposed by business conditions and by the bank's new role as a subsidiary company were reflected in the Mercantile Bank's relatively dull performance in the early 1960s. Charles Pow, in particular, found frustration in this situation and he was acutely conscious of any change which signalled the loss of the bank's independence. Moreover, his relationship with Jake Saunders, chief manager of the Hongkong Bank, was not as comfortable as the dealings between Wardle and Turner in the immediate aftermath of the acquisition. Pow himself had a strong presence and a keen sense of Mercantile traditions, whereas Saunders was equally proud of the Hongkong Bank's heritage and its growing weight in the banking world. Saunders was blunt about the relationship which he expected between the two banks. In 1964, for example, he suggested to Pow that the Mercantile Bank should stop publishing its own profit and loss account because 'by next year it may be even more desirable to withhold information as to the extent of the drop in your profits'.[75] Similarly, in 1962 Saunders had sent A. Mack, Hongkong Bank's chief inspector, to London to report on Mercantile's systems and procedures. Mack's final report criticized Mercantile for being too bureaucratic and 'board bound'.[76] Pow reacted angrily to such conclusions, refuting Mack's report and dismissing any criticisms of the bank's policy and staff: 'our managers are certainly not the small beer some of you people seem to think'.[77]

Although Pow was especially sensitive on the issue of the bank's performance and the independence of its management, elsewhere in the Mercantile the process of integration continued to move forward in a constructive fashion. Members of the bank's staff were sometimes further along the road to integration than their masters realized. As a small example, Stuart Muirhead later recalled that certain Mercantile staff had expected to share in the centenary bonus which was due to the Hongkong Bank staff in 1965 and 'some of us had already spent the money in anticipation!' This was not to be the outcome, however, and 'many years later I learnt that the reason for this was that such things were decided at Board level and at that stage the Board of Mercantile Bank made independent decisions on matters of this sort'.[78] In this case neither of the two banks' boards were being inclusive towards the group's staff. Clearly independence could be a mixed blessing; the time and opportunity for such nice distinctions would soon come to an end.

CHAPTER EIGHT

Removals, 1966–84

In the early 1960s managers and staff throughout the Mercantile Bank were understandably preoccupied with the question of how fully their bank would be integrated into the Hongkong Bank. Many Mercantile officers, especially in the younger generation, saw the dovetailing of business and careers as an inevitable, continuing process. Others, particularly at board and senior management level, were less sure and less enthusiastic about the integration of the two banks. Similar preoccupations affected the British Bank of the Middle East, which had also been acquired by the Hongkong Bank in 1959, with the result that integration was a matter for debate and comparison throughout the group.

In the topmost reaches of management in the Hongkong Bank – finally the only level at which the issue could be decided – there is little evidence that Michael Turner and then Jake Saunders were working to an exact, step-by-step plan of integration. Certainly they were keen to create opportunities and savings wherever possible, but this did not mean that they or their advisers had a fixed view of the end result. Indeed, they had emphasized the Mercantile's distinct identity during and after the acquisition. In the case of the Nagoya branch in Japan and in their planning for the Indian branches, for example, they continued to treat the Mercantile as a bank in its own name and in its own right. As Turner and G. O. W. Stewart pointed out to Frank King, the bank's historian, 'they knew little about mergers at the time, they learned as they progressed'.[1] The extent of integration would be shaped and adapted *en route* rather than following a predetermined path.

A potent influence on this process was the announcement in September 1965 that the head office of the Mercantile Bank would be removed to Hong Kong. Turner and his team at the Hongkong Bank, in the earlier stages of the discussions with the Mercantile in 1957 and 1958, had originally intended to relocate the Mercantile in this way, mainly in order to benefit from the more favourable tax position in Hong Kong. That plan had been abandoned in the later stages of the negotiations (see above, page 138). By 1965, however, other considerations had come into play. Taxation and regulation factors had moved back in favour of a Hong Kong base. At that stage London – as seen from the dynamic business community of Hong Kong – was perceived as a high-tax, over-regulated economic environment. Threats to the value of sterling and the new Labour government's commitment to price and income controls reduced the attractions of a London base.[2] The knowledge that the Mercantile's branch in Hong Kong was one of its strongest performers, and yet was contributing heavily to the tax bill in the United Kingdom for the bank's worldwide earnings, reinforced the taxation argument for transferring to Hong Kong. An additional influence may have been the likelihood that any future changes in the status or role of the Mercantile would be more easily accomplished in Hong Kong than in London.

Saunders and his team, after several years' experience of working with the Hongkong Bank's new subsidiaries, were also much more aware of the problems of controlling and co-ordinating the group's business. This was not a significant issue in the case of the British Bank of the Middle East, as there was little or no overlap between its strong regional presence in the Middle East and the branches, business and expertise of the Hongkong Bank itself. The Mercantile's business was a different matter. In most of their markets the two banks overlapped and had until recently been in competition. There were exceptions such as Mauritius, where the Mercantile was the sole group bank, or Indonesia and the Philippines, where the Hongkong Bank provided the only group representation. There were also differences of degree, notably in the Hongkong Bank's home territory, where it was by far the largest bank, and in India, where the Mercantile was the group's most prominent bank. In the majority of their markets, however, the Hongkong Bank and the Mercantile were neighbours. In each case their business was mainly in the East, yet their branches were controlled by two separate head offices in Hong Kong and London respectively.

Co-ordination of such an arrangement was not impossible but it was certainly difficult at such long range. In the first years after the acquisition the extra burden of co-ordination affected not only questions of policy and personnel but also the more humble tasks of communication and administration. Was this burden really necessary? The preservation of two head offices for what was, in all essentials, one single business increasingly appeared to be a luxury, particularly from the Hong Kong viewpoint.

Other more personal factors had come into play by the mid-1960s. The Mercantile's board of directors was now an ancient institution in every respect. By 1964 the average length of service of its members was over thirteen years, with Sir John Hay having continued for no less than 24 years on the board. In addition the age profile of the board had shifted well beyond normal retirement age; Hay was 80 when he died in office in 1964; Dunlop, Miller, Bunbury, Jones and Morse were all over 70 at that time.[3] Clearly this board would need an inflow of new or replacement members. When that time came, the pooling of interests and experience with the parent bank would simplify the direction of the wider group.

The chief managership of the Mercantile Bank was also a growing influence on the relationship between the two banks. At a personal level Saunders in Hong Kong and Pow in London were not soul-mates. Both men had a strong personal presence and a fierce pride in their own organizations. Pow, nine years older than Saunders, was expected to retire when or soon after he completed 40 years' service in 1965. John Elgar and Stewart Kirk, his senior London managers, were due to retire by the end of the same year. If closer integration were to follow, then these retirements would provide a natural break. Simultaneously, at management level, a change in the status or the location of the chief executive of the Mercantile would overcome one of the Hongkong Bank's specific concerns over its London representation.[4] The role of London manager was important in the Hongkong Bank's business structure but, in name and scope, it appeared to be outranked by the positions of the chief managers of the Mercantile Bank and the British Bank of the Middle East. G. O. W. Stewart in particular was keenly aware of this question when he became London manager of the Hongkong Bank in 1961; the issue was only partly resolved when the title was changed to 'senior manager and manager for Europe' in 1963.

These different factors altered the picture which the two banks had envisaged at the time of the negotiations between 1957 and 1959, and now swung the balance in favour of relocating the Mercantile's head office to Hong Kong. In the course of 1964 Saunders asked Sir Kenneth Mealing, the Mercantile chairman, to think over the timing and other implications of the move.[5] Mealing did not consult his colleagues at that stage and the plan came as a great surprise to them and to Pow when they were informed in the spring of 1965. By June 1965, however, the directors and Pow were discussing a definite proposal. Pow was given the task of obtaining Treasury permission for the change of residence for tax purposes, and he was also asked to recommend a successor as chief manager.

Management succession was a pivotal aspect of the relocation plan. Initially Pow explored the possibility of John Gregoire taking over as chief manager. Gregoire, though honoured by the invitation, did not wish to transfer to Hong Kong for any great length of time. For the longer-term succession, Pow turned instead to Ian Herridge. His previous experience included appointments throughout the sub-continent, in Burma, Malaya and Hong Kong, and at this time he was manager at Singapore branch. Herridge was a close contemporary of Jake Saunders and 'saw a lot of him when they were juniors in London'.[6] Saunders accepted the recommendation, on the understanding that John Gregoire would spend up to a year as general manager in Hong Kong while Herridge toured the branches and investigated ways of bringing the two banks' local business closer together. Herridge would then become general manager at the beginning of 1967, when Gregoire would return to the United Kingdom as Mercantile's senior manager in London.

While the succession planning moved forward, decisions were also needed as to the future of the Mercantile's board. The existing composition of the board, with its high average age, was not a long-term option. In addition there was a pressing need to avoid double taxation of the bank in the United Kingdom and in Hong Kong. E. R. Udal, the Hongkong Bank's legal adviser and a former Treasury Counsel, argued that there should be a complete severance with the London board and management after the relocation. Otherwise the Inland Revenue in the United Kingdom would be able to claim that the bank had dual residence for tax purposes. 'In view of the importance of what we are doing,' Saunders concluded, 'there is clearly no case for taking any chances'.[7] As a result it would be necessary for the board and chief manager *en bloc* either to relocate to Hong Kong or to retire. Relocation was not viable, especially in view of Pow's imminent retirement, and the Mercantile board therefore agreed to stand down immediately after the transfer of the head office. The existing directors would be replaced by a new Hong Kong-based board with the same directorate as the Hongkong Bank. For the sake of continuity (and also to retain their business influence), the former directors and Charles Pow would form a London advisory committee. This new body, like the Hongkong Bank's own London committee, would not attract 'dual residence' taxation of the bank. The Mercantile would also be able to retain its registration as a United Kingdom company.

These main elements of the relocation plan were announced by Pow to the Mercantile staff on 1 September 1965:[8]

NOTICE TO STAFF
H.M. Treasury have approved the transfer of the 'residence' of Mercantile Bank Limited from London to Hong Kong.
This move will take place on the 30th March, 1966 from which date a new Head Office and General Management will be set up in Hong Kong. Branch Offices in London, namely at 15, Gracechurch Street and 123, Pall Mall, will carry on their business in exactly the same manner as before.
The members of the present board of Directors have indicated their willingness to serve on a London Advisory Committee which it is proposed to establish in April next. I have accepted an invitation to join this Committee.

In addition, Pow wrote to all the foreign staff on the same day, explaining that conditions had changed greatly since the acquisition by the

Hongkong Bank and that 'it is no longer desirable to operate two banks trading in the same areas with their Head Offices separated by such a long distance'.[9] A similar press release and a letter to the correspondent banks and regulators was circulated in early November with the more generalized explanation that 'these arrangements are being made for ease of administration within the Hongkong Bank Group, but the present policy regarding [customers] will be continued'.[10]

These brief announcements produced little reaction either from the staff or from the outside world. After posting the notice to staff, Pow found that 'the reaction ... has so far been entirely negative so perhaps we were bothering ourselves too much'; likewise in November 'there has been little or no reaction to our press announcement'.[11] The decision to relocate, like many other planning decisions in business history, seemed momentous to those most closely involved, but in the event generated relatively little excitement in the wider community. In the bank's own markets the outbreak of war between India and Pakistan in September 1965 dominated the headlines. Even within the Hongkong Bank group, the orderly transfer of the Mercantile's headquarters was overshadowed by other developments. More immediate attention was being given to the group's entry into entirely new fields. In April 1965, for example, Hongkong Bank acquired a majority share in Hang Seng Bank after the local banking crisis in Hong Kong, while in September the announcement that electronic data processing was to be introduced throughout the group created special interest and expectation.[12]

Once the arguments for relocation had been circulated and apparently accepted, Pow and his colleagues in London faced an exacting timetable for meeting the deadline of March 1966. The Hongkong Bank shared fully in the work. In October 1965, O. P. Edwards, 'one of the H. & S.B.C.'s organisation experts',[13] was seconded to the Mercantile in London to prepare for the transfer of staff, information and systems. Edwards reported to F. J. Knightly, the Hongkong Bank's deputy chief manager, and involvement at this level ensured that delays and distractions were kept to a minimum.

The planning and timing of communications over the transition period was high on the agenda of the London management, together with the more mundane tasks of arranging office space in Hong Kong and shipping the key sets of records. Most of these issues had been settled by the New Year. Edwards then returned to Hong Kong in January, followed early in February by the Mercantile team which was already 'shadowing' the new head office – Michael Langley as manager with James Anderson and John Drake as assistants. James Baird as manager in charge of the bank's books, Ian Macdonald as sub-manager, and then John Gregoire as general manager arrived in time for the opening of the new headquarters on the first floor of the Hongkong Bank's own head office at 1 Queen's Road Central on 31 March. In London Norman Paton Smith (as senior manager) and Hamish Stewart (as manager) remained in London 'to continue to provide a link with City financial institutions and U.K. customers ... and to advise on propositions put forward by U.K. based customers'. Stewart had been selected to stay on after normal retirement age in view of his experience of the sub-continent: as Pow told him, 'we badly need a strong Indian man on the team here'.[14]

Under this supervision the transfer was completed smoothly, on schedule, and without disruption to the business on 30 and 31 March 1966. The final board meeting and an extraordinary general meeting were held in London as planned on 30 March, and the general meeting passed the resolutions which altered the bank's articles of association to reflect the change of residence. The general meeting also appointed Saunders, Knightly and S. J. Cooke (the Hongkong Bank's deputy chairman) to the board of the Mercantile. On the following day – actually less than twelve hours after the London meetings – the first board meeting in Hong Kong was attended by Saunders, Knightly and Cooke, with John Gregoire, Ian Macdonald and E. R. Udal in attendance. This meeting elected Saunders as chairman and accepted the resignations of Mealing and the other London directors. The new board also elected the other remaining directors of the Hongkong Bank to the Mercantile board.[15] In practice, as Ian Herridge later recalled, the meetings of the board in Hong Kong were 'pretty perfunctory'.[16]

The control of the bank now passed to an 'executive committee' comprising Saunders, Knightly and Gregoire. This key group met for the first time on 7 April 1966 and delegated certain lending powers to Gregoire. Previously the chief manager was able to authorize up to £25 000 in new facilities and £50 000 in renewals. The new mandate, which allowed the Mercantile's general manager and also his London manager to renew lending limits of up to £100 000 and to grant new limits of up to £50 000, was typical of the Hongkong Bank's preference for local responsibility and initiative. The first facilities under these new arrangements were signed off by Gregoire in April 1966; they included overdrafts, trust receipts and import loans for customers in traditional Mercantile strongholds such as Bombay, Calcutta, Singapore, Bangkok, Ipoh, Penang and Hong Kong itself.[17] In the meantime, at management level, the Mercantile team was quickly into its stride and the Hongkong Bank's staff spoke highly of the way in which Langley and his team set up and then maintained lines of communication in their new surroundings.[18]

At the London end of the relocation, it was necessary that the arrangements were transitional rather than permanent. Norman Paton Smith and Hamish Stewart continued only until their retirements in June and December 1967, and John Gregoire returned as planned in the role of London manager at the beginning of 1967. The London advisory committee also proved to be a temporary fixture. The committee, comprising the former directors of the Mercantile with the addition of Charles Pow, met each month under the chairmanship of G. O. W. Stewart as from April 1966. However, Gregoire discovered that the costs of the Mercantile's London operations were actually rising during 1966 and 1967, representing 15 per cent of the bank's total costs during that time. He concluded that the advisory committee had served its purpose and would be disbanded when G. O. W. Stewart retired in June 1968. The directors' luncheon room at Gracechurch Street, one of the last ornaments of the old administration, would close at the same time.[19] These decisions and other economies immediately produced an improvement in the working results of the bank's London business.

The dispersal of the former directorate was soon followed by the physical integration of the London offices of the two banks. This merger, announced to customers in October 1968, required the transfer of the Mercantile's London office from 15 Gracechurch Street to the Hongkong Bank's office next door at 9 Gracechurch Street. The move was to be spread over two years and, significantly, would mean that 'the staff of both banks [would] be interchangeable' when dealing with customers' business. John Gregoire hastened to add that 'it is not intended that Mercantile Bank Limited will lose its identity', and to that end the two banks continued to operate their own departmental units (such as the bills offices and the letters of credit departments) at 9 Gracechurch Street. Despite this assurance, a strong current of rationalization was now moving in the direction of a single City office for the group. Paul Lamb, who had been controller of overseas operations in Herridge's team in Hong Kong, returned to London in 1970 to co-ordinate this integration. As a result the two banks in London treated new lending and other facilities as 'combined operations' in this period, leading to the transfer of customer accounts into the name of the Hongkong Bank. The former headquarters at 15 Gracechurch Street, home to the Mercantile since 1914, were eventually sold to Barclays Bank in 1977. Elsewhere within London's responsibilities, the Longmoor training centre had been closed in 1968; Barcote Manor in Berkshire, which had been acquired in 1951 at the height of the cold war to serve as an emergency evacuation site, was sold in 1970; and in the West End the Mercantile's Pall Mall branch was taken over by the Hongkong Bank in 1970.[20]

By the end of 1968 the Mercantile Bank was presenting an entirely new face to the world. Its head office had moved half-way round the world. Its former board of directors, even in an advisory non-executive role, had been entirely replaced and its old London address was closing. The bank was also operating under a new team of executives who had earned their management credentials in the 1950s and 1960s. On these counts the process of integration with the Hongkong Bank may have seemed to be a one-way street, in which each new initiative rode over the identity of the Mercantile Bank. Again, however, the philosophy which lay behind these developments was not so relentless as it may have appeared. At this stage of the process – in the three years to 1968 – the Mercantile retained a recognized role in the expansion of the group as a whole. In India, especially, the Mercantile was treated as the flag-bearer. Jake Saunders himself argued in 1965 that 'our objective in India is that Mercantile should eventually take over our [the Hongkong Bank's] business'; a year later he was reminding G. O. W. Stewart that the 'ultimate aim is for Mercantile Bank to take us over in India when the time is right'.[21]

The Mercantile's experience and expertise in Indian banking were certainly given careful consideration in the wider group. Late in 1965, for example, G. O. W. Stewart invited Charles Pow to give his assessment of the outlook in India. Pow was confident of the long-term future of the business, provided that the Mercantile could increase its deposit base and reduce its reliance on inter-bank borrowing. He and Stewart looked for the gain of 'substantial deposits' rather than just the increase in business from the new sub-branches in Bombay and Calcutta. He also pointed out that, despite the rising costs of salaries and taxation, the Indian business of both the Mercantile and its competitor National and Grindlays was still generating a higher proportion of the two banks' total profits relative to their Indian branches' shares of the banks' total deposits.[22]

Similarly Herridge, as his first priority when he was designated as Gregoire's successor as general manager, was entrusted with a detailed review of the group's operations in India. His tour of Indian branches in April and May 1966 was intended not only to deepen his knowledge of their business but also to look for ways of bringing the group's business together under the Mercantile banner. In early 1966 the group was represented by nine Mercantile branches, the two Hongkong Bank branches at Calcutta and Bombay, and the Bombay branch of the British Bank of the Middle East.[23] Herridge recommended that the Mercantile itself needed an immediate cut in its borrowings from other banks, together with a more rigorous approach to overstaffing at some of the branches. He believed that lending at Bombay and Calcutta had become overreliant on a handful of large agency houses. Herridge and Saunders also agreed that a general manager was needed to supervise 'the affairs of the Hongkong Bank Group in India'. Mowbray Mackie, formerly the Mercantile's manager in Bombay, was appointed to this role in December 1966 with the task of co-ordinating the activities of the group's three banks in India and generating as much new business as possible without employing scarce sterling reserves.[24] As to the longer-term options in India, Herridge envisaged higher costs for staff and taxation and even the possibility of nationalization. He was prepared to consider the radical steps of closing or selling either the Mercantile's branches or the Hongkong Bank's business in India, which was suffering from a number of bad debts. However, after he and Norman Bennett (assistant to Saunders) visited Calcutta in the summer of 1968, Herridge and Saunders decided against fundamental changes of that kind; they felt the costs of withdrawal, particularly in the form of staff settlements, would be disproportionate to the risks which Herridge had listed.[25]

While Herridge and Saunders pondered these strategic questions, the Mercantile enjoyed a period of steady expansion in the Indian market. This was a major achievement at a time when the economy was suffering from the combined effects of the 1965 war with Pakistan, the effective devaluation of the rupee in 1966, the great drought of 1967 and the resulting high rate of price inflation. The bank pressed forward by taking up the sub-branch licences which had been secured from the Reserve Bank of India and, between 1966 and 1969, five new offices were opened in Bombay and another six were opened in Calcutta (see Table 8.1). The net gain of ten offices (the Gandhidham sub-branch was shut in 1967) was an impressive response to the long-held ambition to seek out new deposits through branch expansion. By the end of 1968 deposits of Rs 50 million, or approximately £3.7 million, had been gathered in this way and at the end of 1971 this total had swollen to Rs 150 million.[26] Although salary increases and bad debts at New Delhi held back profitability until the early 1970s, the bank's gross income from India rose markedly from £832 000 in 1967 to £1.45 million in 1971. India was, as it always had been, the bank's premier market. Its complement of 150 000 customers (including 100 000 savings accounts) and 1550 staff in 1971 easily exceeded the equivalent totals for all other areas of the Mercantile's activities.[27]

During these years the nationalization of Indian-owned banks in 1969 and the government's 'social control' policy – which sought to direct lending to priority sectors such as agriculture and small business – created an arduous climate for foreign banks.[28] The Mercantile's progress and its reputation in these conditions helped to ensure that the bank could continue to operate in India in its own name. Guy Sayer,

Table 8.1   Mercantile Bank: branch openings and closures, 1966–79

Branch	Country	Date opened	Date closed
Osaka	Japan		1966
Bombay, Tardeo Road	India	1966	
Bombay, Vile Parle	India	1966	
Calcutta, New Alipore	India	1966	
Calcutta, Gariahat Road	India	1966	
Calcutta, Sealdah	India	1966	
Dacca	Pakistan	1966	
Hong Kong, Cameron Road, Kowloon	Hong Kong	1966	
Bombay, Chembur	India	1967	
Singapore, High Street	Singapore	1967	
Quatre Bornes	Mauritius	1967	
Rose Hill	Mauritius	1967	
Gandhidham	India		1967
Bombay, Bandra	India	1968	
Calcutta, Kadamtala	India	1968	
Calcutta, Shakespeare Sarani	India	1968	
Bombay, Andheri	India	1969	
Calcutta, Nimtolla Ghat	India	1969	
Hong Kong, Marble Road, North Point	Hong Kong	1970	
Madras, Sowcarpet	India		1970
Port Louis, Lai Min	Mauritius	1971	
Mahebourg	Mauritius	1972	
Beau Bassin	Mauritius	1972	
Hong Kong, Hennessy Road, Wanchai	Hong Kong	1972	
Bombay, Borivli	India	1977	
Centre de Flacq	Mauritius	1977	
Goodlands	Mauritius	1978	
Vacoas	Mauritius	1978	
Vila	New Hebrides	1978	
Plaine Verte	Mauritius	1979	

who succeeded Jake Saunders as chief manager of the Hongkong Bank in 1972, was originally keen to promote the Hongkong Bank to become the principal group bank in India. However, when the bank approached the Reserve Bank of India to discuss the integration of the Hongkong and Mercantile businesses, the governor of the Central Bank had 'expressed his pleasure that a bank with a name so well-known in India [as the Mercantile] was being permitted to act for the group'.[29] In response, Sayer reversed the proposal and announced that the Hongkong Bank's business and branches would be acquired by the Mercantile as from October 1972. This transfer had been planned by Saunders in the mid-1960s but it also underlined the argument – which had been rehearsed since 1959 – that the Mercantile's identity had special value in India. The bank responded with a strong increase in its business and income. From June 1973 (already after the merger of the Hongkong Bank offices), total assets in India surged from Rs 755 million to Rs 955 million in June 1975. In the same period half-yearly profits before tax and provisions jumped from Rs 1.3 million to Rs 8.3 million.[30]

Other parts of the Mercantile network also flourished in the late 1960s and early 1970s. Mauritius, which gained independence in 1968, was still a small and specialist market for banking. For the bank, it was a unique opportunity to develop in its own name. The original branch at Port Louis, its sub-branch at Curepipe and the mobile bank were now reinforced by new offices at Quatre Bornes and Rose Hill in 1967, Lai Min (1971), Mahebourg and Beau Bassin (1972). The volume of business was not large in comparison with other Mercantile territories, but its income grew steadily, especially after the International Sugar Agreement of 1969 raised and stabilized the price of sugar in world markets. The group dimension was also valuable, as the island's export zone and tourism industry had begun to attract business from Hong Kong.[31] The Mauritius command remained one of the most popular postings available to the managers and staff of the bank, perhaps because it was the only country where the Mercantile was the group's sole representative.

The most unusual example of continuing success in the Mercantile's own name was the performance of the branch at Nagoya, which had been opened as recently as 1963. After 1966 this office was the bank's only remaining presence in Japan. By the late 1960s the Nagoya office was building up an important business in Eurodollars, or US dollars borrowed and traded in the European market. Japanese customers – many from much further afield than the city of Nagoya – turned to the branch to borrow Eurodollars to use in their own expanding trade with Europe and the US. The Mercantile was able to provide this business at favourable rates as the Nagoya office could draw on Eurodollars obtained by the bank's London office; local customers or even the Nagoya branch itself would have found it difficult and expensive to borrow Eurodollars in their own names. This demand pushed Nagoya's earnings to very high levels, well above any other Mercantile branch's earnings, in 1971 and 1972 (Figure 8.1).

Hong Kong itself was important to the continuation of the Mercantile as a bank in its own right. Even in the heartland of its parent company, the bank was expanding in the late 1960s and early 1970s. New offices at Cameron Road, Kowloon (1966), Marble Road, North Point (1970) and Hennessy Road, Wanchai (1972) were the bank's first sub-branches in Hong Kong. This branch expansion should be kept in perspective, as inevitably the Mercantile was overshadowed by the Hongkong Bank (with 68 offices in Hong Kong in 1971) and the Chartered Bank (with 33 local offices). Yet the Mercantile's business grew consistently between 1966 and 1970, making Hong Kong the single most profitable branch in the network over those years. As London office's own business remained relatively robust after the transfer, much of the strong growth of the bank's Hong Kong branch can have come only from booming growth in the local economy. In parallel with this growth, the Hong Kong branch rather than London now became the testbed for new systems or types of business: in 1967, for example, it had the distinction of being the first office in the entire Hongkong Bank group to undergo the computerization of savings accounts.

While the Mercantile maintained momentum in these areas, it was operating on an increasingly narrow base of business. In the course of the 1960s, restrictions on overseas banks in the East multiplied rapidly. Nationalization in Burma and intervention in Ceylon had directly affected the Mercantile in the early 1960s (see above, page 148), while in Thailand new banking regulations in 1962 prevented any foreign banks from opening branches outside Bangkok. Prohibitions on opening any new branches were then introduced in Malaysia in 1965 and Singapore in 1968.[32] These regulations were major disincentives in regions where both the Mercantile and the Hongkong Bank were strongly represented. Guy Sayer, who had become general manager responsible for the Hongkong Bank's subsidiaries in 1970 and succeeded Saunders as chief manager in 1972, accepted that there was little realistic prospect of expansion in the names of both banks. As the Hongkong Bank maintained a larger overall business in both countries – even though Singapore was one of the most prominent and profitable Mercantile branches – it was agreed that the Mercantile's business would be acquired by the parent bank. These transfers were completed in July 1973 in Singapore and in January 1974 in Malaysia, ending the Mercantile's direct presence in the region which dated back to the Chartered Mercantile Bank's arrival in Singapore in 1856.[33]

The Malaysian business was particularly valuable to the larger group. As a measure of the regional importance of Malaysia within the

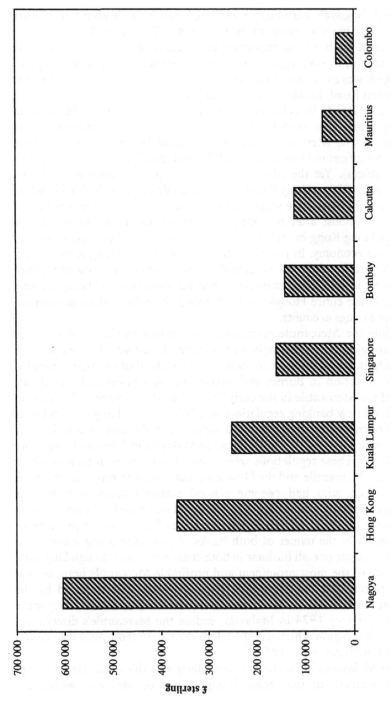

8.1 Mercantile Bank: net profits of principal Eastern branches, 1971

Table 8.2   Mercantile Bank: profile of branch activity, June 1973

Branch/ region	Number of:			Number of staff:		
	Current accounts	Savings accounts	Fixed deposits	Eastern	Regional	Local
Bombay	4 582	28 759	6 614	4	14	552
Calcutta	7 777	79 296	16 872	5	17	691
Madras	968	2 379	494	1	3	142
New Delhi	1 649	5 696	2 087	1	5	115
Malaysia	12 255	44 167	6 507	12	35	413
Mauritius	2 716	24 071	1 460	2	4	120
Singapore	5 469	8 475	5 588	6	6	196
Sri Lanka	4 290	1 549	665	2	7	199

Source: MBH 1853, branch statistics, June 1973.

Mercantile, the total staff of over 450 was exceeded only by the Indian branches.

The bank had over 70 000 customers in Malaysia, a total which included nearly 50 000 savings accounts and also major customers such as the Guthrie group, Lever and Mitsui. The value of the business was vividly demonstrated by record levels of performance in the final year of 1973. The commodity price boom that year helped the branches increase net profits by 82 per cent to over M$ 2 million. The bank's last report on Malaysia pointed out that it was passing on 'a fine network of branches' to the group, ending on the positive note that 'integrated operations will create a very much stronger entity that should play an even more decisive role in Malaysia'.[34]

Restrictions on new branches clearly limited the group's opportunities for expansion and accelerated its integration in these markets. The most that the group could aim for in these conditions was to retain the combined business and earnings of the two banks.

In Pakistan, in contrast, there was an actual loss of business. Since the mid 1950s the overseas banks had been discouraged from expanding into the interior of the country.[35] New branches were still permitted at port towns and cities but, after the opening of the Mercantile's Dacca branch in 1966, the Pakistan banking authorities refused permission for the Mercantile to open any further offices. This ruling ended any serious hopes of developing the local deposit base as the bank was then doing in India. Moreover, the existing branches in East Pakistan – at Chittagong,

Khulna and Dacca – were making losses in the later 1960s. These losses were triggered mainly by the Indo-Pakistan war of 1965, when the assets of Indian jute exporters in Pakistan had been blocked, and the bank's customers were amongst those affected by the dislocation of business.[36] In West Pakistan the Mercantile's position was only marginally stronger. The Karachi office was diligently repairing the damage done by a single advance earlier in the decade. This transaction, relating to a major engineering contract, eventually required the bank to install one of its own officers in the debtor company to oversee its financial operations. Overheads of staff costs and taxation also remained high.

By 1969 the pressures of official restrictions, political uncertainty and poor performance persuaded Herridge and Saunders to pull the Mercantile out of Pakistan. Herridge later admitted that he 'could see no daylight there'.[37] Rather than close the branches, however, they succeeded in selling the entire business to National and Grindlays Bank, which with its eighteen branches was a much larger operation in Pakistan. National and Grindlays agreed to assume the Mercantile's liabilities in Pakistan; in addition £100 000 was payable to the Mercantile in London, while in Pakistan branch-by-branch adjustments were to be decided by the two banks' auditors.[38] The attraction for National and Grindlays was that acquisition of existing branches would not contravene the restriction on new branches; it would also inherit the trained and experienced local staff of the Mercantile offices.[39]

Herridge announced the news to his managers and staff in July 1969. The sale would take effect from 2 September, when the branches would change their name to National and Grindlays and accounts would be transferred to the new owners. He insisted that there would be no loss of jobs from either the local or Eastern staff. National and Grindlays guaranteed the jobs and conditions of local staff while the Mercantile redeployed the eight Eastern staff in the four branches. 'Undoubtedly', Herridge added, there would be 'rumours circulating that Pakistan is only the start but I must emphasise most strongly that our negotiations with N & G relate only to the Pakistan business and there is absolutely no question of any other territory being involved.'[40] The transfer was accomplished without any interruption to the local business and for an initial period the Hongkong Bank group placed its correspondent banking business in Pakistan with National and Grindlays.[41]

Local banking regulations also led to a net loss of representation in Ceylon. In 1961, as part of the island's package of banking regulations and taxation, foreign banks such as the Mercantile, Hongkong Bank and the Chartered had been prohibited from accepting deposits from Ceylonese nationals. Although this was a serious handicap to the banks' plans for business expansion, they continued to provide special facilities for trade finance for the island, and consequently in 1969 the government agreed to remove the prohibition on deposit-taking. The price of the repeal, however, included an agreement that the Mercantile would transfer its up-country offices at Kandy, Galle and Jaffna to the Commercial Bank of Ceylon.[42] The Commercial Bank was a new concern which had been formed as part of the 1969 deal; it also took over the Colombo business of the Eastern Bank, a subsidiary of the Chartered Bank since 1957. Although the up-country branches did not actually change hands until June 1973, the agreement was to leave the Mercantile with only its Colombo and Pettah offices.

In Sri Lanka (as Ceylon was renamed when it became a republic in 1972) conditions for foreign banks did not improve in the early 1970s. The increase in deposits which the banks had hoped would follow from the 1969 agreement did not continue beyond 1971. Guthrie Atterbury, the Mercantile's manager in Colombo, firmly recommended the withdrawal of both of the group's banks, and in 1972 he was supported by a special committee in the Hongkong Bank's head office which was investigating the position. Atterbury's views carried weight, as the Mercantile was the larger of the two group banks on the island. In 1973, for example, the bank's local assets of Rs 151 million outreached the Rs 91 million of the Hongkong Bank's Colombo branch and the business included large and long-standing customers such as the Colombo Commercial group, Liptons, and Harrisons and Crosfield.[43] Guy Sayer, however, was not prepared to cut out the Hongkong Bank's branch while both that office and the Mercantile were still basically profitable; he argued that the Mercantile's future in Sri Lanka was a matter for Herridge and his team. The Mercantile's head office opted for withdrawal from Sri Lanka and in 1974 the two branches were sold to the local Hatton National Bank. Even though most of the local staff of nearly 200 transferred to the Hatton Bank, as King noted in his history of the Hongkong Bank, the sale 'was not a popular decision in Sri Lanka'.[44]

This major series of transfers and closures in the late 1960s and early 1970s did not diminish the balance sheet and earnings of the slimmed-down Mercantile Bank as might have been expected. Total assets, having fallen back to below £100 million in 1966, surged to £195 million in 1973. After a downward 'blip' in the oil crisis years of 1974 and 1975 the growth in business was resumed in 1976. Published profits moved in step with this expansion, more than doubling from £405 000 in 1966 to £1 056 000 in 1973. Clearly the Mercantile's rate of growth was not as high as that of the Chartered (which merged with the Standard Bank in 1969), National and Grindlays or its own parent bank (Figure 8.2) but its performance was not left distantly behind, as it had been in the early 1960s.

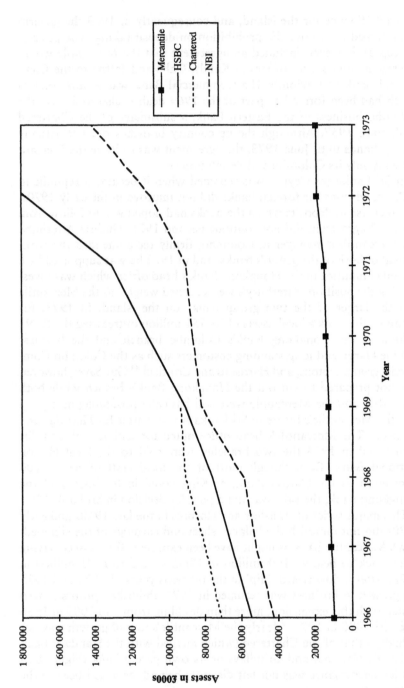

8.2 Eastern banks: total assets, 1966–73

The financial results of the Mercantile, like all international banks, were also given an artificial boost by worldwide price inflation. The bank's business and earnings were nevertheless strong enough to generate increased dividends for the first time since the capital reorganization of 1957. Dividends paid to the Hongkong Bank, the sole shareholder, were raised from the old rate of 12.5 per cent in 1968 to 15 per cent in 1969, followed by further progressive increases to 24 per cent in 1973.

This performance was one of the most sustained and impressive periods of growth in the bank's history. The achievement was doubly remarkable. On the one hand it was obtained at a time when the business base of the bank – in terms of the number of national markets which it served – was narrower than at any time in the life of the Mercantile. On the other hand the bank was generating impressive results at a time when it was changing its character from a fully fledged bank into a banking name or brand which was deployed in specified markets.

This change became visible between about 1972 and 1976 and was accomplished at several different levels. First, in London, the merger of the bank's business with the City office of the Hongkong Bank was completed in 1973. Paul Lamb, who had supervised the integration since 1970, retired in that year and was promptly re-engaged by the Hongkong Bank to prepare for moving the London offices of all the group companies into a new building at 99 Bishopsgate. The removal from Gracechurch Street, where the Hongkong Bank and the Mercantile had been such long-standing residents, was completed in 1976. At the new address a Mercantile nameplate was still needed as a registered address and as an office to handle the London end of transactions with the remaining Mercantile branches, but in practice this business was carried on by the London staff of the Hongkong Bank or the British Bank of the Middle East.

Second, the loss of the London focus affected the traditional pattern of recruitment and training. After the removal of the head office in 1966, juniors were no longer recruited in London and then sent east for their first postings;[45] regional officers continued to be recruited in the East and trained in London. This system ended after the integration of the London offices of the Mercantile and the Hongkong Bank, which included the closure of the Longmoor accommodation for trainees in 1969. From 1971 the Mercantile halted the recruitment of regional and local staff in its own name. Thenceforward the staff of the Hongkong and Mercantile banks were integrated and interchangeable, so that officials from the Hongkong Bank could be posted to Mercantile branches and vice versa without any formal secondments or transfers of contracts. The integration was reflected in the 'staff list' – a prized document in the life of both banks, as these annual lists showed seniority, current appointments and leave entitlements of each member of staff. The publication of a separate staff list for the Mercantile ended in 1971. A combined list showing both the Hongkong Bank and Mercantile staff was produced in the following four years, but after 1976 the list was for the Hongkong Bank only and did not distinguish between the employees' original affiliations.[46]

Third, and decisively, in Hong Kong the head office functions of the Mercantile were subsumed into the head office of the Hongkong Bank in 1972 and early 1973. The two key elements in this process were the winding up of the executive committee and the termination of the post of general manager of the Mercantile. Since 1966 the executive committee had proved to be a compact and effective unit. Although Saunders was a member, he rarely attended meetings, and the supervision of the bank was left to Herridge and the current representative of the Hongkong Bank. Norman Bennett, who represented the Hongkong Bank as a director on the Mercantile board and as a member of the executive committee between 1968 and 1971, was particularly helpful to Herridge.[47] The two men occupied adjoining offices at the south-facing 'shallow end' of the first floor of 1 Queen's Road Central (the Hongkong Bank's senior executives occupied the 'deep end', on the same floor looking north to the harbour). They could complete their business in 'roughly an hour every day'. As Bennett later recalled,

> Herridge and I used to meet every day at noon, and in fact it was a very good way of running a bank ... If there was anything that needed to be discussed in more detail, Macdonald or Lamb would be called in, and we'd thrash it out ... when you're living in the next office to somebody, if anything blows up, it's just a question of walking across the passage and talking about it. It wasn't any real problem.[48]

Workable as this arrangement proved, it did not fit easily into the role which Guy Sayer was developing for the headquarters of the Hongkong Bank in the early 1970s. Appointed general manager with responsibility for the group's subsidiaries in 1970, Sayer was keen to move the group forward from the traditional and almost exclusive reliance on the chief manager in making head office decisions and providing direct feedback to the branches. He wished to see the head office as a control centre, receiving and acting on a much more detailed range of information about the group's business, exposure to risk and overall performance. This would require 'a small caucus of very senior executives' at head office, playing an active role in the effective management of resources.[49] This larger headquarters team was introduced gradually after Sayers succeeded Saunders as chairman of the Hongkong Bank in 1972. In this context the new and more coherent head office of the group was well positioned to carry out the remaining functions of the Mercantile's headquarters, particularly in the evaluation of lending. As a result the executive committee was wound up. Its final meeting, attended by Herridge (in the chair), Sayer and P. A. Hirst, was held on 12 December 1972.[50]

Similarly, as the strengthened head office team was providing group-wide management, there was no further need for a general manager responsible for the Mercantile alone. Ian Herridge, the bank's general manager since 1967, had succeeded Saunders as chairman of the Mercantile in April 1972 (the first and only time that a serving officer had filled the chair[51]). He then continued in the dual role of chairman and general manager until March 1973, when he retired from both posts and was not replaced; his staff of five officers moved across to new posts in the Hongkong Bank.[52] Herridge himself returned to London as 'chairman's representative' until his retirement in 1980. In the latter role, significantly, he acted as ambassador for Sayer's efforts to improve group-wide information and control, particularly in the relationship between Hong Kong and the management of the British Bank of the Middle East.[53]

The integration of the Mercantile's central functions between 1972 and 1976 brought to an end the distinct corporate life of the bank. The vacation of the chief manager's post, in particular, ended the sequence of leadership which had been such a great influence on the bank's fortunes over the previous 80 years. The business which now continued in the Mercantile's name was essentially the responsibility of the enlarged and reinforced head office of the Hongkong Bank.

The name and value of the Mercantile Bank nevertheless survived this loss of leadership and headquarters. Continuity was maintained in two important areas – in the use of the bank's identity and branch offices, and in the contribution which ex-Mercantile staff made to the development of the larger group. In the first of these areas the trading name of the Mercantile remained valuable in specific markets. The preservation of a presence, especially in India and Mauritius, recognized that at that time the Mercantile label was more meaningful at local level than the group's other business names. This continuity was akin to the use of corporate brands elsewhere in the business world. For example, 'badge engineering' was in favour in the American and British motor industries in the 1960s and 1970s, allowing large conglomerates to use old-established marque names for particular markets and groups of customers. In the British insurance industry, which underwent a succession of major amalgamations in the late 1960s and early 1970s, long-standing company names were retained even though their staff, systems and addresses were being provided by the new giants of that industry. There were also examples in international banking. The Chartered Bank retained the name of the Eastern Bank (which it had acquired in 1957) until 1971. The Bank of London and South America, in which Lloyds Bank first took a majority shareholding in 1918, survived in its own name until 1970 and in abbreviated form as Lloyds and Bolsa International until 1974.

The Mercantile enjoyed considerable success in its role as a bank brand. Between 1973 and 1982 total assets rose from £195 million to £322 million. Published profits increased substantially from £1.06 million to £1.97 million in the same period, allowing the Mercantile to pay to its single shareholder dividends of 43 per cent in 1977–78, 44 per cent in 1980, and a massive 99 per cent in 1982. This performance was formally noted in the bank's annual reports, approved and signed by a directorate which was drawn from the board of the Hongkong Bank.

At the heart of this performance was the encouraging achievement of the Mercantile's branches in India. There was even room for expansion in the bank's own name. In 1977, for example, a new sub-branch was opened at Borivli, Bombay, and a specialist merchant banking division was established in Bombay.[54] The drive for increased deposits continued and, high taxation notwithstanding, the bank was producing 'most satisfactory' results in India by 1981. The Mercantile name also continued as the group's only local identity in Mauritius. The volume of business was small in comparison with the Indian branches, but the bank was still able to expand on the island. New sub-branches were opened at Centre de Flacq in 1977, Goodlands and Vacoas in 1978, and Plaine Verte in 1979. These new additions gave the Mercantile a total of eleven offices in Mauritius, placing it on a comparable footing to other major banks on the island.

The Mercantile even shared in the huge development of offshore banking in the 1970s. Private and institutional customers, in an era of high inflation, were seeking homes for large savings which would not attract high taxation or high administration charges. The Hongkong Bank itself responded to this demand by providing offshore banking offices in the Solomon Islands in 1973 and at St Helier, Jersey, in 1976.[55] Likewise in January 1977 the Mercantile board agreed to apply for a licence in the Bahamas. Although this initiative was not pursued, a new offshore office was opened in the Mercantile's own name at Vila, capital of the New Hebrides (Vanuatu) in the Pacific in 1978.

The effective use of the Mercantile's name in these markets was matched by the orderly transition of the Mercantile staff into the employment and pension arrangements of the Hongkong Bank. Inevitably, as with any merger of personnel from different traditions, there were some anxieties and some hard words. Guy Sayer, who had a grandstand view of the integration process, was impatient with any rivalries of that kind. 'There are still people', he remembered, 'who say he's ex-Mercantile, he's ex-Hongkong, he's ex-BBME, but basically they're people like us. Some say that their people are sub-standard. I don't believe that. I found it was the other way round, if anything.'[56]

In general the progress of the Mercantile's staff within the larger group was achieved fairly and amicably. It is striking that, in the voluminous interviews recorded by Frank King and his team in the Hongkong Bank history project, neither the Mercantile nor the Hongkong Bank interviewees cite examples of officers whose careers were impeded by the integration. On the contrary, there are plentiful examples of Mercantile staff who thrived in the broader landscape of the larger group. The business and career opportunities were on an entirely different scale. For instance, Mike Langley and Ian Macdonald, who had been part of the first Mercantile head office team in Hong Kong, both rose to positions of importance within the Hongkong Bank group. Langley enjoyed a variety of high-profile jobs – after a spell as acting managing director of Wardley he was given the task of opening the new office of the Hongkong Bank in Manchester and then returned east to manage the Mongkok and main Hong Kong branches. After his retirement he was instrumental in establishing the bank's representative office in Beijing and then returned to London as consultant manager, China. Macdonald became general manager, India, and oversaw the integration of the two banks in 1972. In 1973 he returned to head office in Hong Kong as general manager, overseas operations, and was a major figure in the Hongkong Bank's development of a global strategy and in the acquisiton of Marine Midland Bank in the US. After retirement his appointments included chief executive of TSB Scotland.

By the early 1980s former staff of the Mercantile Bank held a wide range of appointments in group offices scattered across the globe. The 1984 Hongkong Bank list of group executive staff included at least 50 men who joined Mercantile either in London as members of the Eastern staff, or in the East as regional officers.[57] The highest proportion of these were based in head office in Hong Kong, including four in the audit department; eight were posted in Europe, including the managers of the Hongkong Bank in Ireland and Amsterdam; and seven were managing branches or departments in the Middle East. In addition to managing branches in the traditional Mercantile sphere of operations such as India, Sri Lanka, Mauritius and Malaysia, the ex-Mercantile men could also be found in some of the busier locations such as Mongkok and Macau, and in some of the more exotic locations such as Nassau in the Bahamas, Busan in Korea and Kuala Belait in Brunei.

The life of the Mercantile Bank as a trading name finally drew to a close in the early 1980s. This outcome was not the result of any failure of the Mercantile brand or of its legacy of branches and staff. It was the consequence, instead, of the fundamental change in the character of the Hongkong Bank in these years. Through its acquisition of the Mercantile, the British Bank of the Middle East and the Hang Seng Bank, it had become a major overseas bank with pronounced regional strengths. By its purchase of the Marine Midland Bank of New York State, US, in 1980, and then by its bid for the Royal Bank of Scotland in 1982, the Hongkong Bank signalled its ambition to become a multinational bank of a quite different order, with a capacity to operate in all the major financial markets of the world.[58]

Within this framework there was a limit to the number of different entities and business names which the group could retain. The diversification of banking into new territories and new types of business was also helping to proliferate and complicate the number of trading names in use by the group. Michael Sandberg, who had succeeded Sayer as chairman in 1977, and his head office team took a pragmatic approach to this multiplicity of group identities. Where the group was not the sole owner of a subsidiary or associated company, the existing company name would remain. Where there were business, fiscal or regulatory advantages in the *status quo*, the existing names would again be retained. Where there was already full ownership, however, and where the group could reduce the number of linked names and addresses, then the subsidiary company would be fully converted to use the standardized names of the Hongkong Bank or its foremost local companies. The residuary business of the Mercantile Bank clearly came into the latter category.

In these changed conditions and in the quest for simplicity, the group wound down the remaining operations of the Mercantile in a gradual and careful programme of transfers and disposals. The three sub-branches in Hong Kong itself had been transferred to the parent bank in August 1976, leaving only the main branch at 7 Queen's Road Central; two years later the Hong Kong note issue, with its authorized limit of HK$ 30 million, was cancelled and the Hongkong Bank's own authorized note issue was increased by an equivalent amount. However, the main element in the 'Mercantile Bank rationalization' – as the exercise now became known – was the conversion of the Indian branches. In July 1982 a court order was obtained in the United Kingdom permitting the Mercantile to reduce its capital from £4 million to £3 050 515 in anticipation of transferring its business in India to the Hongkong Bank. The return of the Hongkong Bank name to India was notified to customers and staff later that year and in December the High Court in

Bombay approved the transfer of business and branches. From January 1983 Indian branches operated under the Hongkong Bank name and the Mercantile's title, after 130 years in its different variations, was no longer in use in India. Nagoya office, the bank's sole branch in Japan, also transferred to the Hongkong Bank in January 1983, and six months later the Mauritius branches and banking licence were converted in the same way. The offshore business at Vila, Vanuatu, was also transferred in the course of 1983 (Table 8.3).

The situation in Thailand was more complex. At the end of 1982 the main business of the Mercantile's branches in Bangkok was transferred to the Hongkong Bank, leaving a licence and skeleton business. Citibank, underrepresented in Thailand, agreed in August 1983 to buy the Mercantile's two offices in Bangkok. The sale appeared to have fallen through when Citibank did not obtain a new banking licence by the end of 1983 (which had been a condition of the sale). A more radical solution was found in March 1984 when the group and Citibank reached a new agreement for the sale of the shares of the Mercantile to Citibank. The acquisition included the Mercantile's business and licences in Thailand and its licence in Hong Kong; the remaining Hong Kong operations were excluded, however, and the Mercantile office in Hong Kong (which had recently moved to New Henry House, Ice House Street), would revert to the parent bank. This became a formal agreement in May 1984, which was approved by the Bank of England and the Commissioner of Banking in Hong Kong in July. The proceeds of the sale exceeded the net asset value of the Mercantile Bank – HK$ 104 million or £9.45 million – at that time.

The Mercantile's passage out of the group was completed quietly and without fuss. Neil Reypert, the bank's manager in Hong Kong, wrote to his customers on 21 May to announce the Citibank agreement and to explain that their accounts would be transferred to the Hongkong Bank in the near future unless they requested otherwise. 'There will be no interruption in the banking facilities offered and service will be provided by existing staff.'[59] The conversion of the branch into the 'Victoria Office' of the Hongkong Bank, including the change of systems and codes, was completed on 23 July 1984. Two days later the Hongkong Bank published a press announcement of the completion of the sale of the Mercantile to Citibank, the transfer of the branches in Thailand to Citibank, and the conversion of the Hong Kong branch.[60] For enquiry purposes the bank continued to be listed in the *Bankers' Almanac* and other directories but by then its telegraphic address – PARADISE, Hong Kong – was the only survivor of its old name and address.

The integration was now complete. It was a process which had spread over 25 years, since the acquisition of 1959. In certain respects the

Table 8.3   Mercantile Bank: branch closures and transfers, 1971–84

Country	Branch / branches	Date closed or transferred	Business transferred to:
Pakistan	4 offices	September 1969	National & Grindlays Bank
Singapore	4 offices	July 1973	Hongkong Bank
Malaysia	14 offices	January 1974	Hongkong Bank
Sri Lanka	Galle, Jaffna, Kandy	June 1973	Commercial Bank of Ceylon
Sri Lanka	Colombo, Pettah	1974	Hatton National Bank
Hong Kong	3 offices	August 1976	Hongkong Bank
India	20 offices	January 1983	Hongkong Bank
Japan	Nagoya	January 1983	Hongkong Bank
Mauritius	11 offices	July 1983	Hongkong Bank
Vanuatu	Vila	1983	Hongkong Bank
Thailand	2 offices	July 1984	Citibank
Hong Kong	Hong Kong	July 1984	Hongkong Bank

outcome was inevitable, even as soon as the early 1960s. It was always unlikely that the enlarged group would be able to maintain two banks alongside each other in markets such as Malaysia, Singapore and Japan; the British Bank of Middle East, in contrast, was then the sole group bank in most of its markets and its identity was not at issue. The consolidation of the Mercantile and the Hongkong Banks in these areas of overlap offered to provide savings in administration, overheads and – not least – would reduce the possibility of confusion of the banks' identity. The only surprise, certainly to some of the younger generation in both banks, was that this overlap survived until the early 1970s.

In other respects the process of integration was not so inevitable. The Mercantile had been the Hongkong Bank's first major acquisition and the subsequent relationship between the two banks was experimental in terms of business, management, and even the pace of change. Initially the Hongkong Bank preferred the retention of the full Mercantile identity, particularly in markets such as India where the Mercantile was the stronger member of the partnership. Even when the bank's headquarters was removed to Hong Kong, Gregoire, Herridge and their small teams demonstrated that an effective business could be maintained with an extremely simple and compact management structure. When that structure was disbanded in 1972, however, and when the Mercantile was no longer recruiting in its own name, then full integration was the obvious outcome. While the name of the Mercantile was put to productive use in its traditional markets such as India and Mauritius into the late 1970s and early 1980s, the assimilation of business and staff was by then moving forward in a steady sequence. That the transition of the business and the name of the Mercantile were given such care by its owners, however, is a measure of the achievements and the resilience of the bank, its management and staff over the long history of the Mercantile in Eastern banking.

CHAPTER NINE

Review, 1893–1984

In the history of finance there are times and places at which a single bank might enjoy prominence, advantage and even fame. Location, market conditions, political climate and the quality of staff and services can come together to place a company ahead of its competitors in business and reputation. In overseas banking, examples of such good position in the field include the Rothschilds' success in government loans in Europe after the Napoleonic Wars; the acquisition of the Turkish railway concessions by the Belgian banker Baron de Hirsch ('Türkenhirsch') in 1869; the French banks' strong showing in Russia after 1887; and the Hongkong Bank's success in the commercial and industrial boom in Hong Kong after the Second World War.

The Mercantile Bank of India rarely enjoyed such favourable positioning. It found itself in the wrong place at the wrong time at frequent intervals in its long history. External factors and events – in addition to the political and economic risks which affected all the Eastern banks – repeatedly put the bank at a disadvantage. Hence whenever the bank was relatively strong in a particular market, the impact of external factors proved to be comparatively heavy. Business in India, still the bank's main area of activity in the 1950s and 1960s, incurred increasingly heavy costs in staff and taxation. Also in the 1950s and the early 1960s the Indian authorities' unwillingness to grant licences to overseas banks to open new branches had impeded the Mercantile at one of the rare moments when the bank was in expansive mood and keen to attract new deposits in India. Ceylon, another market where the Mercantile held a long-standing share of business, was subject to trade restrictions and heavy taxation from the 1960s, while in Burma the nationalization of the banks in 1963 ended the most successful decade in the history of the bank's Rangoon branch since its reopening in 1909.

These setbacks were not foreseen by previous generations of the bank's managers and directors. In the Second World War and its immediate aftermath, for example, which was the lowest point in the fortunes of the British banks in the East, the Mercantile's strength on the Indian sub-continent appeared much more promising as a long-term position than the heavy involvement of other banks in China and Japan. Even when the obstacles to future development did become obvious, the bank's existing commitments were too substantial to allow any sudden retreat or withdrawal. The Mercantile's departure from the Dutch East

Indies in 1931/32 and the sale of the Pakistan branches in 1969 were the only examples where the bank withdrew voluntarily in the face of external business and political pressures.

The Mercantile Bank, despite an almost habitual experience of unfortunate timing and location, was a remarkably durable and successful exponent of Eastern banking for nearly a century after its renewal in 1892. In Bombay, to take the example of the Chartered Mercantile's place of birth, the bank was one of fifteen banks in the city at the beginning of the twentieth century. Most of these banks were British overseas banks, with the exception of the two presidency banks of Bengal and Bombay and the Comptoir National d'Escompte de Paris. Eighty years later, shortly before the transfer of its Indian branches to the Hongkong Bank in 1983, the Mercantile was one of only five British banks with full branches in the city. By then Indian banks such as the Bank of Baroda, the Central, Syndicate and Union Banks dominated local banking, while there was also competition from American, French and Japanese banks.[1] The bank showed similar staying power in its other principal markets.

In terms of performance, the bank produced impressively solid results in the inter-war period when many of its contemporaries were suffering losses and disruption. It generated spectacular success in pre-war Shanghai under the management of Huxter, one of the true originals in exchange banking in the 1930s and 1940s. The Mercantile was also able to produce strong performances in the 1950s and again in the 1970s, in its final years as a bank name in its own right. This chapter reviews this survival, endurance and success by assessing four aspects of the bank's history: the business profile of the Mercantile; the changing nature of overseas banking; the special character or corporate culture of the Mercantile; and, last, the contribution of the bank to its own world of business and banking.

As a business institution the Mercantile Bank did not aspire to a high profile. Throughout its history after the reconstruction in 1893 the size of the business (in total assets) held station behind the Hongkong Bank, the National Bank of India and the Chartered Bank, but ahead of the Eastern Bank and competitors in the earlier twentieth century such as the Delhi and London Bank and the P&O Banking Corporation.[2] It was dwarfed by the major London clearing banks and by leading international banks from the US, Europe and Japan. In 1913, for instance, the Mercantile's total assets of £8.2 million were less than one-tenth of those of the Deutsche Bank, Crédit Lyonnais, Société Générale or any of the three largest clearing banks in London. Even the London and River Plate Bank, which like the Mercantile was primarily an overseas bank, was four times as large as the bank at that time.[3] On the other hand the

Mercantile produced strong and steady growth in its balance sheet, taking total assets from £3.5 million in 1900 to £72.5 million in 1960 and nearly £250 million by 1980. The multiple of 21 between 1900 and 1960 was well ahead of the fourfold inflation in sterling prices in those years. Admittedly this is an arbitrary time-scale for comparison but the multiple shows a similar pace of progress to that of banks such as the Chartered (with a multiple of 25) and National and Grindlays (19),

Similarly, the published profits of the bank in absolute terms were lower than those of its larger neighbours. Between the two world wars, for example, the bank's results were rather less than half of those of the Chartered and the National Bank of India and no more than one-fifth of the published profits of the Hongkong Bank. The quality of earnings, however, compared well with the performance of other overseas banks. The Mercantile's profitability (that is, the ratio of profits to shareholders' funds) was ahead of most British overseas banks between about 1910 and 1960, joining the other Eastern banks at the top of this measure of earnings (Table 9.1).

The earnings which were passed on to shareholders also compared well with those of other overseas banks. For a shareholder who remained with the 'new' bank, there was a lengthy period of meagre returns while James Campbell re-established the bank's position in the 1890s and early 1900s. Dividends did not exceed 5 per cent until 1907 but thereafter they recovered strongly to a level of 16 per cent in the 1920s (Appendix Two). Dividend rates were cut back in the 1930s and 1940s, in common with the rest of the banking community, but then recovered to 14 per cent for all three classes of shares in the 1950s. After the capital reorganization of 1957 and the acquisition of the bank by the Hongkong Bank in 1959, dividends on the new shares settled at 12.5 per cent before rising to very high levels in the 1970s. The yield on the shares was also relatively high, particularly from the period of the First World War onwards. Table 9.1 shows the average profitability of the bank, average dividends and the average yield (the dividend per share divided by the price of the bank's shares). Using yield as a measure of return, the Mercantile actually headed the rankings of British overseas banks in the years between 1947 and 1955 – a reflection of the bank's rugged performance and recovery in the years of war and partition.

The bank itself benefited from the sustained growth of earnings. Published profits, in tune with the results of all British banks until full 'disclosure' was required in 1969, were generally well below the level of actual profits. This difference between real and published profits allowed the bank to accumulate strong reserve funds. It was a practice which gave the Mercantile considerable security against the high risks which prevailed in many of its markets and levelled out the volatile

Table 9.1 Measures of performance of the Mercantile Bank, 1896–1959

Date*	Profitability		Average dividends		Yield		Comparison
	Ratio, net profits to shareholders' funds	Rank	Average dividends, % nominal capital	Rank	Ratio, dividend per share to share price	Rank	Number of British overseas banks
1896–1913	7.7	13=	5.3	16=	4.6	15=	19
1914–20	11.3	4	12.0	10	5.5	12=	18
1921–29	10.0	6=	16.0	4	6.5	4	19
1930–38	7.6	5	12.4	5	5.4	6=	17
1939–46	7.0	4	8.4	5	4.6	6=	16
1947–55	7.2	4	12.6	4	7.1	1	16
1956–59	6.1		12.7		5.7		16

Note: *Time periods selected in Jones, *Multinational Banking*, Appendix 5. Rankings for 1956–59 not applicable.

Source: G. Jones, *British Multinational Banking 1830–1990* (Oxford, 1993), Appendix 5.

earnings from exchange banking. In the Mercantile's case the difference became significant from 1919–20 onwards. The only variations from this pattern occurred in 1924–26 and 1930–31, when the bank posted profits which were actually higher than real profits and which smoothed out the effects of exchange losses in the early 1920s and the onset of the worldwide slump in 1929. By the 1950s, however, the bank's board was continuing to build up these hidden reserves to an unnecessary extent. By 1956 inner reserves reached nearly £4.5 million, or £1 million more than the total paid-up capital and published reserves; the inner reserves of the Chartered Bank, by comparison, were only one-half of its paid-up capital and published reserves at the same period. Shareholders might have claimed that the real profits could have been used to make substantial increases in the Mercantile's dividend payments, that published reserves could have been strengthened, or (as George Marden contended) that the bank could have used its resources more vigorously in expanding the business. In reply, the directors could argue that shareholders were not disadvantaged by the high level of inner reserves. The shares produced relatively high earnings and in 1959 the Hongkong Bank paid shareholders a full price which reflected the value of the bank's reserves. A charge of conservatism would have carried more weight, as the deployment of inner reserves in the expansion of the business was the opportunity for even higher levels of earnings.

The conservative instincts of the bank on this question of reserves, especially in the post-war period, were characteristic of the overseas banking sector. The impact of two world wars, political turmoil in the East and the weakening position of sterling after the Second World War combined to discourage risk and enterprise.[4] In the Mercantile's own case such caution limited the chances for challenging its larger competitors. A deep aversion to risk also impeded the development of a strategy for expansion. Survival and piecemeal gains were the priorities in a bank which was perhaps fundamentally too small for a strategic approach. There was a strategic element to the ideas for moving into entirely new markets in the inter-war period, Mealing's search for new, more distant markets in the 1950s, and the extension of branches on the sub-continent to attract new deposits in the 1960s. With these exceptions any meaningful experience of wide-ranging strategy was delayed until after the bank became a member of the Hongkong Bank group. In the larger group, strategic issues – such as the evaluation of markets for entry or exit and the development of new or existing companies for specific markets and activities – greatly affected the positioning of the Mercantile Bank after 1959. In its business in India and Japan, for instance, the bank was part of banking strategy on a much larger scale than would have been possible in its old independent form.

Ultimately a conservative and tactical approach to overseas banking did not prevent the Mercantile from achieving success and longevity. It survived wars, revolutions and the rise of nationalism in the East. It survived worldwide depression between the wars and monetary upheavals in Eastern markets. It delivered a reliable international service to its customers and gave value to its shareholders and (after 1959) its sole owner. Few overseas banks could make such a claim. Certainly there are few companies in international banking which have faced closure, as the Mercantile did in 1892, and yet were able to stage such a spirited long-term recovery and to develop such a durable banking business.

The experience of the Mercantile Bank throws light on the changing character of overseas banking in the twentieth century. Again, the size of the bank is a central concern. One of the bank's main business attributes was its willingness to provide a full range of services in a wide range of different locations and currencies. In the mid-1950s, in the final years of its independent ownership, the bank was represented in twelve countries (including the New York office) and was trading and accounting in the same number of currencies. This width was vital in overseas banking; a full service could not be provided *unless* the bank was far-flung in its activities. In particular, customers on the sub-continent, the bank's home ground, needed facilities for trade finance throughout the East. Hence the finance needed by these customers was a significant factor in the bank's presence in Hong Kong and Japan, where Indian merchant houses shared in the trade booms of the post-war period.

As to the services which it offered, the Mercantile also needed to offer a wide and adaptable range to its customers. Banking commentators in the late twentieth century have often assumed that, in comparison with modern financial products and services, traditional banking was simple and narrow in its range, offering little more than current accounts, deposit accounts and a limited range of trustee and safe custody services. This was certainly not the case in the banking markets where Mercantile carried on its business. Exchange banking was a complex and skilful service, demanding good communications and an almost instinctive understanding of currency movements, the maturity of bills and guarantees, and the niceties of local cash transactions. In the Mercantile's case there was also the additional dimension of bank note issue in Hong Kong and acting as banker to Malayan states. Even the ordinary current account was a complex product when placed in an overseas setting. The reports of Mercantile's inspectors in the post-war era give a picture of the variety of borrowing which was possible on current account. At Penang in May 1957, for example, borrowing included overdrafts secured by letters of guarantee; borrowing by limited companies and partnerships; borrowing limits sanctioned by the board, regional or local manager; advances secured by mortgage bonds; advances secured by 'moveables' (usually rubber in the case of Penang); and advances against stocks and shares.[5] Each of these services was a distinct banking 'product' in the sense that it required its own documentation and legal status. In lending on moveables, the bank's officers were also required to inspect and assess the quality and condition of stocks of goods which were pledged to the bank and held in local godowns.

This multiplicity of skills and services was essential to the work of overseas bankers. Yet in its different locations and in its range of services, the Mercantile was thinly spread. Even where the bank was relatively strong – notably on the Indian sub-continent and Malaysia – it faced larger competitors such as the Chartered Bank and National Bank of India. In other cases, as in Burma, Japan and Thailand, it was confined to single branches or small numbers of offices which were required to provide the full range of international banking services. This thin representation suggests that the Mercantile was above the minimum size for an independent bank but below the optimum size for overseas banking. Although this condition was present throughout the bank's history, it was not a major obstacle to profitable business and growth as long as British overseas banks dominated trade finance in their chosen markets in the earlier twentieth century. In the post-war setting, however, such banks faced serious competition from local and international banks. As the population of competing banks increased, optimal size became more apparent. By the mid-1950s that optimum required a strong set of favourable factors. These advantages included a dominant position in one or more markets (such as the Hongkong Bank in Hong Kong or the Standard Bank in South Africa), a branch network of 50 or more offices (such as the Chartered Bank or the Bank of London and South America (BOLSA)), a supply of experienced officers available for new or sudden assignments, and total assets of at least £100 million.[6] It was these banks which had the capacity to grow in the face of increased competition. They also operated on a sufficiently large scale to participate in the 'internationalization' of banking, particularly the growth of the Eurodollar markets in which banks such as BOLSA were especially active from the late 1950s onwards. The Mercantile Bank and the British Bank of the Middle East, which became sisters in the Hongkong Bank group in 1959, were both below these optimum levels. The important difference here was that the BBME's business was concentrated in the niche market of the Middle East, where the bank had a prominence which the Mercantile could not match in its far-flung markets. In this context the acquisition of the Mercantile in 1959 was well timed, as the scale of its business was by then nearer to minimal than optimal for an independent bank. As part of the larger group, the problem of thin coverage of markets and services was quickly removed.

The character and culture of the Mercantile were also deeply influenced by its relatively small size. At no time in its history after 1893 could a new recruit mistake his new employer for one of the giants of the financial world. The bank's addresses and buildings in London, Calcutta, Bombay and Singapore, for example, were impressive specimens of overseas banking but they were modest in comparison with the palaces of finance of the London clearing banks, the Edinburgh and Glasgow headquarters of the Scottish banks where many recruits had begun their careers, or the splendid buildings with which the Hongkong Bank dominated the waterfronts of Hong Kong and Shanghai. The new recruit also found that the Mercantile, unlike many larger banks, was not heavily involved with representative and professional bodies in banking. Even in life outside work the bank took a low-key role in social and sporting activity. Sport was an important ingredient in the life of the overseas branches but, in comparison with larger banks, it was enjoyed without the luxuries of sports grounds, pavilions, sports secretaries and groundsmen.

The bank's somewhat modest profile may have been a disappointment to the most ambitious recruits, but it was not necessarily a disadvantage. Many of the bank's customers preferred to attach to a small British bank, in the same way that private banks keep a constituency long after their services are more widely and cheaply available elsewhere. Likewise the limited scale of operations could be an attraction for staff and even directors. Here the Scottish tradition within the bank was an additional bond in establishing and retaining loyalty. In the twentieth century the bank was not monopolized by Scots-trained bankers and it certainly did not deserve the tag of 'Mercantile Bank of Scotland'.[7] Yet Scots bankers still contributed some 37 per cent of the 396 foreign staff recruited between 1893 and 1965 whose origins are recorded.

The limited size of the bank could also be a business advantage. One of the strongest characteristics of the bank was the intimacy of its business life. This intimacy operated at several levels. For the foreign staff of the bank the low numbers of personnel meant that any one officer would know most of his contemporaries and many of his seniors. News of promotions, postings and leave entitlements was eagerly awaited and highly valued throughout the bank. In the preparation of this history the authors have been struck by the fine details of colleagues' appointments which former Mercantile staff have recalled 20 or even 30 years after leaving the bank. This knowledge was not merely a matter of personal curiosity. It was information which enabled an officer to assess the experience and expertise of colleagues in distant branches and to have confidence in the type of service which his own branch or his customers would receive.

As the counterpart to this personal knowledge, the size of the bank meant that during their careers members of the foreign staff would serve in many of the Mercantile's key branches. For officers and their families, this required great adaptability, resilience of character and tolerance of the many different cultures and climates in which they found themselves. The average number of postings was eight, but some members of staff could boast an encyclopaedic knowledge of the branch network – William Hobbin, for example, served at seventeen different branches between 1925 and 1954. Additionally, certain head office officials, particularly the inspectors, would be required to tour all of the bank's branches. There were individuals who developed specializations. Fairly, and sometimes unfairly, within the bank they might also become popularly associated with particular branches. James Steuart, a future general manager, held no less than six appointments in Ceylon; Jackie Huxter was synonymous with the Shanghai business. In general, however, wide experience of the branches was a usual and desirable feature, particularly in the careers of the most senior staff. If a senior manager did not have such broad experience (as in the case of Ian Herridge's relatively brief time on the sub-continent before becoming the designated chief manager in 1966), then efforts were made to accelerate his knowledge of regions where he had not served.

Throughout the history of the Mercantile, the bank was in this way producing officers who could understand from personal or close knowledge the full extent of the bank's business. At the customer level, the intimate character of the bank was also an advantage in building and maintaining business relationships. Customers such as the British agency houses and Indian and Singapore trading companies were operating in most of the markets where the Mercantile Bank was represented. Geographical continuity of this kind ensured that the bank's officers, even after being posted thousands of miles from their last sighting of a customer, were familiar with the scale and importance of that customer's business. This was not the type of information that could be conveyed by instruction or formula. It required familiarity with the customer's special requirements, the timing of his payments and receipts, and the usual destinations of his shipments and settlements. This familiarity was ingrained in the Mercantile's staff and management in a fashion not possible in a larger bank. The Scots origin of many Mercantile staff again came into play, as it provided a informal link to customers in the tea and rubber plantations or the raw jute industry, where Scottish ownership and management were a distinctive feature of business life in the late nineteenth and early twentieth centuries.

Familiarity and close knowledge were invaluable in the front line of the bank's management, staff and customer relations. Yet that pattern had a flaw. Throughout the Mercantile's history there was segregation between the realities of overseas banking in the field and the authority of the distant headquarters in London. This separation produced tension and even dissatisfaction among overseas managers and staff in their attitude to the decisions and procedures of the London board and management. This, a persistent theme of the oral history interviews with Mercantile staff which were carried out in 1980–81,[8] was a problem both of practicalities and ideas. In day-to-day business the requirement to refer decisions to London seemed excessive. Low-level lending decisions, staff matters and insignificant purchases of equipment or furniture were passed to head office for clearance. The London office was also responsible for detailed checking of branch returns on a regular fortnightly basis. In the first half of the twentieth century, when a decision might spend ten weeks in transit from submission to authorization, the Mercantile's local managers were frequently frustrated or unable to respond to on-the-spot decisions made by their competitors. All overseas banks faced problems of delay or breakdown in communication, but for the Mercantile the difficulty lay in the lack of authority and initiative which was allowed to local managers. When a decision or comment eventually arrived, the peremptory tone of instructions from London (especially in the late 1940s and 1950s) did not ease the tension. Furthermore, members of the overseas staff cited the rarity of visits by board members, and even the reluctance of some directors to introduce business to the bank, as examples of the great divide between London and the branches.

The disengagement between the head office and the branches extended to larger questions of policy and planning. From the perspective of the East, the directors and managers in London appeared unwilling or slow to respond to the pace and direction of change in overseas markets. By the time that they reached the top of the bank, chief managers had been away from the East for many years, while the expertise of many of the directors was confined to a single market or a single commodity. The rejection of Donovan Benson's proposals for expansion in Hong Kong – even when the signs of the city's post-war boom were self-evident – was cited as an example of London's indifference to new or sudden developments. The bank followed rather than led new developments in Eastern banking. There were moments when the branches themselves showed a lack of foresight (for example the unwillingness to take up new opportunities for trade between India and

Japan in the late 1920s), but more commonly the branches were well ahead of the London board and management in their ideas for new business in the East.

Tension between headquarters and branches is a feature of the history of all varieties of business, in some cases bred by a head office's obstruction of local progress and in other cases the result of branches being driven too hard or being given impossible targets by their head offices. In the Mercantile's experience, the conservative approach more often derived from the London head office than from the branches. It was only in the final years of London's status as a head office, ironically, that the segregation was significantly reduced. As chief manager between 1958 and 1962, Towkay Wardle made great efforts to visit and inform the branches of the business opportunities which were then becoming available in the larger Hongkong Bank group. His successor Charles Pow, chief manager from 1963 to 1966, took the process further by enhancing communications between London and the overseas offices. His newsletters, introduced in 1962 and continued by later chief executives until 1972, were a serious attempt to advise the branches of current business and performance throughout the network. The newsletters also provided a clearer view of the overall position and prospects of the bank.

The transfer of the bank's head office to Hong Kong in 1966 effectively marked the end of any remaining segregation between branches and their headquarters. The transfer of decision making from a board in London to a three-man executive committee in Hong Kong immediately reduced the time and paperwork required for the larger decisions. At the same time the integration of the bank's branches into the larger group brought lending decisions and procedures into closer line with the Hongkong Bank's emphasis on local responsibility, thereby removing the long-standing grievance that the Mercantile's procedures were over-elaborate and overcentralized.

If the segregation of the head office and branches was virtually a constant feature of the Mercantile's business culture, it was not necessarily a long-term disadvantage to the survival and progress of the bank. The board and management in London had sound reasons for retaining direct control of relatively small decisions and for knowingly accepting delays in the delivery of decisions. The misfortunes of the old Chartered Mercantile left an indelible mark on the outlook and behaviour of the bank, particularly in the first generation after the 1893 reconstruction. James Campbell and his successors placed caution high on their list of priorities. The tradition of checking fortnightly returns and reviewing each application was perceived as the only sure protection against error or abuse of the bank's procedures. The result of this prudence was that the Mercantile, throughout its later history, was a remarkably safe bank. There were very few misjudgements which threatened to engulf the business of individual branches, let alone the bank as a whole. Bad debts, the sums which the bank did not expect to recover from loans or other customer facilities, were kept tightly in check. Between 1950 and 1959, for which consolidated figures are available, the bank actually made provision for large amounts of bad debts, but in the event the amounts written off in those years never exceeded 9.6 per cent of the Mercantile's real profits in any one year and averaged less than 5 per cent over the whole period (Table 9.2). Comparisons with other banks are difficult, as few historians or archivists have paid much attention to this aspect of performance, but it is probable that the Mercantile's bad debt ratio was well below the average for overseas banks. Likewise the bank escaped crippling failures amongst its large corporate customers on the scale of the Beyts, Craig and Co. failure which had brought down the Chartered Mercantile in 1892. The size of the bank in the twentieth century precluded it from exposures of that kind, but safety was driven mainly by the prudent attitude – deliberate and not popular with managers and staff in the field – of the London board and management.

The relationship between the Mercantile's head office and its branches was embedded in the bank's personality and performance. In contrast,

Table 9.2 Mercantile Bank: bad debts provided for and written off, 1950–59

Year	Bad debt provision (£)	Bad debts written off (£) (a)	Real profits (£) (b)	(a) as per cent of (b)
1950	155 713	12 528	585 542	2.14
1951	80 756	14 730	878 361	1.68
1952	298 483	31 925	648 688	4.92
1953	200 873	20 873	537 687	3.88
1954	109 689	35 140	510 824	6.88
1955	65 620	29 241	704 423	4.15
1956	96 965	66 638	777 484	8.57
1957	85 913	6 893	685 699	1.01
1958	130 776	18 723	561 267	3.34
1959	66 052	41 152	429 566	9.58
Total	1 290 840	277 843	6 319 541	4.40

Source: Contingent bad debt account file, MBH 2398.

its business and its personnel were the main elements in the long-term achievements of the bank. What did the Mercantile add or contribute to the world in which it operated? What would have been missing from Eastern markets and from banking development if the Mercantile Bank had not been rescued and reconstructed in 1892? The role of overseas banks and multinationals in general is a topic of continuing debate among economists, political scientists and environmentalists as well as among historians, all searching to show whether these international enterprises added value to or removed value from their local markets. Cumulatively the contribution of overseas banks may have made some impact on this balance. While small banks such as the Mercantile are not candidates for changing the course of economic history, none the less there are areas where the bank was able to leave a lasting impression.

Consistently throughout its history the Mercantile provided a reliable service in the finance of international trade. That service was employed not only in commerce between the United Kingdom and the major ports of the East, but also in the entrepôt trade between the Eastern markets and in Eastern trade with Europe and North America. As an illustration of the sheer scale of that commitment and the volume of business between the bank's branches, Table 9.3 gives the dimensions of the main activities of Bombay branch in a single half-year period. By that stage the heavy volume of bill transactions for trade finance was being supplemented in the form of loans and overdrafts for industrial and development projects.

While the Mercantile was not prominent in introducing banking to entirely new territories, there were examples where it was an early arrival. The new offices on the east coast of Malaya in the late 1920s were the first in those territories and the Mercantile was the first overseas bank in Osaka (in 1949) and Nagoya (1963) in Japan. Yet these were exceptions. The bank's principal contribution in all its markets was to provide an additional layer of choice and competition. The Mercantile, smaller in scale than Eastern banks such as the Hongkong, Chartered and National Banks, was substantial enough to offer alternative terms and facilities and to take a share of the business of large agency houses and multinationals. Significantly, even if it could not capture a large aggregate share of this business, the bank did attract a relatively high proportion of small to medium-sized business accounts. Analysis is not available for the whole of the bank's history, but in the later 1920s and 1930s a growing number and value of the Mercantile's credits was directed to locally owned export business in comparison with the traditional emphasis on British and other overseas customers. From the recollections of former members of staff, this process was

Table 9.3   Mercantile Bank: Bombay branch, key indicators, July–
December 1954

Business	Value (Rs lakhs)	Value (£000s)	Number of transactions
Current account deposits	336	2520	
Fixed deposits	231		
Loans	329		
Overdrafts	288		
Investments (government securities)	179		
Bills for collection			
receivable from London	43		1564
receivable direct	270		3527
Bills remitted			
to branches	460		3509
to banks	187		2501
Telegraphic transfers			
from branches	524		
to branches	537		

Note: Exchange rate: 1rupee = 1s. 6d. (7.5p).

Source: Half-yearly returns, July–Dec. 1954, MBH 2309.22.

carried further at the Mercantile than in other overseas banks. In addition the bank had a long tradition of lending to local bankers, such as the chettiar bankers in Malaya and Ceylon, who were in turn an important link in the cycle of credit for local business development. In these areas the bank was filling a need which was not a priority for other overseas banks and yet could not be met by local banks alone.

The Mercantile also joined other banks in India (but was ahead of other Eastern banks) in improving the recruitment and promotion opportunities for local staff. On Lord Catto's initiative, from 1936 the bank was active in developing a cadre of Indian staff who could take the place of the Eastern staff. Increased responsibilities were gradually transferred to these regional staff, many of whom later held senior positions in the Hongkong Bank group. An outstanding example was Aman Mehta, who joined the Mercantile Bank in 1970 in Bombay as a regional officer and after a series of group appointments became chief executive of the Hongkong Bank in 1998. This policy was a lasting contribution to the regions where the bank operated, as it added to the pool of trained and experienced bankers. It was also part of the bank's legacy even where the Mercantile's business eventually passed into other hands, as in Pakistan and Sri Lanka.

These contributions continued after the Mercantile became part of the larger Hongkong Bank group in 1959, adding to the character and progress of the group in a number of directions. Many of its former branches provided business, staff and buildings for the continuing business of the group; the successful integration of the Mercantile meant that its local business was not lost to the group. In India, in particular, the modern business of the HSBC Group is built on the foundations laid by the Mercantile, as neither the Hongkong Bank nor the British Bank of the Middle East ever operated on the same scale on the sub-continent.

The most substantial of the Mercantile's contributions to the larger group was its own personnel. In sheer numbers the bank brought approximately 3000 members of staff into the group: this figure is based on the total payroll in the mid-1960s, before any appreciable number of secondments and transfers was under way.[9] It was a large contingent at a time when the Hongkong Bank's total workforce was no more than about 6500. The Mercantile's Eastern executive staff of 141 officers was also a substantial presence in comparison with the Hongkong Bank's 278 Eastern staff in 1962.[10] This presence was not eroded in the process of integration which then followed. The disposal of the bank's business in Pakistan in 1969 and Sri Lanka in the early 1970s required the transfer of local staff to employment by the new owners, but elsewhere the staff continued en bloc. By 1972, when the Eastern staffs of the Hongkong and Mercantile banks were combined, the 79 Eastern staff of the Mercantile still represented 21 per cent of the combined staff.[11]

The Mercantile presence amounted to more than staff numbers. It also comprised the skills and experience of individual members of staff. Intimate knowledge of their business, commercial initiative, reliability and loyalty were qualities which ensured that many Mercantile staff flourished and continue to flourish in the enlarged group. Those who had recognized the acquisition of the bank in 1959 as an opportunity for business and career were fully vindicated and their contribution continued long after the Mercantile name finally disappeared from the Hongkong Bank group in 1984. At the time of writing (in 1999) this contribution and commitment is still maintained by staff of the modern HSBC Group who were recruited by the Mercantile and by the close-knit clan of HSBC pensioners who spent all or most of their careers with the Mercantile Bank.

The abilities and positive attitude of the Mercantile staff contributed to the larger group in the process of merger and integration. The Hongkong Bank, as Michael Turner and his contemporaries pointed out, had no experience of mergers and acquisitions when the purchase of the Mercantile was being planned and completed in the late 1950s. Similarly there was no compelling blueprint for how the acquired bank could be integrated into the operations of a larger banking group. This was not such an immediate concern with the British Bank of the Middle East, which was also acquired in 1959; that bank's specialization in the Middle East did not overlap with the Hongkong Bank and did not provide internal competition. With the Mercantile, in contrast, there was obvious overlap and competition. The challenge for the group was to manage the integration of the Mercantile in a way that would retain and then enhance the business of both the Hongkong and Mercantile Banks.

The integration process – and other external factors which intervened – has been described in detail in Chapter Eight. In assessing the process, however, we should note that it held a wider significance for the Hongkong Bank. The integration was the Hongkong Bank's first prolonged experience of engineering the structure of, and then operating, a group of companies. That this was completed in a constructive and orderly way was of signal importance in the later history of the HSBC Group, as the group became known in 1991. In the 1980s and 1990s the HSBC Group has emerged as one of the pre-eminent multinational banks in the world.[12] That position owed a great deal to its programme of acquisitions and investments around the world. The expansion of the HSBC Group included ground-breaking acquisitions such as the Marine Midland Bank of New York State in 1980 and the Midland Bank, one of the largest British clearing banks, in 1992. In each case acquisition was followed by a process of integration and harmonization over a number of years. As with the earlier experience with the Mercantile, that process required exchange and secondments of staff, commonality of procedures and systems, and careful planning of the group's representation in particular markets and services.

Clearly the integration of the Mercantile Bank did not provide an exact model for these extensions of the larger group. There was no conscious effort to reproduce the conditions of the 1959 acquisitions in the induction of later members of the group. None the less the Mercantile *did* set a precedent. It set the Hongkong Bank group on its way in a long and momentous series of acquisitions and alliances. The experience gave the directors and executives the confidence that their bank in Hong Kong could manage change on a significant scale and could bring different businesses and different company cultures into a single whole. This experience, and the assurance which it generated, was contributing to the group well before the flurry of other mergers in British overseas banking (the union of Standard and Chartered in 1969, for example) and the amalgamations in domestic banking such as the Westminster/ National Provincial and Barclays/Martins mergers of 1968.

Finally, and not least, the integration of the Mercantile left a more personal legacy to later acquisitions by the Hongkong Bank group. Mercantile bankers who had seen the integration process at close quarters were later entrusted with important roles in later mergers and group reorganizations. Ian Macdonald, who played a central part in the Marine Midland negotiations,[13] had been in the front line of the Mercantile's transfer to Hong Kong in 1966. Peter Fletcher, who was appointed with special responsibilities at the Saudi British Bank in the early 1980s, had been involved in the integration in Malaysia in the early 1970s and had served on the Mercantile board between 1982 and 1984. In these cases experience in the Mercantile provided both precedent and a practical contribution to the multi-bank expansion of an international group.

Business historians and management theorists have used the concept of 'life cycle' to depict the stages of development of companies and banks.[14] This can be a useful device for identifying the birth, youthful ambitions, maturity and decline of business institutions, particularly when there is a good view of the entire history of a company. Not all companies fit the life-cycle pattern, however, and in many cases the pattern ignores the continuities of business life. In the example of the Mercantile Bank, the bank launched in 1893 was a rehabilitation rather than a birth or rebirth; there was no distinct period of youthful experiment and innovation. In its final years in its own name the bank was gaining from and making a lasting contribution to a larger banking group rather than slipping into decline. A more useful metaphor for the Mercantile might be the history of a house or building. The 1893 bank can be understood as a building inherited from previous owners, many of whom stayed on under the new ownership; the building continued to perform the same functions as the old house, but extensions and outhouses were needed to cope with new residents or new activities which the owners were keen to encourage. The building survived the storm damage of war and political turmoil, and parts of the house needed rebuilding or, when they no longer served a meaningful purpose, demolition. The building needed major modernization in the 1950s but it was increasingly difficult to keep it in independent ownership. New owners moved in, making it possible for the building to continue to function and to prosper, with further extensions and modernization. The name of the building changed in 1984 but it continued to perform its traditional role, with the same occupants and visitors and with a lasting place in its local landscape.

The building analogy allows for the continuities, man-made changes and external events which shape the existence of a business such as the Mercantile. The change of ownership in 1959 was particularly decisive in the upkeep of the business. In the view of Michael Langley, who saw the transformation at close hand, the acquisition was 'probably the best thing that ever happened to the Mercantile ... Otherwise I feel that we would have slipped back and probably been gobbled up by somebody else.'[15] As a bank on a relatively small scale, it was doubtful whether the Mercantile would have secured a long-term independent future, especially when opportunities for British overseas banks narrowed in the age of nationalism after the Second World War. In this sense its passage into the Hongkong Bank group was well timed and well chosen on both sides, as the new owners were attuned to similar markets and traditions. In this setting the Mercantile was able to expand its business and make a positive contribution to the larger whole. That contribution and its distinctive culture is part of the inheritance of the modern HSBC Group and of the wider community of international banking. As Ian Macdonald, one of its most experienced bankers, recalled, 'It was a good little bank: I enjoyed it'.[16] It is an image and attitude which recurs throughout the records of the bank and in the recollections of those who worked for the Mercantile or shared its long and diverse experience.

Appendices

APPENDIX ONE

Mercantile Bank: capital, reserves and total assets, 1893–1983

Date	Nominal capital £	Paid-up capital £	Published reserves £	Inner reserves £[a]	Total assets £
1893	1 500 000	554 908	nil	nil	3 128 343
1894	1 500 000	555 938	nil	nil	2 576 359
1895	1 500 000	557 313	nil	nil	2 911 383
1896	1 500 000	562 500	10 000	nil	2 808 187
1897	1 500 000	562 500	10 000	22 363	3 084 384
1898	1 500 000	562 500	20 000	23 046	3 094 443
1899	1 500 000	562 500	30 000	23 226	3 621 689
1900	1 500 000	562 500	40 000	44 675	3 515 932
1901	1 500 000	562 500	50 000	54 928	3 780 192
1902	1 500 000	562 500	60 000	48 115	3 449 292
1903	1 500 000	562 500	80 000	59 961	4 122 922
1904	1 500 000	562 500	110 000	76 500	4 386 010
1905	1 500 000	562 500	135 000	87 745	4 486 098
1906	1 500 000	562 500	170 000	113 051	5 903 142
1907	1 500 000	562 500	210 000	146 311	6 156 773
1908	1 500 000	562 500	250 000	138 289	5 535 657
1909	1 500 000	562 500	285 000	140 822	6 498 106
1910	1 500 000	562 500	325 000	132 350	7 587 400
1911	1 500 000	562 500	365 000	142 560	7 928 013
1912	1 500 000	562 500	415 000	162 046	8 368 315
1913	1 500 000	562 500	465 000	188 032	8 187 487
1914	1 500 000	562 500	500 000	243 718	7 901 553
1915	1 500 000	562 500	550 000	214 004	9 023 778
1916	1 500 000	562 500	600 000	213 976	11 265 674
1917	1 500 000	562 500	650 000	233 963	12 807 941
1918	1 500 000	562 500	700 000	267 969	15 302 126
1919	1 500 000	750 000	750 000	462 963	22 450 927
1920	3 000 000	1 050 000	1 100 000	868 963	20 157 778
1921	3 000 000	1 050 000	1 150 000	868 963	16 429 435
1922	3 000 000	1 050 000	1 200 000	719 054	16 643 701
1923	3 000 000	1 050 000	1 250 000	632 912	16 599 678
1924	3 000 000	1 050 000	1 300 000	565 373	16 460 755
1925	3 000 000	1 050 000	1 350 000	552 470	18 418 528
1926	3 000 000	1 050 000	1 385 000	506 022	18 800 720
1927	3 000 000	1 050 000	1 420 000	540 778	18 387 226
1928	3 000 000	1 050 000	1 450 000	758 372	18 989 409
1929	3 000 000	1 050 000	1 480 000	771 108	17 857 416
1930	3 000 000	1 050 000	1 500 000	763 154	17 643 624
1931	3 000 000	1 050 000	1 050 000	283 905	14 668 281
1932	3 000 000	1 050 000	1 075 000	623 592	16 211 689

Mercantile Bank: capital, reserves and total assets, 1893–1983
continued

Date	Nominal capital £	Paid-up capital £	Published reserves £	Inner reserves £[a]	Total assets £
1933	3 000 000	1 050 000	1 075 000	620 215	15 291 862
1934	3 000 000	1 050 000	1 075 000	774 568	16 730 419
1935	3 000 000	1 050 000	1 075 000	870 818	17 160 163
1936	3 000 000	1 050 000	1 075 000	983 964	18 468 464
1937	3 000 000	1 050 000	1 075 000	944 855	19 673 948
1938	3 000 000	1 050 000	1 075 000	1 080 518	18 400 660
1939	3 000 000	1 050 000	1 075 000	1 281 188	22 025 002
1940	3 000 000	1 050 000	1 075 000	1 351 559	24 923 500
1941	3 000 000	1 050 000	1 075 000	1 142 199	28 632 069
1942	3 000 000	1 050 000	1 075 000	1 227 778	28 318 370
1943	3 000 000	1 050 000	1 075 000	1 451 965	30 298 482
1944	3 000 000	1 050 000	1 075 000	1 549 671	33 150 254
1945	3 000 000	1 050 000	1 075 000	1 666 514	36 701 950
1946	3 000 000	1 050 000	1 075 000	1 813 004	44 016 133
1947	3 000 000	1 050 000	1 075 000	2 226 747	45 073 759
1948	3 000 000	1 050 000	1 200 000	2 302 914	49 550 860
1949	3 000 000	1 050 000	1 200 000	2 479 658	54 093 343
1950	3 000 000	1 050 000	1 350 000	2 973 853	67 041 587
1951	3 000 000	1 050 000	1 500 000	3 239 351	74 153 595
1952	3 000 000	1 050 000	1 500 000	3 677 237	73 654 579
1953	3 000 000	1 050 000	1 500 000	4 365 152	63 634 427
1954	3 000 000	1 470 000	1 750 000	4 257 803	68 594 152
1955	3 000 000	1 470 000	1 750 000	3 992 653	72 065 153
1956	3 000 000	1 470 000	2 000 000	4 458 872	74 897 385
1957	4 000 000	2 940 000	2 100 000	3 204 849	76 273 108
1958	4 000 000	2 940 000	2 200 000	3 983 332	71 027 431
1959	4 000 000	2 940 000	2 200 000	4 071 583	71 083 661
1960	4 000 000	2 940 000	2 200 000	4 237 041	72 555 791
1961	4 000 000	2 940 000	2 200 000	5 362 489	87 024 796
1962	4 000 000	2 940 000	2 200 000	5 474 073	109 139 509
1963	4 000 000	2 940 000	2 200 000	5 746 362	107 896 155
1964	4 000 000	2 940 000	2 200 000	5 311 803	118 232 565
1965	4 000 000	2 940 000	2 200 000	5 392 494	109 614 142
1966	4 000 000	2 940 000	2 200 000	5 209 803	97 799 873
1967	4 000 000	2 940 000	2 200 000	6 264 723	112 985 277
1968	4 000 000	2 940 000	2 200 000	6 479 407	126 480 382
1969	4 000 000	2 940 000	2 250 000	8 023 847	127 240 748
1970	4 000 000	2 940 000	2 400 000	8 659 468	140 844 256
1971	4 000 000	2 940 000	3 000 000	8 823 744	150 167 321
1972	4 000 000	2 940 000	5 750 000	7 417 521	190 846 432
1973	4 000 000	2 940 000	6 100 000	9 915 926	194 563 236
1974	4 000 000	2 940 000	6 400 000	10 941 079	154 381 087
1975	4 000 000	2 940 000	6 500 000	6 999 447	152 063 502
1976	4 000 000	2 940 000	6 600 000	7 470 894	197 708 239

Mercantile Bank: capital, reserves and total assets, 1893–1983
concluded

Date	Nominal capital £	Paid-up capital £	Published reserves £	Inner reserves £[a]	Total assets £
1977	4 000 000	2 940 000	6 700 000		248 290 000
1978	4 000 000	2 940 000	6 800 000		291 990 000
1979	4 000 000	2 940 000	6 900 000		273 038 000
1980	4 000 000	2 940 000	6 900 000		249 090 000
1981	4 000 000	2 940 000	6 900 000		308 213 000
1982	3 050 515	1 990 515	6 900 000		322 382 000
1983	3 050 515	1 990 515	6 900 000		52 160 000

Note: [a] Inner reserves comprise contingency funds, surplus provision for taxation, investment suspense accounts, unquoted investment reserves, and bank property reserves. These separate reserves were transferred to the Hongkong Bank in 1976.

Sources: MBH 2369–70, statements of general balances, 1879–1957; MBH 2374, contingent account ledger, 1893–1934; MBH 2397, 'Data supplied to the board', 1947–65; MBH 2402, papers re alteration of capital, 1938–53.

APPENDIX TWO

Mercantile Bank: profits and dividends, 1893–1983

| Date | Published net profits £ | Real net profits £[a] | Dividends per cent by share type | | | |
			A	B	C	New
1893	21 713	21 713	5	nil		
1894	16 880	16 880	5	nil		
1895	16 263	16 263	5	2		
1896	23 141	23 141	5	3		
1897	21 110	25 110	5	3		
1898	31 129	33 129	5	3		
1899	31 166	36 166	5	3		
1900	35 843	45 843	5	4		
1901	36 423	43 423	5	4		
1902	35 008	35 008	5	4		
1903	46 434	58 434	5	5		
1904	60 675	77 175	5	5		
1905	59 461	70 461	5	5		
1906	71 364	93 364	5	5		
1907	80 300	107 800	6	6		
1908	76 528	76 528	6	6		
1909	71 401	71 401	6	6		
1910	82 867	93 217	7	7		
1911	84 993	94 493	7	7		
1912	98 965	118 465	8	8		
1913	111 499	137 499	8	8		
1914	101 620	157 320	8	8		
1915	100 328	122 328	10	10		
1916	133 375	167 375	12	12		
1917	176 005	196 005	14	14		
1918	181 112	181 112	14	14		
1919	215 636	410 636	16	16		
1920	260 208	666 208	16	16	8	
1921	263 033	313 033	16	16	16	
1922	267 434	353 434	16	16	16	
1923	258 707	258 707	16	16	16	
1924	243 410	235 410	16	16	16	
1925	257 663	237 663	16	16	16	
1926	250 782	190 782	16	16	16	
1927	257 180	257 180	16	16	16	
1928	250 201	255 201	16	16	16	
1929	257 459	267 459	16	16	16	
1930	213 340	144 340	16	16	16	
1931	152 081	38 581	12	12	12	
1932	179 808	179 808	12	12	12	
1933	161 697	178 697	12	12	12	
1934	173 398	180 398	12	12	12	
1935	174 266	184 266	12	12	12	
1936	181 732	215 732	12	12	12	

Mercantile Bank: profits and dividends, 1893–1983 continued

Date	Published net profits £	Real net profits £[a]	Dividends per cent by share type			
			A	B	C	New
1937	183 497	195 497	12	12	12	
1938	192 443	267 443	12	12	12	
1939	195 869	307 532	12	12	12	
1940	196 106	200 606	12	12	12	
1941	173 023	275 403	9	9	9	
1942	131 916	149 006	6	6	6	
1943	133 239	198 739	6	6	6	
1944	133 581	217 581	6	6	6	
1945	132 991	194 991	6	6	6	
1946	180 837	254 837	8	8	8	
1947	183 152	296 152	10	10	10	
1948	189 238	255 238	12	12	12	
1949	191 805	413 805	12	12	12	
1950	193 542	585 542	12	12	12	
1951	195 361	878 361	12	12	12	
1952	195 188	648 688	14	14	14	
1953	194 687	537 687	14	14	14	
1954	194 324	510 824	14	14	14	
1955	235 423	704 423	14	14	14	
1956	236 484	777 484	14	14	14	
1957	331 243	685 699				12.5
1958	324 267	561 267				12.5
1959	300 566	429 566				12.5
1960	326 103	612 103				12.5
1961	340 659	780 659				12.5
1962	325 685	461 685				12.5
1963	301 008	403 008				12.5
1964	260 087	376 431				12.5
1965	251 394	335 394				12.5
1966	405 416					12.5
1967	369 905					12.5
1968	381 823					12.5
1969	505 128					15
1970	600 806					15
1971	714 772					17
1972	825 330					20
1973	1 055 654					24
1974	1 088 411					30
1975	1 098 438					33
1976	1 294 840					40
1977	1 376 000					43
1978	1 348 000					43
1979	1 035 000					32
1980	1 408 000					44
1981	1 697 000					57

Mercantile Bank: profits and dividends, 1893–1983 concluded

Date	Published net profits £	Real net profits £[a]	Dividends per cent by share type			
			A	B	C	New
1982	1 974 000					99
1983	855 000					42

Note: [a] Real profits comprise published profits plus undisclosed transfers to inner reserves or special reserves, including contingency accounts, investment suspense accounts and property reserves. The bank's tax position was assessed on real profits rather than published profits. Comparable figures are not available after 1965.

Sources: MBH 573A, annual reports, 1893–1983; MBH 2374, contingent account ledger, 1893–1934; MBH 2377, abstracts of profit and loss accounts, 1893–1965.

APPENDIX THREE

Mercantile Bank: composition of earnings, 1893–1959

The pattern of earnings is a neglected area of banking history. Studies of major commercial banks and international banks rarely throw light on changes in the source of a bank's business. Yet these are changes which can decisively influence the growth and profitability of a business and changes in the composition of earnings are also a measure of the relative success of a bank in its chosen sectors of service.

Table A.3 and Figure A.3 show fluctuations in the principal sources of the Mercantile Bank's earnings – exchange, interest, commission and discount. *Exchange* earnings were the original *raison d'être* of the Chartered Mercantile Bank in the nineteenth century. These earnings were derived from the currency exchange profit on the finance of foreign trade. The types of finance which earned this exchange profit included buying and selling bills of exchange, bankers' drafts and rupee securities; telegraphic remittances of funds in sterling and other currencies; and foreign exchange and bullion transactions in local currencies. *Interest* earnings came from the bank's loans and overdrafts to current account customers. Much of this income came from lending to producers (such as tea and cotton estates and rubber plantations) which also used the bank for the finance of their exports. Customers for loans and overdrafts also included importers bringing or trans-shipping manufactures to Eastern ports. *Commission* income, mainly in the form of bank charges for routine payment services, was also derived from these current account customers. *Discount* income, in contrast, was earned primarily from inter-bank trading in bills, in which the bank's London office, operating in the City money market, was the key component.

Exchange earnings, a highly volatile form of income, had dominated the performance of the old Chartered Mercantile Bank in its first two decades (see above, Figure 1.1, page 16). The fall of silver values from the mid-1870s changed that pattern. As exchange income fell away (and even vanished in 1881, 1886 and 1888), the Mercantile was able to replace some of these earnings by the steady expansion of its interest and discount business. This trend was maintained in the longer term after the reconstruction of the bank in 1893. After an initial period in the 1890s when exchange earnings revived as the largest category of income, from 1899–1900 onwards income from interest moved ahead decisively. Thereafter exchange only provided the largest share of income in the exceptional years between 1917 and 1920, when the appreciation of silver and the post-war boom provided huge opportunities for exchange profits. Exchange business continued to be an essential and characteristic element in the bank's operations for the remainder of its history. As Figure A.3 shows, however, it was a volatile source of income, peaking only during unusual opportunities such as the Shanghai market before the Second World War and the Far Eastern markets during the Korean war.

Discount business, which in the nineteenth century had provided income to counterbalance fluctuations in exchange business, fell in importance to the bank as exchange lost its primacy as the main source of earnings. After a brief surge in the post-First World War period, discount became a negligible part of the bank's income after 1922. Interest and commission, however, increased their contribution to the bank's performance after the First World War. Interest income, especially, provided a platform for the bank's relatively strong showing in the 1920s and 1930s and for the robust growth of published and real earnings in the late 1940s and 1950s.

By the latter period the Mercantile's loans and overdrafts were its foremost service in the finance of trade. The change in emphasis reflected shifts in demand from its customers (particularly their growing preference for longer-term, non-specific credit) but it also reflected the expansion of the bank's own branch system since the 1920s. The larger branch network increased the relative importance of the bank's current account operations *vis-à-vis* trade finance. The surviving figures do not show comparable figures for the period after 1959 but the trend towards greater use of lending, with exchange operations in a subsidiary role, certainly continued into the 1960s and 1970s. The transformation was a necessary part of the Mercantile's journey from the traditions of Eastern exchange banking to the broader discipline of modern international banking.

Table A.3   Mercantile Bank: composition of earnings, 1893–1959

Date	Exchange	Interest	Discount	Commission
1893	50 310	31 386	22 054	2 978
1894	67 797	27 756	25 269	3 229
1895	42 464	21 864	25 507	3 178
1896	64 791	21 121	13 937	3 667
1897	56 756	21 390	3 409	3 710
1898	61 813	35 158	3 258	3 589
1899	41 059	48 675	4 720	3 734
1900	27 200	70 471	4 943	4 118
1901	16 760	87 807	5 270	4 509
1902	33 127	67 709	5 039	5 350
1903	51 552	62 867	8 879	3 952
1904	74 906	75 685	7 118	5 053
1905	60 122	85 336	6 583	6 389
1906	56 943	113 140	6 448	6 884
1907	51 000	141 133	7 442	8 220
1908	60 152	129 759	7 552	9 283
1909	48 654	104 213	7 413	11 058
1910	71 586	122 813	8 268	12 755
1911	80 095	124 896	7 991	11 577
1912	72 196	158 317	9 173	12 571
1913	39 806	227 610	13 674	14 641
1914	100 267	192 900	10 208	15 545
1915	141 900	144 475	5 373	14 290
1916	179 935	208 713	14 138	19 879
1917	337 002	229 178	25 642	20 387
1918	250 958	249 263	41 141	20 258
1919	495 554	276 157	54 619	29 920
1920	791 818	682 626	106 267	75 002
1921	348 317	461 306	56 675	77 588
1922	265 373	399 374	56 944	44 205
1923	154 026	358 678	23 323	34 107

Table A.3 Mercantile Bank: composition of earnings, 1893–1959
concluded

Date	Exchange	Interest	Discount	Commission
1924	142 587	360 175	15 318	32 660
1925	123 162	390 001	16 187	39 742
1926	148 329	420 053	10 927	39 814
1927	122 979	492 658	11 572	41 392
1928	100 365	507 285	15 114	40 990
1929	126 760	548 753	9 739	50 234
1930	201 564	453 757	17 232	40 916
1931	84 174	426 269	5 663	34 012
1932	178 715	345 758	3 088	33 353
1933	112 503	373 470	2 715	43 399
1934	93 156	421 711	2 544	41 536
1935	110 112	419 671	1 935	44 850
1936	116 269	424 594	1 554	43 629
1937	115 578	464 487	1 268	49 922
1938	189 868	457 968	1 265	49 995
1939	343 321	457 558	1 298	49 238
1940	458 046	474 158	1 644	50 236
1941	338 188	442 944	819	52 057
1942	158 412	432 251	455	37 228
1943	178 632	493 219	153	40 603
1944	169 871	524 128	235	46 889
1945	169 580	592 064	423	59 492
1946	571 445	933 024	355	172 959
1947	507 434	894 989	884	191 283
1948	324 936	1 086 788	3 966	235 491
1949	814 277	1 169 142	10 028	268 635
1950	1 001 335	1 296 269	5 957	439 958
1951	1 452 702	1 525 391	5 593	525 403
1952	1 197 843	1 745 563	10 791	435 486
1953	1 098 242	1 377 918	12 972	326 782
1954	950 606	1 414 234	12 737	311 188
1955	1 138 183	1 703 988	15 771	334 417
1956	1 195 006	1 835 069	17 913	342 808
1957	1 222 527	1 895 560	19 814	351 236
1958	1 116 226	1 830 947	10 224	300 957
1959	1 077 737	1 838 124	16 659	348 044
TOTAL	21 644 909	35 451 714	863 089	6 038 460

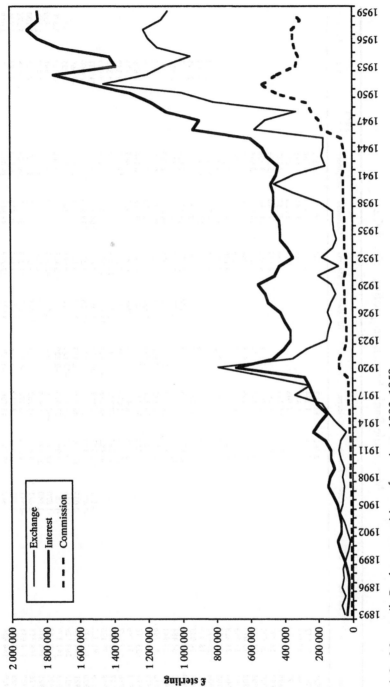

A.3 Mercantile Bank: composition of earnings, 1893–1959

APPENDIX FOUR

Mercantile Bank: branch net profits, 1894–1972

Date	London	West End	City	New York	Bombay	Calcutta	Karachi	Rangoon	Madras	Colombo	Singapore	Kuala Lumpur	Penang	Bangkok
1894	-2 762				-2 462	12 962			10 341	-2 250	16 251			
1895	15 952				-7 551	1 244			2 834	440	5 738			
1896	13 684				259	5 676			4 859	5 654	4 015			
1897	30				5 384	13 508			-1 745	5 503	246			
1898	2 788				7 364	11 238			934	8 257	2 727			
1899	18 797				-2 052	7 210			4 119	7 740	5 554			
1900	20 401				-814	6 006	-1 374		4 352	11 180	8 808			
1901	22 203				4 259	14 471	24		2 287	10 071	-3 694			
1902	15 079				3 145	-1 058	448		3 084	10 138	9 924			
1903	13 769				3 610	6 582	1 339		3 058	10 046	23 814			
1904	21 228				9 049	4 337	2 343		4 140	15 560	23 177			
1905	24 907				8 860	25 395	3 026		2 647	15 693	19 760		-42	
1906	35 412				7 688	25 376	281		-3 151	19 886	23 358		2 355	
1907	46 009				8 566	35 872	1 866		1 976	25 359	14 889		1 204	
1908	24 055				14 099	35 392	3 130		2 904	25 840	-22 077		2 015	
1909	32 912				10 871	13 195	3 459	-178	2 651	27 999	5 804		7	
1910	34 484				11 905	18 277	2 542	-757	1 962	44 836	9 347		425	
1911	30 941				11 465	28 583	2 676	1 120	2 085	44 811	-2 063		545	
1912	47 786				8 553	29 185	4 606	2 705	560	39 647	15 948		862	
1913	66 748				11 722	33 389	5 839	5 557	1 741	42 520	1 382		-786	
1914	53 616				12 360	38 507	7 551	7 842	4 745	49 742	6 176		6 679	
1915	51 796				6 165	16 419	3 734	6 989	4 909	39 900	21 445		5 934	
1916	7 727				19 096	51 074	3 818	6 294	10 107	46 146	18 107		3 359	
1917	90 609				57 865	87 392	14 690	15 824	18 878	69 462	-507		4 379	
1918	78 125				40 482	86 218	-15 113	18 198	-3 748	20 545	22 159		9 039	
1919	81 323			-501	162 342	311 803	54 089	31 704	13 876	-108 194	61 366		11 331	
1920	163 932			-2 471	2 479	115 546	1 173	10 355	33 253	219 885	101 325		16 060	
1921	264 170			-2 059	87 134	48 570	2 993	-12 192	3 157	7 861	16 400		-3 966	
1922	269 526			-1 846	-9 700	-3 084	-13 121	6 068	9 085	-2 563	-10 923		-7 905	-730
1923	141 359			-1 787	2 094	-22 083	-2 920	7 350	3 153	-5 394	5 666		-2 317	2 670
1924	148 409			-1 870	19 679	-62 866	-4 070	2 456	-2 651	20 010	24 144		-961	450
1925	148 316			-2 240	20 495	18 935	-4 505	540	2 016	20 482	48 769		2 458	2 331
1926	164 358			-2 421	7 804	-5 752	-5 161	-21 465	6 643	20 315	59 107		8 131	2 100
1927	171 655			-2 541	6 293	3 570	-4 928	1 157	11 088	36 221	36 639		2 618	5 673
1928	173 986			-2 571	-576	14 811	-3 368	2 603	2 163	30 625	36 003		4 058	2 704
1929	184 624			-2 602	-19 761	15 590	-4 479	3 821	-27 259	48 565	36 001		11 117	2 019

Year														
1930	172 438			-2 796	-6 359	8 153	-2 760	2 245	1 339	2 802	-41 418	2 673	-20 789	1 660
1931	155 356			-3 235	-6 197	-10 681	-5 360	1 053	-2 672	6 743	-12 390	403	-8 574	-50 891
1932	149 216			-3 055	12 532	14 552	-765	1 930	2 113	11 618	-5 900	3 128	-6 931	37 197
1933	145 600			-2 742	8 566	16 234	6	1 513	4 361	14 729	4 480	3 079	-6 178	-610
1934	139 994			-2 936	8 043	13 859	-841	-46	1 929	18 031	14 880	2 010	-1 081	78
1935	116 978			-3 053	43 033	15 721	1 175	2 875	1 089	-11 818	11 949	3 557	2 424	3 288
1936	112 909			-2 910	32 914	24 981	952	4 786	1 905	-6 378	30 448	5 171	2 628	2 734
1937	113 846			-3 231	56 108	27 511	3 852	10 192	2 294	-8 971	45 220	11 410	10 746	5 360
1938	112 237			-3 066	48 227	31 710	2 362	7 560	4 228	-4 735	19 800	6 811	6 254	1 238
1939	91 309			-3 513	52 522	41 221	1 418	7 256	5 144	-6 036	46 910	5 804	4 950	4 517
1940	67 496			-3 855	52 274	29 725	861	5 193	3 080	-4 564	60 534	10 152	4 833	3 268
1941	57 699			-5 676	66 939	34 595	494	12 556	4 057	-4 683	38 468	7 258	6 892	4 650
1942	86 955			-6 356	50 456	19 342	583	-2 380	-1 426	18 118	0	0	0	0
1943	105 364			-6 988	56 376	62 144	-1 679	-3 222	3 530	16 626	0	0	0	0
1944	87 486			-5 584	47 973	29 794	534	-2 088	600	12 875	0	0	0	0
1945	101 973			-5 625	56 539	33 679	366	-5 580	4 411	14 079	-16 220	-8 606	-8 606	0
1946	191 879			-6 827	134 219	73 387	11 571	1 295	6 648	18 124	123 114	42 829	43 877	-5 354
1947	135 167			-6 553	55 231	64 157	9 040	-9 136	9 677	38 946	43 292	3 670	13 014	-6 400
1948	102 462			-8 987	77 798	64 448	35 623	3 801	9 807	32 945	80 662	16 470	44 234	10 117
1949	101 629			-12 472	87 288	71 601	39 559	-444	21 277	46 586	72 554	21 154	36 786	32 687
1950	72 073			-14 468	42 039	28 307	84 887	13 396	9 815	49 047	184 833	42 506	45 454	44 011
1951	142 268			-12 426	79 227	86 494	44 049	10 767	21 624	74 457	304 208	57 176	81 531	62 050
1952	182 122			-12 948	61 840	63 657	-2 766	20 047	8 890	44 187	280 585	61 984	62 443	103 211
1953	192 339			-13 544	32 049	47 804	57 053	24 296	10 926	35 821	120 730	55 007	28 095	70 973
1954	164 012			-13 012	61 175	35 908	29 014	20 707	8 753	36 378	74 693	37 723	11 770	49 134
1955	279 198			-14 117	63 517	50 869	38 999	17 296	12 027	44 085	188 996	89 880	31 693	41 840
1956	249 542	-15 523		-14 712	61 386	42 999	30 922	14 401	16 920	36 424	242 121	101 200	32 364	31 861
1957	241 834	-15 116		-13 198	56 225	80 285	36 108	16 138	17 654	50 283	203 341	113 855	36 153	21 210
1958	250 793	-15 922		-13 697	-330	40 881	33 543	2 800	-551	41 956	145 472	101 694	13 543	10 624
1959	381 944	-15 272		-12 902	34 667	25 593	36 066	8 652	8 749	56 777	70 694	66 045	20 737	3 823
1960	246 857	-12 879		-15 226	79 188	71 966	72 524	13 068	12 858	67 660	110 165	77 704	39 901	-41 630
1961	259 039	-7 124		-16 610	229 155	44 778	54 692	9 843	8 079	100 023	134 295	77 099	32 942	32 965
1962	252 222	-8 563		-9 143	56 848	54 532	17 988	15 439	12 051	112 804	115 953	76 537	36 034	10 810
1963	138 653	-6 453	16 053		84 785	54 131	49 193		11 773	38 576	67 375	29 353	9 797	11 540
1964	135 159	-1 586	-2 037		107 060	56 146	41 230		6 413	23 054	140 610	53 706	-2 758	17 049
1965	162 653	4 394	16 933		177 812	40 902	-11 073		-33 642	0	71 597	63 201	-42 177	25 064
1966	336 777		-67 427		-34 900	44 711	18 770		45 009	35 401	114 599	62 475	-32 437	37 988
1967	485 884		19 425		40 582	41 710	20 785		-3 673	46 935	112 501	39 681	30 369	33 189
1968	495 985		99 561		30 159	79 519			-10 673	25 062	75 316	114 804	-1 584	-6 579
1969	608 113		224 042		80 813	61 090			-7 278	58 552	188 144	274 177	176	71 422
1970	650 685		177 418		187 974	103 957			-44 866	92 112	102 143	237 987	38 900	-5 914
1971	585 735		301 168		142 902	122 166			-24 450	36 000	159 489	252 410	17 110	10 911
1972	851 643		-20 534		110 494	98 914			-22 880	41 904	41 690	234 240	-294	-15 492
Total	12 391 477	-94 044	764 602	-298 372	3 247 320	3 084 942	981 115	322 200	287 972	2 235 073	4 410 718	2 457 417	701 025	680 816

Mercantile Bank: branch net profits, 1894–1972 concluded

Date	Batavia	Surabaya	Hong Kong	Shanghai	Mauritius	Chittagong	Tokyo	Osaka	Khulna	Ipoh	Nagoya	New Delhi	Dacca	Total
1894			2 929	-8 472										26 337
1895			1 250	-5 729										14 178
1896			-1 696	-1 933										30 518
1897			-553	-528										21 845
1898			3 753	-469										36 592
1899			-40	-549										40 779
1900			2 914	-750										50 723
1901			-129	-645										48 847
1902			-6 520	-561										33 679
1903			1 175	-766										62 627
1904			3 136	-787										103 241
1905			2 855	-749										81 294
1906			52	-450										110 807
1907			-7 643	-297										127 801
1908			-1 244	-18										86 255
1909			-4 191	-616										89 754
1910			-9 210	-818										112 993
1911			-6 853	-893										112 417
1912			-9 508	-855										139 489
1913			-974	-648										166 490
1914			184	-490										186 912
1915			5 218	-2234										160 275
1916			8 110	11 504	32 500									217 842
1917			6 205	20 909	47 517									433 223
1918			-102	20 042	34 393									310 238
1919			44 259	89 194	8 078									760 670
1920			20 408	-41 302	91 443									732 086
1921			9 088	-154 108	87 561									354 609
1922			7 447	-64 180	44 995									223 069
1923	-5 031		9 446	-20 037	31 925									143 657
1924	-13 303	-437	4 039	-12 133	27 699									138 574
1925	-6 363	-10 458	11 411	-2 131	18 803									267 835
1926	-8 050	-11 482	6 051	2 731	-9 822									219 787
1927	-3 515	-4 782	6 246	5 390	15 564									287 140
1928	-1 122	-3 990	2 009	14 137	-6 214									265 623
1929	-81	-3 625	17 621	17 411	16 786									296 476
1930	-2 368	-2 897	32 821	9 009	19 664									173 294
1931	-45 846	-3 020	38 933	20 276	6 232									45 813
1932	-12 269	-37 337	14 450	3 128	4 742									206 630
1933	-29	-19 056	3 713	22 806	6 408									220 320
1934		-1 616	7 237	29 737	2 195									233 089
1935			13 526	11 075	6 850									218 669
1936			-1 153	22 362	16 178									247 727

Year													
1937		-2 236	-28 921	4 523									247 703
1938		1 671	63 989	2 182									300 468
1939		10 835	194 276	4 195									460 808
1940		14 529	218 862	8 484									480 872
1941		5 127	75 818	6 587									310 781
1942			0	3 484									168 776
1943			0	9 121									241 272
1944			0	9 585									181 175
1945		-4 111	-6 957	14 371									169 713
1946		63 288	129 242	13 952									841 244
1947		110 079	53 715	18 939									532 838
1948		153 147	44 520	28 925	-4 296		-3 800						691 676
1949		138 355	-15 547	32 594	4 537	-7 199	11 041						667 145
1950		197 201	2 796	32 252	31 022	-1 346	24 414						872 247
1951		288 821	-41 726	40 973	34 026	996	46 107						1 339 767
1952		174 848	-34 002	31 551	15 100	-1 726	31 057						1 151 945
1953		124 454	-37 707	41 948	8 992	-6 151	30 706	-7 833					756 490
1954		135 957	-15 302	42 668	12 376	700	15 815	1 735					753 134
1955		137 513	-4 002	36 818	16 681	2 201	18						1 039 342
1956		98 060	-1 694	52 605	12 293	-5 277	8 689	6 819	5 016				1 014 493
1957		164 121		61 668	11 615	-3 929	23 431	6 644	2 289	-10 257			1 105 425
1958		159 393		67 997	10 185	-11 770	17 737	5 087	-7 564	11 807			854 441
1959		140 529		57 702	15 663	-24 348	13 156	2 898	-2 229	10 053			876 164
1960		125 822		54 789	17 892	-4 982	18 374	8 122	6 229				923 751
1961		109 589		92 006	24 555	9 873	27 260	11 673	3 489				1 282 246
1962		94 484		75 018	22 372	30 629	57 630	5 097	564	8 518			1 092 360
1963		45 740		66 104	12 902	-21 528	72 097	2 589	-5 305	-9 550	-7 824		665 500
1964		89 600		52 772	18 898		122 879	-387	-19 459	-1 588	29 319		842 838
1965		116 140		61 977	7 256		58 618	-5 378	-70 577	-9 213	32 169		726 922
1966		162 700		39 225	-15 543		-20 797	3 202	-16 983	9 118	70 633	-27 043	787 938
1967		169 882		32 288	-2 778		-61 102	21 418	-71 041	19 719	55 117	-25 519	973 514
1968		243 748		15 625	-11 014			-3 506	-38 155	28 884	-17 169	-27 037	1 111 716
1969		296 479		8 447	-2 181			-634	-85 644	44 699	16 844	-13 565	1 844 481
1970		406 359		-524					-42 355	12 833	120 262		2 036 971
1971		366 863		64 666					-66 012	32 920	604 536		2 606 414
1972		422 536		73 982					-25 938	21 401	885 151		2 696 817
Total	-97 977	-98 700	573 923	1 762 996	240 553	-43 857	493 312	57 564	-433 675	169 344	1 789 038	-93 164	4 998 193

Note: This table shows annual branch net profits before head office deductions for transfers to and from: the profit and loss account; published and inner reserves; provisions and recoveries for bad debts; and other adjustments for the bank as a whole. Branch profit figures are provided for each year when a branch was open. When a branch temporarily closed (notably during the Second World War) or was not remitting profits, a zero figure is supplied.

Sources: MBH 2369–70, statements of general balances, 1879–1957; MBH 2377, abstracts of profit and loss accounts, 1893–1965; MBH 2434, head office quarterly papers, 1966–73; MBH 2437, private ledger, 1962–73.

APPENDIX FIVE

Mercantile Bank: chairmen and chief managers, 1893–1984

Chairman	Period of office
Sir Alexander Wilson	1893–1906
Sir Robert Black	1906–25
John Ryrie	1925–35
Lord Catto of Cairncatto	1935–38
Sir Charles Innes	1938–52
Sir Kenneth Mealing	1952–66
J. A. H. Saunders	1966–72
Ian Herridge	1972–73
G. M. Sayer	1973–77
M. G. R. Sandberg	1977–84

Chief manager	Period of office
James Campbell	1893–1913
Percy Mould	1913–23
James Steuart	1923–35
James Crichton	1935–47
Eric Paton	1947–50
Robert Drake	1950–58
Colin Wardle	1958–62
Charles Pow	1962–66
John Gregoire	1966–67
Ian Herridge	1967–73

APPENDIX SIX

The note issue of the Mercantile Bank, 1912–78

Throughout most of its history the Mercantile Bank issued and circulated its own bank notes in Hong Kong and Shanghai. Bank notes were an additional means of attracting funds to the bank and they were treated as one of its ordinary balance sheet liabilities. Although these liabilities were small in comparison with other liability funds such as current and deposit accounts, they served an important additional role as a form of advertisement and marketing. The circulation of the bank's notes was a visible reminder of the name and presence of the bank in the Far East.

The Mercantile's forerunner, the Chartered Mercantile Bank of India, London and China, had issued bank notes at many of its overseas branches. The right to issue bank notes was built into the Royal Charter granted to the bank in 1857.[1] At different intervals between 1858 and 1892 the bank's notes were printed in the United Kingdom and then issued and circulated at Colombo, Kandy and Galle; at Hong Kong, Shanghai, Hankow and Yokohama; and at Singapore, Penang and Malacca. These notes were issued in the local currencies in use at the branches, as for example the Chinese tael and Mexican dollar notes issued at Shanghai branch between 1881 and 1892.[2] The total value of notes in circulation was as high as £732 000 in 1883 and was still over £500 000 in the early 1890s.[3]

The printing, issue and circulation of the Chartered Mercantile Bank's notes ended when the bank was reconstructed in 1893, as the liquidation of the old company specified that the right to issue notes should be surrendered. The old bank's notes were sent to the Bank of England for confidential destruction and by 1898 the outstanding liability for Chartered Mercantile notes was reduced to only £2207.[4] Notes of the Chartered Mercantile were still being presented for payment (and were duly paid out) as late as 1954.[5]

The Mercantile Bank itself obtained permission to issue notes at its Hong Kong branch in 1911 and began to issue notes there in 1912. In return the bank was required to place securities to the equivalent value with the Hong Kong authorities in order to guarantee payment of the notes. The initial series of notes – denominated in HK$ 5, HK$ 10, and HK$ 100 – was printed by Waterlow and notes with a total value of over £107 000 were in circulation by 1915. From 1916 the Mercantile also issued notes at its Shanghai branch, also printed by Waterlow. The circulation of notes was much lower than the Hong Kong issue and the notes were withdrawn when the Shanghai business was being wound down in the late 1940s.

The issue of the Mercantile's notes, which carried the shortened name of Mercantile Bank Limited after 1957, was maintained after the acquisition of the bank by the Hongkong Bank in 1959. In 1966, however, following the transfer of the Mercantile's headquarters to Hong Kong, management responsibility for the note issue was transferred to the Hongkong Bank. Thereafter the note issue was limited to the HK$ 100 denomination, but the value of the amount in circulation was greatly increased to nearly £2 million by 1970 (see Table A.6). The issue of these notes continued until 1978, when the authorised limit of HK$ 30 million was cancelled and the issue limit of the Hongkong Bank was increased by the same amount.

By the 1970s the Mercantile's notes represented less than one per cent of currency in circulation in Hong Kong but they represented a note-issuing tradition which reached back for 120 years. The last Mercantile bank notes still bore the Chinese characters for Yau Lei Ngan Hong, or 'Profitable Bank', which had first appeared on the Chartered Mercantile Bank's notes in Shanghai in 1859.

Table A.6   The note issue of the Mercantile Bank of India, 1912–78
(Notes in circulation at five yearly intervals [£])

Date	Hong Kong	Shanghai	Total
1912	65 980		65 980
1915	107 377		107 377
1920	100 406	56 900	157 306
1925	181 628	19 343	200 971
1930	267 902	7 325	275 227
1935	157 690	2 722	160 412
1940	273 366	413	273 779
1945	228 435	404	228 839
1950	282 374		282 374
1955	259 138		259 138
1960	206 353		206 353
1965	286 139		286 139
1970	1 944 687		1 944 687
1975	2 813 130		2 813 130

APPENDIX SEVEN

The Bank of Mauritius, 1894–1916
'The Star and the Key of the Indian Ocean'[1]
by Rachel Huskinson

The Bank of Mauritius, founded in London in 1894, achieved prominence on the island as one of the main financiers of the sugar industry and banker to the British government in Mauritius. Despite its dependence on the fortunes of the sugar industry, the bank made steady but cautious progress. Ultimately its development was restricted primarily by its inability to find employment for surplus funds and in 1916, following shareholder pressure, the bank was purchased by the Mercantile Bank of India.

The island of Mauritius was dubbed 'the star and key of the Indian Ocean' by the British who colonized the island in the early nineteenth century. Situated in the south-west Indian Ocean off the east coast of Madagascar, Mauritius was an important station on the trading route which linked Europe, via the Cape of Good Hope, to India, South-East Asia and Australia. The island had been discovered by the Portuguese in 1500 and subsequently occupied by the Dutch and the French. When the British captured it from the French in 1810, they acquired one of the busiest trading centres in the southern hemisphere.

Mauritius developed a new significance under the British, who were quick to realize the economic potential of the island's main commodity: sugar. Sugar cane had been introduced to Mauritius by the Dutch in the seventeenth century and flourished as one of the few crops hardy enough to survive the island's cyclonic climate. The British began cultivation and production on a large scale and introduced Mauritian sugar to the London markets in 1825. By then sugar production had reached over 10 000 tons (compared to 3000 tons in 1801).[2] All sugar was exported to Britain until the 1860s when the availability of cheaper European sugar beet forced Mauritius to turn to the Indian markets. This shift was influenced by the opening of the Suez Canal in 1869, which pushed the island out of the European trading route into the orbit of India and the East. Mauritius's close relationship with India was further strengthened in 1877 when it adopted the rupee as its sole standard currency.

Banking did not become a permanent feature of the island's economy until the 1830s. There had been earlier attempts to establish banks, such as the Colonial Bank of Mauritius, Bourbon & Dependencies (1812–13) and a Bank of Mauritius (1813–25), but these ventures generated little confidence. The financial climate changed when Mauritian sugar became competitive on the London markets in 1825 and the island became an attractive investment for London trading firms. This influx of capital was, on the whole, welcomed by the sugar industry, particularly after the abolition of slavery in 1833, when planters replaced their workforce with indentured labour from India. But the British mercantile community did not always find its financial interests compatible with those of the planters, of whom a significant proportion were French in origin. In 1838 a group of merchants established the Mauritius Commercial Bank, apparently to counteract the pro-planter tendencies of the revived Bank of Mauritius (1832–48). Overseas banks, including the Chartered Mercantile Bank of India,[3] also opened offices on the island during the prosperous decades of the 1850s and 1860s, but struggled to build a profitable business. Of these, the Oriental Banking Corporation's branch, which had been opened in 1852, was the most successful. It survived the failure of the bank in 1884 to continue as a branch of the New Oriental Banking Corporation until this bank suspended payment in 1892, leaving the Mauritius Commercial Bank as the main bank in Mauritius.

The 1890s was a difficult decade for Mauritius. The failure of the New Oriental Banking Company, combined with a disastrous cyclone in 1892, brought hard times to both investors and planters. At the same time the sugar industry embarked on a programme of specialization and mechanization in a drive to make Mauritian sugar more competitive. The funding of this development put an increasing strain on the resources of the Mauritius Commercial Bank; it also provided the impetus for a new Bank of Mauritius.

The Bank of Mauritius was incorporated in London on 2 October 1894. Its head office at 10 George Yard, Lombard Street, opened on 19 November, followed on 10 December by the branch in Port Louis. It began business with an authorized capital of £200 000, of which £125 550 was subscribed in fully paid shares of £10 each. The bank's chairman and main instigator was Lord Stanmore, who had been governor of Mauritius from 1871 to 1874. Stanmore had begun his career as private secretary to his father Lord Aberdeen, who had been prime minister from 1852 to 1855.

The bank was governed by a board of directors in London and an advisory local board in Mauritius. Both boards represented the interests of London trading firms in Mauritius and, as such, established the character of the bank. In 1894 the London board consisted of George W. Davidson of Ireland, Fraser & Co., W. Graham Loyd of H. H. Vivian & Co. and Maurice Ulcoq of Chalmers, Guthrie & Co. This association with H. H. Vivian & Co. and Chalmers, Guthrie & Co. continued throughout the lifetime of the bank. The local board, from its establishment, similarly included partners from two of the leading trading firms on the island – Ireland, Fraser & Co. and Scott & Co. These two firms dominated the local board until 1908, when the London board recruited Pierre Adam from Adam & Co. At various periods during the bank's history the local board also included representatives of influential Mauritian families and plantation owners, for example, Sir Celicourt Antelme, who was a member of the executive council and 'one of the oldest and best known families in Mauritius'.[4] He was a member of the board from 1894 until his death in 1899. His son continued this association from 1901 to 1907.

Another element in the constitution of the Bank of Mauritius was its commitment 'to adopt and carry out' an agreement between the bank's London manager John Alexander Ferguson and the liquidator of the New Oriental Banking Corporation made on 13 March 1894. This allowed the new bank to step into the shoes of the former New Oriental Banking Corporation's branch in Mauritius, specifically by occupying the branch premises in 'La Place d'Armes', Port Louis. The bank also gained the experience of the branch staff: the former manager Alex Wemyss and accountant George Dickson resumed their positions in the new branch.[5] This experience was vital to the bank's successful launch and during the first shareholder meeting, held on 29 January 1895, the London board was able to report that the branch had already gained 230 current accounts amounting to Rs 1 million and had achieved 'considerable transactions in exchange and loans'. Lord Stanmore also informed the shareholders that the British government had chosen the Bank of Mauritius as its banker on the island and was to open an account in April. This association, which was formalized on 9 April 1895,[6] continued until 1916 when it was renewed by the Mercantile Bank of India.

The government account was an important credential for the Bank of Mauritius as it demonstrated confidence in the new bank. Certainly this association appealed to the British investor as insurance against Mauritius's poor reputation for banking. The majority of investors in the Bank of Mauritius were British: of the £125 550 capital fully paid in 1894, only £3036 had been raised in Mauritius.[7] By far the largest contributors were the trading firms represented on the London and local boards of directors and other mercantile connections such as the Mavrogordato family (associated with the London based firm P. P. Rodocanachi & Co.), whose shareholding was to have particular significance in 1916. However, the bank's share registers also demonstrate the bank's strong appeal to small investors, particularly in Mauritius. Local shareholders included storeowners, chemists and clerks as well as estate proprietors and merchants. The bank also found support in the French community: the share registers reveal a significant group of shareholders from Paris who had commercial and private interests in Mauritius.

Local confidence contributed to the bank's successful start. The balance sheet for 1895 reported net profits of £14 165 and total assets of £360 402. A year later, profits had risen to £16 298 and assets amounted to £420 000.[8] The bank, however, was cautious about its progress. At the 1895 general meeting, Stanmore explained that most of the £60 000 in cash 'kept at Mauritius and with bankers' was kept on the island because of its 'particularly isolated position'; in the event of emergency it would take two weeks to import rupees from Bombay. The bank was also concerned to build a strong reserve fund. A total of £5000 was assigned to the reserve fund in 1895, followed by £10 000 in 1896. These sums were set against a low dividend to shareholders, who received returns of 4 per cent in 1895 and 5 per cent in 1896. During the second annual general meeting, Stanmore informed the shareholders that such cautious measures were essential to the security 'of so young an Institution'. As the years passed, it became clear that these were not temporary measures. Large holdings of cash, large allocations to the reserve fund and low dividends became regular features of the bank's balance sheet.

The question of security preoccupied the directors throughout the bank's lifetime. Memories of the failure of previous banks on the island were brought home in 1898 when the bank faced its first crisis. A poor sugar crop, combined with rock-bottom prices, had resulted in the failure of some of the smaller firms on the island which involved heavy losses for the bank. Whilst reporting net profits of £4283 for the year, Stanmore acknowledged the 'prejudicial' effects of a depression in sugar to 'the whole community' and to 'this Bank, in common with most others engaged in business in the Island'. The fact that the bank's profits were hostage to the fortunes of the Mauritian sugar industry raised the issue of maintaining confidence in the bank's long-term progress. Stanmore continued his report to the shareholders with a reference to his presidency of the Anti-Bounty League, which included 'among its members the most influential firms and individuals interested in the sugar industry of the West Indies, Mauritius, India and Queensland'. The League, which Stanmore helped to set up in 1896, aimed to persuade the British government to repeal the bounties which encouraged trade in European sugar beet at the expense of colonial producers. It eventually achieved this in 1902 but the treaty, which came into effect on 1 September 1903, failed to bring long-term benefits to the Mauritian sugar industry. For the time being, however, Stanmore's leadership of the League demonstrated a personal commitment to the future of the sugar industry and to the success of the trading firms which had invested in the bank.

The bank's profits improved with the fortunes of the sugar industry in 1899, warranting a rise in dividend to 6 per cent. The island's prosperity, however, exposed new problems for the bank. A low demand for advances and the discounting of bills resulted in the dramatic increase of cash balances in London and Mauritius from £71 709 in December 1899 to £222 322 in December 1900. The bank's struggle to find profitable employment for its funds contributed to a slump in profits and, while the bank continued to pay a dividend of 6 per cent, nothing was transferred to the reserve fund in 1900 and 1901. The fickle nature of the economy provided relief in 1902 when sugar prices reached the 'lowest level on record'[9] and planters and merchants once again turned to the bank for financial support. From then on the bank made steady progress, achieving its highest profits yet in 1905.[10] The bank's inability to find employment for surplus funds, however, was a recurrent problem, which left the bank vulnerable when business was slow and exposed in times of crisis.

Crisis was never too far away. In 1907 drought, a poor crop and prices which were 'barely remunerative' reduced the colony to 'a critical state', causing the bank 'a few bad and doubtful debts': published net profits fell by over £7000 to £8237.[11] The bank, however, had taken care to transfer £3000 of the real profits to an inner reserve fund.[12] So severe was the depression on the island that the legislative council petitioned the government for a loan of £20 000. When this was refused the council asked for a Royal Commission to investigate the financial position of the island.

The appointment of the Royal Commission in 1908 encouraged speculation about the credibility of the Bank of Mauritius. The local press reported on the lack of capital for trade and agriculture and fuelled public opinion against the bank. As tensions inherent in Mauritian society simmered, the bank was challenged with accusations of 'La Banque Anglaise'. In real terms this lack of confidence in the Bank of Mauritius revealed itself in an alarming drop in advances and bills discounted between 1907 and 1909 which fell to an all-time low of £71 218.[13] Internally, the bank was weakened by the retirement of Leopold Antelme from the local board in 1907 'due to financial difficulties',[14] and the London board, during the annual general meeting held on 23 February 1909, came under the fire of shareholders who complained about the consistently low dividend.

The bank responded positively to this criticism. Pierre Adam of Adam & Co., 'a gentleman of position and popularity in Mauritius', was appointed to the local board in 1908 to 'bring the Bank much more into touch with the French element in the Colony with which he is closely connected'.[15] Further board changes early in 1910 optimized experience within the bank when Ferguson retired from his position as London manager and was appointed a London director, and F. P. Murray, who had been secretary since the bank's establishment, was also promoted to the London board in the new appointment of managing director. In March 1910 shareholder loyalty was boosted by a rise in dividend to 7 per cent (including a bonus of 1 per cent) and the announcement that in future smaller sums were to be transferred to the reserve fund. Confidence was also encouraged by the report of the Royal Commission which, while regretting that no large banking company with business throughout the East was represented on the island, reported favourably on the practices of the Bank of Mauritius.

The Bank of Mauritius successfully weathered the storm of 1907 to 1909. At the end of 1910 the bank was able to report record net profits of £18 818. The 'erratic price of sugar' had led to a significant rise in advances and a decrease of £13 000 in cash. The shareholders' patience was rewarded with a dividend of 8 per cent. Moreover, the bank appeared to have emerged from the crisis in a stronger position. In 1911 it coped with the failure of Hossen Cassim, a leading merchant on the island. Due to its cautious policy of 'not advancing too much in any one firm regardless of a firm's reputation',[16] the bank was spared heavy losses. Then, on 16 October 1911, the bank took the ambitious step of opening a branch at Mahé in the Seychelles. This was a risky venture, as Maurice Ulcoq, who had succeeded Stanmore as chairman in January 1912, acknowledged at the annual general meeting on 21 February: 'the Colony is small and the volume of business is restricted ... The Seychelles vanilla is of extraordinarily fine quality, though the crop of this always fickle commodity will probably be small this year, having been unusually large last year.'[17] Nevertheless the new branch represented a deliberate effort to find alternative sources of income for the bank.

Over the next few years the bank made steady progress, earning real profits of £17 429 in 1912 and £15 627 in 1913;[18] total assets rose from £578 982 to £599 298 and shareholders saw dividends rise to 10 per cent in 1913.[19] The bank's position was aided by a period of prosperity for the sugar industry which enjoyed an unusual equilibrium due to a serious shortage in European beet and to the installation of new machinery in the main mills. Improved production methods contributed to a crop of record size (275 000 tons) in 1914. The outbreak of war in August 1914 had immediate and favourable consequences for the sugar industry: prices almost doubled, London's traditional sources for beet sugar, Germany and Austria, were cut off and Britain feared a sugar famine. As a result the government decreed that it would purchase all exportable sugar produced in the colonies. The Bank of Mauritius acted as government agent in Mauritius and was responsible for securing 100 000 tons of sugar for shipment to Britain.[20] This role contributed to extraordinary results for the bank: real profits rose by over £19 000 to £35 077, of which £10 000 was transferred to inner reserves.[21] In addition current accounts, at £621 859, had more than doubled over the year.[22]

This sudden boom was over by the end of 1915 when the bank announced net profits of £17 153.[23] To the shareholders these sobering results raised questions about the long-term prospects of the bank. These concerns were exaggerated by the death in April 1915 of the managing director F. P. Murray, who had been the bank's figure-head since the death of Maurice Ulcoq in May 1912. Murray's death was closely followed by the closure of the branch in the Seychelles due to 'the very remote prospect of its ultimate success'.[24]

The Mercantile Bank of India first approached the London board with an offer of amalgamation in January 1916. This offer was briefly considered by the London directors during the board meeting held on 12 January, and was quickly rejected on the grounds that 'the proposed scheme is not such as the bank could recommend to shareholders'.[25] On 25 January the board reconsidered the offer on the request of Geroge M. Mavrogordato, a partner of P. P. Rodocanachi & Co. and a major shareholder in the bank. He had requested that the board present the offer to the shareholders as it was clear that the bank had progressed as far as it could. Eventually the interests of the bank's major investors, the London-based trading firms, carried the day. On 29 February, the bank's 'principal shareholders' agreed to accept the offer.[26] This resolution was passed by eleven shareholders, who included Patrick R. Chalmers, Charles S. Guthrie and Mavrogordato. The local directors were not consulted; in a letter to the local board, drafted on 25 February, the London board explained that 'the leading shareholders' were unanimously in favour of selling and 'the matter was thus, practically, out of our hands'.[27] The argument, which the London board presented to the local board and later to the shareholders at a meeting held on 18 April 1916, focused on the bank's limited prospects for the future. They argued that 'of late' there had 'been little expansion in the bank's business' and they feared that 'the high water mark in this respect' had been reached. They also invoked the report of the Royal Commission of 1909, which had 'deplored the fact that none of the large Indian Exchange Banks had a branch in the Colony', and pointed out the advantages to Mauritius if such a bank was represented on the island.[28]

In fact the Bank of Mauritius was experiencing the same pressures which had brought about the demise of single office banks in Britain during the late nineteenth and early twentieth centuries. This amalgamation movement in domestic banking was now influencing overseas banks as British clearing banks began to pursue opportunities for overseas banking.[29] In this context the Bank of Mauritius had little chance of survival. The inevitability of the takeover was commented on by David Bevan, who had been the bank's stockbroker since its establishment, as he closed the meeting of 18 April. The meeting, however, ended on a congratulatory note which was reminiscent of the failures of the branches previously opened on the island by overseas banks. Bevan concluded: 'I think we have made a very good sale of our property, but I can quite understand that the Mercantile Bank are equally pleased with their bargains because they are able to establish a branch in Mauritius as a going concern.' In due course the Mauritius branch was to prove a great asset to the Mercantile Bank and, in the modern period, to the HSBC Group.

References

Introduction

1. Muirhead, S. (1996), *Crisis Banking in the East: The History of the Chartered Mercantile Bank of India, London and China, 1853–93*, Aldershot: Scolar Press.
2. Green, E. and Kinsey, S. (1996), 'The archives of the HSBC Group', *Financial History Review*, 3, pp. 87–99.
3. King, F. H. H., Cook, C. and King, C. E. (1983), 'The Hongkong Bank Group's oral history projects', in King, F. H. H. (ed.), *Eastern Banking. Essays in the History of the Hongkong and Shanghai Banking Corporation*, London: Athlone Press, pp. 180–93.
4. King, F. H. H., (1987–91), *The History of the Hongkong and Shanghai Banking Corporation*, Cambridge: Cambridge University Press, 4 vols.
5. Jones, G. (1986–87), *The History of the British Bank of the Middle East*, Cambridge: Cambridge University Press, 2 vols.
6. Jones, G. (1993), *British Multinational Banking, 1830–1990*, Oxford: Clarendon Press.
7. Jones, G., 'Postscript', in Muirhead, p. 275.

Chapter One: Reprise, 1853–93

1. The source for this chapter is Muirhead unless otherwise stated.
2. Tomlinson, B. R. (1993), *The Economy of Modern India 1860–1970*, Cambridge: Cambridge University Press, pp. 52–55.
3. MBH 511, Letter book, 6 January 1892.
4. MBH 511, Letter book, 21 December 1892.

Chapter Two: Rehabilitation, 1893–1913

1. Muirhead: pp. 241–3.
2. Jardine Skinner MSS, Cambridge University Library, 6 May 1892, quoted in Chapman, S. D. (1998), 'British free-standing companies and investment groups in India and the Far East', in Wilkins, M. and Schroter, H. (eds), *The Free-Standing Company in the World Economy*, Oxford: Oxford University Press, p. 209.
3. Probyn, L. (1893), 'A gold standard for India', *Journal of the Institute of Bankers*, vol. 14, part 1, p. 6.
4. Giffen, R. (1893), *Essays on Finance*, p. 202.
5. MBH 515, Letter book of J. Campbell, 1 March 1894.
6. Muirhead: pp. 262–8.
7. Muirhead: p. 259.
8. Muirhead: p. 269.
9. MBH 511, Letter book, 3 December 1892.

10. Muirhead: pp. 269–70.
11. *Bankers' Magazine*, vol. 117, p. 876.
12. Muirhead: p. 255.
13. Muirhead: pp. 318–19.
14. Crick, W. F. and Wadsworth, J. E. (1936, 4th edn 1964), *A Hundred Years of Joint Stock Banking*, London: Hodder & Stoughton, pp. 308–24; Holmes, A. R. and Green, E. (1986), *Midland: 150 Years of Banking Business*, London: Batsford, p. 96.
15. MBH 509, Letter book, Chief Manager to Inspector, 19 May 1893.
16. MBH 2308.3, Minutes, 26 June 1894. By 1896 business in Shanghai warranted the opening of a sub-agency.
17. MBH 515, Letter book of J. Campbell, 27 April 1893.
18. MBH 1218, Lease of Threadneedle Street Premises, 1895.
19. MBH 515, Letter book of J. Campbell, 30 March 1893.
20. Ibid., 7 April 1893.
21. Ibid., 25 November 1896.
22. Ibid., 21 April 1893.
23. For details see King I, pp. 208–12.
24. MBH 509, Letter book, 1893.
25. MBH 511, Letter book, 20 October 1893.
26. MBH 510, Letter book of J. Campbell, 15 January 1896.
27. Collins, M. (1988), *Money and Banking in the UK: A History*, Beckenham, Kent: Croom Helm Ltd, pp. 78–81 and Jones, G. (1993), *British Multinational Banking 1830–1990*, Oxford: Clarendon Press, p. 80.
28. Muirhead: pp. 80–85.
29. Muirhead: pp. 206–7.
30. The following analysis is based upon confirmed credits recorded in the bank's board minute books, MBH 2308.3–5.
31. Hornby, O. (1985), 'The Danish shipping industry, 1866–1939', in Yui, T. and Nakagawa, K. (eds), *Business History of Shipping*, Tokyo: University of Tokyo Press, pp. 162–3.
32. Yui, T. (1985), 'Introduction', in Yui and Nakagawa, *Business History of Shipping*, pp. xvi–xvii; Jones, G. (1996), *The Evolution of International Business. An Introduction*, London: Routledge, p. 148.
33. MBH 511, Letter book, 7 December 1905.
34. MBH 2385, Property ledger, 1913.
35. *London and China Express*, 15 February 1914.

Chapter Three: Resurgence, 1913–23

1. MBH 1009, Private letter, 27 July 1914.
2. Ibid., 28 and 29 July 1914.
3. Ibid., 6 August 1914.
4. MBH 2413, General advice, 21 August 1914.
5. MBH 2413, General advice, 11 September 1914.
6. MBH 2413, General advice, 20 November 1914.
7. MBH 2414, General advice, 29 July 1915.
8. MBH 435, Inspector's report, 4 February 1918.
9. MBH 2308.6, Minutes, 21 December 1915.

10. Buchanan, D. H. (1934), *The Development of Capitalistic Enterprise in India*, New York, quoted in Tomlinson, B. R. (1993), *The Economy of Modern India, 1860–1970*, Cambridge: Cambridge University Press, p. 120.
11. MBH 2414, General Advice, 19 April 1917.
12. MBH 507, Inspectors' correspondence, 24 February and 3 March 1915.
13. Jones, G. (1993), *British Multinational Banking 1830–1990*, Oxford: Clarendon Press, pp. 157 and 396.
14. MBH 1009, Manager Calcutta to Mould, April 1914.
15. MBH 578, Minutes of an Extraordinary General Meeting, Bank of Mauritius, 18 February 1916.
16. Ibid.
17. MBH 1191, Bank of Mauritius file, February 1916.
18. Almaula, N. I. (1960), *Operations of the Reserve Bank of India (1935–1954)*, Bombay: Asia Publishing House, p. 10.
19. Jones, *Multinational Banking*, p. 480.
20. MBH 944, Auditors' correspondence, notes by Percy Mould, January 1918.
21. Jones, *Multinational Banking*, Appendix A5.2, pp. 475–6. Geoffrey Jones and Frances Bostock, in their calculations of NPV (net present value), show that between 1914 and 1920 an investment in the Mercantile would have outperformed all British overseas banks except the Anglo-Egyptian Bank and the Anglo-South American Bank.
22. The following analysis is based upon confirmed credits recorded in the bank's board minute books, MBH 2308.7.
23. Barty-King, H. (1977), *The Baltic Exchange: The History of a Unique Market*, London: Hutchinson, p. 104.
24. MBH 435, Inspector's report, February 1922.
25. See also Jones, *Multinational Banking*, pp. 49–50.
26. *Journal of the Institute of Bankers* (February 1920), 48; (May 1920), 173–4.
27. MBH 518, Special Private Letter, July 1917.
28. Auditors' correspondence, 16 February 1924.
29. MBH 442, Inspector's report, January 1915.

Chapter Four: Resilience, 1923–35

1. Sir Bertram Hornsby, whom the Bank of England installed as chairman of both banks to supervise their sale or liquidation, described the two companies as his 'dead dogs'. Jones, G. (1993), *British Multinational Banking 1830–1990*, Oxford: Clarendon Press, p. 231.
2. AGM, March 1929.
3. AGM, April 1925.
4. Bramsen, B. and Wain, K. (1979), *The Hambros, 1779–1979*, London: Michael Joseph, ch. 19.
5. Davenport-Hines, R. P. T. (1984), 'Thomas Sivewright Catto', in *Dictionary of Business Biography*, London: Butterworth, vol. 1, pp. 617–19.
6. Muirhead, pp. 72–3, 171–2, 337.
7. MBH 2352, Ryrie to J. O. Robinson, 14 November 1928; MBH 2381, Bad and doubtful debts committee minutes, 4 March 1941.

8. Winton, J. R. (1982), *Lloyds Bank, 1918–1969*, Oxford: Oxford University Press, p. 23.
9. Tyson, G. (1963), *100 Years of Banking in Asia and Africa*, London: National and Grindlays Bank, p. 199.
10. Winton, *Lloyds Bank*, pp. 22–3.
11. MBH 2352, Robert Horne to David Yule, 18 November 1927.
12. MBH 1190, FMS file, 9 April 1927.
13. MBH 1006, Patterson to Steuart, 9 March 1935.
14. MBH 1190, Steuart to Cromartie, 6 October 1927.
15. MBH 1190, Cromartie to Steuart, December 1927.
16. MBH 1190, Kennedy to Crichton, 11 February 1928 and 9 May 1929.
17. MBH 1190, Benson to Kennedy, 23 April 1929.
18. Muirhead, p. 228.
19. MBH 1188, Japan file, May–June 1927.
20. MBH 1189, China file, January–November 1929.
21. MBH 1187, India file, 19 June 1930.
22. MBH 1006, Cowan to Provis, 23 September 1935.
23. MBH 1006, Ferrier to Steuart, 21 January 1929.
24. MBH 945, Steuart to Dutch Colonial Department, 23 November 1932.
25. J. Shirreff, Oral history.
26. L. Blanks and W. Hobbin, Oral histories.
27. MBH 1002.8, Letter book, 14 August 1926.
28. Green, E. (1979), *Debtors to their Profession. A History of The Institute of Bankers, 1879–1979*, London: Methuen, pp. 134, 222–3.
29. MBH 1002.8, Letter book, 14 August 1926.
30. J. Shirreff, Oral history.
31. Enclosed in MBH 2353, 1930–31.
32. Ralli Brothers were also represented in Shanghai in this period. We are grateful to J. B. Stewart for this information.
33. The following analysis is based upon confirmed credits recorded in the bank's board minute books MBH 2308.8.
34. Tomlinson, B. R. (1993), *The Economy of Modern India, 1860–1970*, Cambridge: Cambridge University Press, pp. 121–2.
35. Rothermund, D. (1993), *An Economic History of India*, London: Routledge, p. 79.
36. Tomlinson, B.R., 'Britain and the Indian currency crisis, 1930–32', *Economic History Review*, new series, 32 (1979), pp. 88–99.
37. Ibid., p. 95.
38. MBH 1006, Kennedy to Steuart, 26 September 1931.
39. Tomlinson, *Economy of Modern India*, pp. 68–70.
40. Ibid., pp. 140–41.
41. MBH 2352, Edlundh to Crichton, 1 May 1931.
42. AGM, March 1932.
43. MBH 850, Staff file, 2 September 1931.
44. MBH 850, Bombay staff file, 27 January 1938.
45. MBH 2352, Anon Bombay to Eastern Exchange Banks Association, September 1930.
46. Figures taken from Reserve Bank of India (1954), *Banking and Monetary Statistics of India*, Bombay, pp. 8–9 and 282.
47. MBH 2349, Memorandum by C. Innes, 1934.

Chapter Five: Ready or not, 1935–47

1. Tyson, G. (1963), *100 Years of Banking in Asia and Africa*, London: National and Grindlays Bank, p. 178.
2. *Stock Exchange Official Yearbook* (1935), London: Thomas Skinner & Co.
3. Verbatim report of Annual General Meeting, *Times*, 24 March 1937.
4. L. Blanks, Oral history.
5. R. Thomas, Oral history.
6. MBH 548/1, Crichton to Cobbold, Bank of England, 15 July 1941; L. Blanks, Oral history.
7. The following analysis is based upon agreed limits for advances and overdrafts recorded in the bank's minutes, MBH 2308.11.
8. Hongkong Bank Archives, K7.2.10, Private letter, 22 March 1939.
9. MBH 950, General advice, 22 September 1939.
10. MBH 950, General advice, 30 August 1939.
11. Ibid., 6 September 1939.
12. Hongkong Bank Archives, K7.2.11, General advice, 5 July 1940.
13. L. Blanks, Oral history.
14. Quoted in King III, p. 425.
15. Fforde, J. (1992), *The Bank of England and Public Policy, 1941–1958*, Cambridge: Cambridge University Press, p. 226n.
16. MBH 548/1, Bolton to Paton, 5 December 1940.
17. Ibid., Paton to Bolton, 7 December 1940.
18. Ibid., Bolton to Paton, 30 October 1940; Fisher to Paton, 21 February 1942.
19. Ibid., Fisher to Buckley, 29 January 1942.
20. Ibid., Crichton to Fisher, 18 August 1942; Fisher to Crichton, 14 March 1946.
21. Hongkong Bank Archives, K7.2.10, Private letter, 22 March 1939.
22. MBH 548/1, Bank of England file, 22 October 1940.
23. R. Thomas, Oral history.
24. This paragraph draws on the oral histories of J. B. Stewart, R. Thomas and L. Blanks and statements of Mr Huxter and Mr Blanks, August 1942, MBH 1420.
25. The following paragraphs on the fate of the bank in Malaya are based on MBH 542, C. R. Wardle's diary; MBH 1002.6, report by S. Stocks; and various letters to Crichton in MBH 1002.6 and 1002.9.
26. I. MacFarlane, Oral history.
27. MBH 548/1, Crichton to Bolton, 21 March 1942. For other examples of inter-bank co-operation during the retreat from Burma and Malaya, see Tyson, *100 Years of Banking in Asia and Africa*, pp. 83–5.
28. MBH 1002.6, Report by S. Stocks, 5 June 1942.
29. MBH 548/1, Bank of England file, 22 July 1942.
30. MBH 2402, Capital file, 1938–53.
31. N. Paton-Smith, oral history.
32. Interview with Mr and Mrs J. B. Stewart, November 1997.
33. MBH 978, Indian assistants file, 19 March 1936.
34. Ibid.
35. Ibid.
36. Ibid.

37. Interview with Mr Sunil Singh Roy, August 1997.
38. MBH 978, Indian assistants file, 16 October 1943.
39. Ibid.
40. MBH 951, Special private letter to branches, 17 August 1945.
41. MBH 1003.5, Ross to Paton, 1 October 1945.
42. Interview with Mr and Mrs J. B. Stewart, November 1997.
43. Spence, J. (1990), *The Search for Modern China*, New York; W. W. Norton.
44. C. Pow, Oral history.
45. MBH 1003.6, Huxter to Paton, 19 October 1946.
46. MBH 1003.6, Huxter to Paton, 23 January 1947; MBH 1003.9, Paton to Huxter, 13 March 1947.
47. MBH 1003.9, Stocks to Paton, 17 September 1945.
48. MBH 951, Special private letter to branches, 17 August 1945.
49. MBH 951, General advice to all branches, 17 August 1945.
50. MBH 1003.9, Paton to Cromartie, 5 July 1946.
51. Ibid., Paton to Benson, 13 July 1945.

Chapter Six: Realignment, 1947–57

1. Alford, B. W. E. (1996), *Britain in the World Economy since 1880*, London: Longman, pp. 199–200, 233–4.
2. MBH 573A, Chairman's statement, February 1952.
3. Jones, G. (1993), *British Multinational Banking 1830–1990*, Oxford: Clarendon Press, p. 247.
4. Tyson, G. (1963), *100 Years of Banking in Asia and Africa*, London: National and Grindlays Bank, pp. 189–90.
5. Winton, J. R. (1982), *Lloyds Bank, 1918–1969*, Oxford: Oxford University Press, p. 125.
6. MBH 989, Summary of overseas taxes, 1955.
7. MBH 573A, Chairman's statement, February 1952. Sir Cyril Jones was an Assistant Under Secretary at the Foreign Office between 1947 and 1950.
8. Jones, *Multinational Banking*, p. 250.
9. MBH 2362, AGM proceedings, 21 March 1953.
10. MBH 1133, List of C shares, 1954.
11. King IV, p. 501.
12. MBH 1133, List of C shares, 1954.
13. MBH 969, Drake to Crichton, 24 June 1947.
14. MBH 1185 Chittagong file, 1947.
15. Information about the closure of the branch in Shanghai can be found in MBH 1095–9, Shanghai closing files; and in MBH 1000.11, Drake's private letters. The closure of Hongkong Bank's branch in the city is covered in King IV, pp. 384–99.
16. MBH 1095, 26 February 1953.
17. For details on Hongkong and Shanghai Bank's situation in Shanghai see King IV, pp. 383–96.
18. MBH 1098, 6 July 1955.
19. MBH 1099, Drake to Swales, 10 May 1956.
20. MBH 2308.29, Board minutes, 7 April 1959.

21. King IV, pp. 102–5.
22. MBH 1000.1, Benson to Drake, 24 June 1948.
23. MBH 3136.7, Memorandum by Mealing, 21 June 1955.
24. J. B. Stewart, Oral history.
25. I. MacFarlane, Oral history.
26. MBH 969, Drake to Duffield Harding, 3 July 1947.
27. MBH 969, Drake to Soul, 8 September 1948. Soul was previously accountant at Ipoh branch.
28. MBH 971, Drake to Wardle, 20 October 1950.
29. MBH 3136.7, Memorandum by Mealing, 21 June 1955.
30. MBH 808, Thomas report on East Africa, 1950.
31. MBH 3135.10 and MBH 3135.11, Drake USA files, 1955.
32. MBH 3136.6, West Africa file, 1955.
33. MBH 2141, Wardle's report, May 1957. 'Towkay' is an eastern term for 'Head Man'.
34. MBH 2119, Wardle to Wilkie, 11 October 1955.
35. MBH 836, Local staff papers, 1955.
36. Ibid.
37. MBH 987, Staff files, 1960–65.
38. MBH 791, Inspection reports by Pow, May and July 1957.
39. MBH 794, Wyatt to Wardle, 4 February 1959.
40. MBH 573A, Chairman's statement, March 1949.
41. King IV, pp. 347–8.
42. MBH 573A, Chairman's statement, February 1952.
43. Anon (1954), *The International Bank for Reconstruction and Development, 1946–1953*, Baltimore: Johns Hopkins Press, pp. 128–31.
44. 'Brief by the Malaysian rubber industry', 1951, Colonial Office, quoted in Van Helten, J. and Jones, G., 'British business in Malaysia and Singapore since the 1870s', in Davenport-Hines, R. P. T. and Jones, G. (eds) (1989), *British Business in Asia since 1860*, Cambridge: Cambridge University Press.
45. MBH 971, Drake to Wardle, 7 December 1950.
46. MBH 966, Inspection report, 1953.
47. Jones, *Multinational Banking*, Appendix 5.
48. MBH 2397, 'data supplied to each member of the board', June 1957.
49. King IV, p. 507.
50. Tyson, *100 Years of Banking in Asia and Africa*, pp. 205–7.

Chapter Seven: Reckoning, 1957–66

1. Hannah, L. (1976), *The Rise of the Corporate Economy*, London: Methuen.
2. Winton, J. R. (1982), *Lloyds Bank, 1918–1969*, Oxford: Oxford University Press, p. 134.
3. Ibid.
4. Jones, G. (1993), *British Multinational Banking 1830–1990*, Oxford: Clarendon Press, pp. 256–9.
5. MBH 2308.27, Board minutes, 11 June 1957.
6. The following account of Marden's career is based on I. Verchère, 'Wheelock Marden: last of the old-style hongs', *Insight* (December 1978), pp. 8–20.

7. L. Blanks, Oral history.
8. Hongkong Bank Archives, J22.8.21, G. Marden to M. Turner, 11 December 1956.
9. King IV, pp. 498–9.
10. MBH 1317, Donn to Drake, 5 April 1956.
11. Ibid., Drake to Donn, 12 April 1956.
12. Hongkong Bank Archives, J22.8.21, G. Marden to M. Turner, 11 December 1956.
13. Bank of England, Cobbold papers, 8 January 1957; G3/117. Bicester was a member of the Court of the Bank of England from 1954 to 1966.
14. GHO 436, Memorandum by Perry-Aldworth, 6 June 1957.
15. Hongkong Bank Archives, J22.8.21, Memorandum by Turner, September 1972.
16. King IV, p. 499.
17. Bank of England, Cobbold papers, 1 May 1957, G3/117.
18. GHO 436, Memorandum by Perry-Aldworth, 6 June 1957.
19. Ibid.
20. Bank of England, Cobbold papers, 11 June 1957, G3/117.
21. GHO 436, Stewart to Turner, 12 June 1957.
22. Bank of England, Cobbold papers, 27 June 1957, G3/117.
23. GHO 436, 18 June 1957.
24. Green, E. and Moss, M. S. (1982), *A Business of National Importance. The Royal Mail Shipping Group, 1902–1937*, London: Methuen, chs 8 and 9.
25. GHO 436, Stewart to Turner, 2 July 1957.
26. Board minutes, 16 July 1957.
27. King IV, p. 503.
28. Bank of England, Cobbold papers, 17 July 1957, G3/118.
29. GHO 436, Perry-Aldworth to Stewart, 20 September 1957.
30. King IV, p. 508.
31. We are grateful to Paul Lamb for this information.
32. GHO 436, Perry-Aldworth to Turner, 6 October 1958.
33. Ibid., Turner to Perry-Aldworth, 14 October 1958; King IV, p. 508.
34. King IV, pp. 509–11.
35. Bank of England, Cobbold papers, 1 November 1957, G3/120.
36. GHO 436, Reid to Turner, 14 November 1958.
37. King IV, p. 510; Bank of England, Cobbold papers, 11 November 1957, 11 December 1957, G3/1208.
38. GHO 436, Reid to Turner, 20 November 1958.
39. Bank of England, Cobbold papers, 7 July 1957, G3/120.
40. King IV, p. 513.
41. GHO 436, Perry-Aldworth to Turner, 16 December 1958.
42. GHO 436, 29 December 1958.
43. King IV, p. 514.
44. Jones, *Multinational Banking*, p. 258; Standard Chartered Bank (1980), *Story Brought Up To Date*, Aldershot, Hants: Scolar Press, p. 6.
45. King IV, p. 509.
46. MBH 573A, Chairman's statement, 24 February 1959.
47. Hongkong Bank Archives, J18.7, HSBC chairman's statement, 1959.
48. GHO 436, F. R. Burch to Reserve Bank of India, 5 December 1958.
49. GHO 436, Turner to Reid, 8 November 1958.
50. King IV, p. 510.

51. Ibid., 515.
52. GHO 436, Notes by Turner, 8 December 1958.
53. King IV, p. 516.
54. MBH 794, Inspector's report, 1958.
55. King IV, p. 515.
56. MBH 1325, Wardle to Turner, 15 January 1959.
57. L. G. Atterbury, quoted in King IV, p. 515.
58. MBH 1304, October 1959.
59. MBH 1305, Circular letter, 14 August 1965.
60. King IV, pp. 550–51.
61. MBH 1321, Saunders to Lydall, 8 March 1962.
62. King IV, pp. 602–3. James Shirreff's career had begun in 1926. He went East in 1930 and subsequently held appointments throughout the East, including managerships at Kuala Lumpur, Karachi, Bombay and Penang .
63. MBH 2164, Pow to Saunders, 26 September 1962.
64. MBH 2164, Nagoya file, 1962–63.
65. MBH 2164, Pow to Liddle, 1 November 1962.
66. MBH 1304, January–September 1960.
67. MBH 1325, Wardle to Turner, 1 March 1961.
68. MBH 985, Pow to Saunders, 22 January 1964.
69. Ibid., Pow to Saunders, 20 January 1966.
70. MBH 2484, Pow, newsletter, January 1963; MBH 985, Pow to Saunders, 22 January 1964.
71. MBH 985, Memos on staff numbers, 31 December 1962 and 31 December 1965.
72. MBH 2484, Dargie to Pow, 29 March 1963.
73. MBH 2484, Pow, newsletter, February 1965.
74. MBH 985. These additions comprise (in 1964) £206 838 in notional profit, £32 810 in tax savings and £40 000 in management charges; and (in 1965) £201 165 in notional profits, approximately £30 000 in tax savings and £40 000 in management charges.
75. MBH 1322, Saunders to Pow, 12 October 1964.
76. MBH 1324 and GHO 1666, Report by Mack, 1962.
77. MBH 1324, Pow to Saunders, 1 September 1965.
78. Hongkong Bank Archives, J22.8.20, Muirhead to Asher, 14 August 1981.

Chapter Eight: Removals, 1966–84

1. King IV, p. 553.
2. King IV, p. 634.
3. This age profile was not unusual in banking history and it was not unprecedented in the Mercantile's own history. E.g. Muirhead, p. 182.
4. King IV, pp. 635–8.
5. King IV, p. 645.
6. MBH 1306, Pow to Gregoire, 30 June 1965.
7. MBH 1313, Memorandum by Saunders, 23 July 1965.
8. MBH 1313, Notice to staff, 1 September 1965.
9. MBH 1316, Pow, confidential letter to covenanted foreign staff, 1 September 1965.

10. Hongkong Bank Archives, J22.8.22, Copy board minutes, 2 November 1965.
11. MBH 1306, Pow to Herridge, 17 September 1965; MBH 1313, Pow to F. J. Knightly, 25 November 1965.
12. King IV, pp. 701–6.
13. MBH 1306, Pow to Gregoire, 2 August 1965.
14. MBH 1316, Circular letter, 8 November 1965; MBH 1306, Pow to Stewart, 4 August 1965.
15. The other new directors were H. J. C. Browne, the Hon J. D. Clague, S. J. Cooke, M. A. R. Young-Herries, L. Kadoorie, I. H. Kendall, F. J. Knightly, J. Dickson Leach, G. M. B. Salmon and P. G. Williams. MBH 1615.
16. I. Herridge, Oral history.
17. Hongkong Bank Archives, L(ME)3, Facilities sanctioned by general manager, 5 April 1996.
18. MBH 1324, Memorandum by J. Gregoire, undated 1967.
19. MBH 2027, Gregoire to Herridge, 12 February 1968.
20. MBH 2159, Longmoor file, 1962–69; MBH 570, Barcote Manor file, 1967–70; King IV, p. 604.
21. MBH 1313, Saunders memo, 23 July 1965.
22. MBH 1323, Pow to G. O. W. Stewart, 9 December 1965.
23. Jones, G. (1987), *Banking and Oil*, Cambridge: Cambridge University Press, pp. 242–9.
24. MBH 2501.1, Executive committee minutes, 30 December 1966; the branch of the British Bank of the Middle East at Bombay remained largely independent of the integration. Jones, *Banking and Oil*, p. 249.
25. Hongkong Bank Archives, Chairman's files, C2.4, Herridge to Saunders, 25 July 1968; Herridge to Mackie, 19 November 1968.
26. MBH 2027, Newsletter, 3 February 1969; Hongkong Bank Archives, J22.8.15, Paul Lamb, 'History of Mercantile Bank Limited' (unpublished typescript, 1972), p. 61.
27. MBH 1919, India report, June 1973.
28. Jones, G. (1993), *British Multinational Banking 1830–1990*, Oxford: Clarendon Press, pp. 292–3.
29. King IV, p. 607.
30. MBH 1919, India report, June 1975.
31. Interview with I. H. Macdonald, 7 July 1997.
32. Jones, *Multinational Banking*, p. 293.
33. Muirhead, p. 45. The Raffles Place office eventually closed in November 1984 (information from Ian Imlach, 15 September 1995).
34. MBH 1926, Malaysia report, December 1973. In comparison the Singapore branches had approximately 20 000 accounts and 208 staff. MBH 1924, Singapore report, December 1972.
35. MBH 1794, Pow, Karachi inspection, 29 March 1956.
36. Hongkong Bank Archives, J22.8.15, Paul Lamb, 'History of Mercantile Bank Limited' (unpublished typescript, 1972), p. 62.
37. I. Herridge, Oral history, 73.
38. MBH 2501.2, Executive committee minutes, August 1969.
39. Hongkong Bank Archives, J22.8.15, Paul Lamb, 'History of Mercantile Bank Limited', p. 63.
40. MBH 1274, Herridge, Circular letter 130, 22 July 1969.
41. In 1982 the Hongkong Bank returned to Pakistan by establishing a new

branch. The group also returned to Bangladesh (as the former East Pakistan had become in 1971), when a representative office was opened in Dacca in 1997. The old Dacca branch of the Mercantile in Motijheel is now the Dhaka Main branch of ANZ Grindlays. The other former Mercantile branches closed in 1969 (Chittagong), 1978 (Khulna) and 1983 (Karachi). We are very grateful to Trevor Hart, Group Archivist, ANZ Group, and his colleagues for this information.

42. Hongkong Bank Archives, J22.8.15, Paul Lamb, 'History of Mercantile Bank Limited', p. 64.
43. MBH 1925, Sri Lanka results, December 1973; King IV, p. 657.
44. King IV, pp. 607, 652–4.
45. Chris Langley was the last to join the foreign staff of the bank in this way.
46. Hongkong Bank Archives, S2.20, S2.24, Staff lists.
47. I. Herridge, Oral history. N. H. T. Bennett was assistant to the chairman and chief manager of the Hongkong Bank in this period.
48. N. Bennett, Oral history, pp. 70–71.
49. King IV, pp. 583–4.
50. MBH 2501.3, Executive committee minutes.
51. Hongkong Bank Archives, J22.8.15, Paul Lamb, 'History of Mercantile Bank Limited', p.64.
52. The bank's head office staff in Hong Kong then comprised Frank Fitzpatrick (controller overseas operations), J. W. Baird and P. A. Hirst (assistant controllers), D. P. Brown and B. C. Gray.
53. King IV, p. 646.
54. The banking licence for Boriuli was transferred from the sub-branch at Veer Nariman Road, which became an office of the British Bank of the Middle East.
55. King IV, pp. 608–9.
56. King IV, p. 646.
57. Hongkong Bank Archives, S2.32, Group Executive Staff List, August 1984.
58. This theme is explored extensively in King IV, chs 15 to 18.
59. MBH 2464, Reypert to Hong Kong customers, 21 May 1984. Neil Reypert had joined the Mercantile in 1957; he retired in 1988.
60. MBH 2464, circular OCL 19 July 1984; press release, 25 July 1984.

Chapter Nine: Review, 1893–1984

1. *Banking Almanac*, passim.
2. Jones, G. (1993), *British Multinational Banking 1830–1990*, Oxford: Clarendon Press, Appendix 1.
3. Cottrell, P. L., 'Aspects of commercial banking in Northern and Central Europe, 1880–1931' in Kinsey, S. and Newton, L. (eds) (1998), *International Banking in an Age of Transition: Globalisation, Automation, Banks and their Archives*, Aldershot: Scolar Press, p. 109.
4. Jones, G. (1987), *Banking and Oil*, Cambridge: Cambridge University Press, pp. 2, 280.
5. MBH 791, Inspection report by Pow, May 1957.
6. British overseas banks with assets of over £100 million in 1950 were (in

descending order) Barclays DCO, Standard, Australia and New Zealand Bank, Chartered, Hongkong Bank, National Bank of India, BOLSA, and English Scottish and Australian Bank. Jones, *British Multinational Banking*, table A1.6.

7. Muirhead, p. 135.
8. Oral histories. We are particularly grateful to Frank Reid for his comments on these records.
9. MBH 985, Correspondence of Pow and HSBC, memorandum on staff numbers, 31 December 1965.
10. King IV, p. 287; Hongkong Bank Archives, S.3.B.1, staff list, December 1967.
11. King IV, p. 663.
12. By 1998 its assets exceeded £291 326 million, it operated in 79 countries and it employed a total of 130 000 staff around the world.
13. King IV, passim.
14. For example, Tamaki, N. (1983), *The Life Cycle of the Union Bank of Scotland, 1830–1954*, Aberdeen: Aberdeen University Press; Jones, *Banking and Oil*, p. 283–5.
15. M. Langley, Oral history.
16. Interview with Ian Macdonald, 7 July 1997.

Appendix Six: The note issue of the Mercantile Bank, 1912–78

1. Muirhead, pp. 62–7.
2. Cribb, J. (1987), *Money in the Bank. An Illustrated Introduction to the Money Collection of the Hongkong Bank*, London: Spink, pp. 148–9.
3. Research notes by Stuart Muirhead for Muirhead.
4. Ibid.
5. *Hongkong Bank Group Magazine* (Summer 1972).

Appendix Seven: The Bank of Mauritius, 1894–1916

1. 'Stella Calvisque Maris Indici' was the shared motto of the Bank of Mauritius and the British colony of Mauritius.
2. Public Relations Office of the Sugar Industry (1997), *Sugar in Mauritius*, ch. 1.
3. Muirhead, p. 85.
4. H210.2, Oriental Banking Corporation Opinion Book, 1891; MBH 779, annual reports of the Bank of Mauritius, 31 December 1899 and 31 December 1907.
5. MBH 1263, Memorandum of Association of the Bank of Mauritius, clause (h). George Dickson was appointed manager of Mauritius branch and he became the Mercantile's first manager in Mauritius in 1916.
6. MBH 1191, Agreement with the Bank of Mauritius as to the transaction of part of the banking business of the Government, 9 April 1895.
7. MBH 575, Minutes of the statutory meeting of the shareholders of the Bank of Mauritius, 29 January 1895.
8. MBH 779, Annual report of the Bank of Mauritius, 31 December 1896.

9. MBH 779, Annual report of the Bank of Mauritius, 31 December 1902.
10. MBH 779, Annual report of the Bank of Mauritius, 31 December 1905: net profits of £17 135.
11. MBH 779, Annual report of the Bank of Mauritius, 31 December 1907.
12. MBH 1191, Bank of Mauritius analysis of profit, 1903 to 1915. This includes inner reserves for 1907, 1912, 1913 and 1914. Real profit has been calculated for these years by adding inner reserve sums to the net profit figure.
13. MBH 779, Annual report of the Bank of Mauritius, 31 December 1909.
14. MBH 779, Annual report of the Bank of Mauritius, 31 December 1907.
15. MBH 779, Annual report of the Bank of Mauritius, 31 December 1908.
16. MBH 779, Annual report of the Bank of Mauritius, 31 December 1911.
17. Ibid.
18. MBH 1191, Bank of Mauritius analysis of profit, 1903 to 1915: £2000 was transferred to inner reserves in 1912 and £500 in 1913.
19. MBH 779, Annual reports of the Bank of Mauritius, 31 December 1912 and 1913.
20. MBH 579, Board minutes of the Bank of Mauritius, 3 September 1914 and 16 October 1914.
21. MBH 1191, Bank of Mauritius analysis of profit, 1903 to 1915.
22. MBH 779, Annual report of the Bank of Mauritius, 31 December 1914.
23. MBH 505, Bank of Mauritius combined balance sheet for London, Mauritius and Seychelles, 31 December 1915.
24. MBH 579, Board minutes of the Bank of Mauritius, 16 November 1915.
25. MBH 579, Board minutes of the Bank of Mauritius, 12 January 1916.
26. MBH 1191, Minutes of a meeting of some of the principal shareholders of the Bank of Mauritius, 29 February 1916.
27. MBH 1191, Draft letter to the Local Board of Directors of the Bank of Mauritius, 25 February 1916.
28. MBH 578, Minutes of an extraordinary general meeting of the shareholders of the Bank of Mauritius, 18 April 1916.
29. Jones, G. (1993), *British Multinational Banking 1830–1990*, Oxford: Clarendon Press, p. 139.

Index

For Product Safety Concerns and Information please contact our
EU representative GPSR@taylorandfrancis.com Taylor & Francis
Verlag GmbH, Kaufingerstraße 24, 80331 München, Germany